Why People Buy Things They Don't Need

Understanding and Predicting Consumer Behavior

PAMELA N. DANZIGER

Dearborn™
Trade Publishing
A **Kaplan Professional** Company

This publication is designed to provide accurate and authoritative information in regard to the subject matter covered. It is sold with the understanding that the publisher is not engaged in rendering legal, accounting, or other professional service. If legal advice or other expert assistance is required, the services of a competent professional should be sought.

Vice President and Publisher: Cynthia A. Zigmund
Acquisitions Editor: Michael Cunningham
Senior Project Editor: Trey Thoelcke
Interior Design: Lucy Jenkins
Cover Design: Design Solutions
Typesetting: the dotted i

Published by Dearborn Trade Publishing
A Kaplan Professional Company

Printed in the United States of America

04 05 06   10 9 8 7 6 5 4 3 2 1

Library of Congress Cataloging-in-Publication Data

Danziger, Pamela N.
    Why people buy things they don't need : understanding and predicting consumer behavior / Pamela N. Danziger.
        p.   cm.
    Includes bibliographical references and index.
    ISBN 0-7931-8602-1
    1. Consumer behavior.   2. Consumers—Research.   3. Marketing research.   I. Title.
    HF5415.32.D36 2004
    658.8′342—dc22

                                                                    2004003269

For Greg and the boys

C o n t e n t s

TO ACCURATELY PREDICT THE FUTURE, YOU'VE GOT TO UNDERSTAND WHY

Conventional wisdom in market research circles holds that the best predictor of future consumer behavior is past consumer behavior. In other words, if you want to know what consumers are likely to do in the future, study what they have done in the past and project the results forward. I learned this lesson well in the many years I worked in marketing research for big corporations. But once I founded Unity Marketing and started working directly with client companies to develop marketing strategies that produce results, I discovered the absolute, utter failing of this conventional wisdom. The simple fact is if you study past consumer behavior, all you learn is what consumers did in the past, not what they are likely to do in the future. But many businesses continue working under the erroneous assumption that you can use the past to predict the future, so they study, quantify, validate, and make predictions and projections on historical but ultimately meaningless data.

Another piece of faulty market research conventional wisdom has to do with consumer motivation. Many researchers say you don't need to understand why consumers behave as they do because it is irrelevant. They believe all you need to understand is the *what, how, where, when,* and *how much* of the consumer equation. The *why* isn't really important, it is reasoned, because if you ask consumers why they do something, they really can't tell you anyway. Bunk! Being an aficionado of the murder mystery genre, I know the only way to solve the mystery is to uncover the motive. All the clues at the scene of the crime may point to one or more suspects—usually red herrings—but the mystery is only solved once the true motive is revealed. So too in market research. While the behavioral data is important to understanding the consumer, the real insight into what drives a consumer to buy is the *why*.

Ultimately, the goal of any market research study is to provide information and insight about consumers to support business decision making. The focus of those business decisions is what will happen in the future, not the past. Market research, therefore, must enlighten and guide corporate *future vision*. You need to know, or at least have a pretty good idea, how specific marketing strategies and new products and services will impact or change the consumer market. In other words, are consumers likely to buy more of what you have to sell because of your strategies?

Hockey great Wayne Gretzky put it best in his apocryphal anecdote. When asked in an interview what made him so much better than the other hockey players on the ice, Gretzky responded, "Everybody else skates to where the puck is. But I skate to where the puck is going." In business our "hockey puck" is the consumer and rather than trying to catch up to where the consumer is today or was yesterday, we need to get out in front and anticipate where the consumer is going and what he or she is going to want when they get there. Unfortunately, this challenge of gaining future vision of the consumer market is getting harder and harder today because the consumers are moving so much faster than they ever did before. Businesses must keep ahead or risk becoming increasingly irrelevant—nonplayers in the consumer market.

In my research work with clients, big and small, over the past ten plus years, I have discovered two secrets of gaining future vision about where the consumer market is going and what companies need to do to be ready for it. The first secret, and the subject of this book, is to understand why people buy. The second secret, and the topic of my next book—entitled *Let Them Eat Cake: Marketing Luxury to the Masses (As Well As the Classes)*, to be published by Dearborn Trade Publishing in early 2005—is to track changes and moves at the luxury end of the market to predict where the mass market will be in the near future. In other words: First the rich do it, then everybody follows.

> Unfortunately, this challenge of gaining future vision of the consumer market is getting harder and harder today because the consumers are moving so much faster than they ever did before.

WHY PEOPLE BUY: A KEY THAT
UNLOCKS MARKETING SUCCESS

Gaining insight into consumer motivation—why people buy—is the best predictor of consumer behavior in a changing, shifting world. While consumer behavior changes as consumers progress through different life stages, the basic consumer personality that guides and directs their behavior is fixed over time. For example, bargain shoppers who religiously clip coupons and are willing to drive 30 minutes to save $5 will always be bargain shoppers—as young adults, as the heads of households of a growing family, as empty-nesters with no more children at home, and as seniors. The type of products those bargain shoppers buy at each of these major life stages will change, the amount of money they may spend will change with changes in income, where they shop will change, but their basic personality as careful, bargain-driven shoppers is fixed. So too for the impulse shopper who gains ultimate satisfaction in the process of shopping and buying. The things he or she buys will change, but the basic motivation and consumer mind-set is fixed.

So by understanding why consumers behave as they do, you have a looking glass into the future. Understanding why helps a company anticipate and prepare for changes in the cultural, economic, and political environment. It provides insight into how predictable changes in consumer demographics will impact consumer behavior. In essence, while the what, how, where, when, and how much of consumer behavior fluctuates, the why remains fixed and can be used to predict how change will impact the other factors of consumer behavior.

"WHY PEOPLE BUY" EVEN MORE IMPORTANT NOW
THAN EVER BEFORE

Not only are consumers moving faster than ever before, they are fueled by a new sense of empowerment in their commercial affairs. Most Americans, even the poorest, participate at some level in the twenty-first-century luxury lifestyle. Where else in the world do you find households that live below the median income level owning cars, color television sets, video recorders linked to cable, air-conditioning, and cellular phones? With the infectious spread of discount retailers like Wal-Mart, Costco, Sam's Club, Dollar General, factory outlets, and the rest, consumers everywhere find more and more options for buying everything they need—

and don't need—at unthinkable discounts. Their consuming choices have exploded and they don't need to buy your "widget" anymore. They can choose from thousands of perfectly acceptable alternatives sold at any price point in hundreds of different retailers accessible directly from home or within a five-mile proximity.

The fulcrum of power in the consumer marketplace has shifted from the marketer and retailer to the consumer. Too many companies across the commercial landscape have yet to discover that they no longer hold all the cards. Today the consumer, rich and poor, is in control and it is *never* going back to the way it was before. Just open any edition of the *Wall Street Journal* and you'll find story after story of companies in their death spiral because they failed to understand the new consumer balance of power.

In only the first couple of years of the twenty-first century, marketers have felt the effects of this dramatic shift in power. The tragic events of September 11 sent businesses into a tailspin and the economy into a mild recession. This was followed by the war in Iraq, which created more confusion and uncertainty in the consumers' mind-set. These events, totally beyond anyone's control, have a dramatic and long-lasting impact on consumers and how they behave. Businesses dependent upon consumers need better tools to help them predict and prepare for the future.

Ever since the unexpected attack on September 11 and the question of what our leaders really knew about the presence of weapons of mass destruction (WMD) in Iraq, we've all learned, thanks to the CNN effect, the critical importance of "human intelligence" in the political and military arena. Many analysts and pundits have laid the blame for the terrorist attack and our subsequent intervention in Iraq on the fact that our country allowed its human intelligence capability to decline, while relying more and more on satellite, communications, and technically oriented data collection.

Like the government, many businesses and marketing executives have let their "consumer intelligence" slide, while relying too heavily upon factual point-of-purchase, real-time, computer-generated and supplied data. They want to see the future, yet they ignore the very information— the consumer intelligence—that will enable them to see it. Why? Because it doesn't graph nicely, and it requires a human being—an expensive, intelligent one with some real-world experience—to process it instead of a computer.

In this book, *Why People Buy Things They Don't Need*, you will gain insight and understanding about why consumers behave the way they do. By understanding the *why*, your business strategy will be grounded and supported by *consumer intelligence*, not just historical facts and figures. You'll find a lot of statistics, facts, and figures here, but you will also discover a new way to look at your consumers, not as a point on a data graph, but as real, complex, irrational but strangely predictable human beings who love and fear and strive and feel pain. They are wonder-

> By understanding the why, your business strategy will be grounded and supported by consumer intelligence, not just historical facts and figures.

ful. They are frustrating. They are awe-inspiring. They are fascinating. Moreover, they are our customers. We desperately need them. And we must respect them. That is why you as a business and marketing execu-tive need this book, because without the consumer your business is des-tined to become history.

1

WHY DO PEOPLE BUY THINGS THEY DON'T NEED?

Because they do need!

That is the simple answer to a profoundly challenging question. Consumers buy things to satisfy a concrete, distinctly felt need. Many consumer marketers go little further than this: uncover the need, target it in advertising, and, voila, products get sold. But in today's diverse, networked, information-crowded marketplace, it is hard to rise above the background noise of commerce with practical, needs-based advertising.

What do any of us really need? More fundamentally, how do you reach a mass-consumer market where my need is so different from your need and your need is so different from that of each of your neighbors? What about where the need cannot be defined in conscious, rationally based criteria, but is ephemeral, based on emotions and feelings? Any psychologist will tell you that each of our individual needs extends so much deeper than the simple physical subsistence level. In today's consumer-driven society, satisfying consumer needs has less to do with the practical meeting of physical needs and everything to do with gratifying desires based upon emotions. The act of consuming, rather than the item being consumed, satisfies the need. This is the subject of this book.

WHAT DO CONTEMPORARY AMERICANS NEED?

Economists and social scientists who study the realm of consumer spending can tell us much about what consumers buy, where they buy it, when they buy, and how much they spend. They chart it, graph it, and measure it. However, the flood of numbers emanating from this research cannot reveal the *why* that ultimately drives consumer behavior. Yet, by understanding the why, practicing marketers can communicate with potential consumers to entice them to buy products using the emotionally based, right-brain-inspired language.

The overall message of so many books that explore modern American consumerism is to shake their fingers at our wasteful consumer behavior and call on consumers to stop their unnecessary, throwaway spending. Think if Americans directed their economic might toward the public good and infrastructure, rather than the extravagant weekly, even daily, shopping trips to the malls, armed with credit cards and insatiable consumer appetites. For example, Juliet Schor, of Harvard University, writes:

> The intensification of competitive spending has affected more than family finances. There is also a boomerang effect on the public purse and collective consumption. As the pressures on private spending have escalated, support for public goods and for paying taxes has eroded. Education, social services, public safety, recreation, and culture are being squeezed. The deterioration of public goods then adds even more pressure to spend privately. People respond to inadequate public services by enrolling their children in private schools, buying security systems, and spending time at Discovery Zone rather than the local playground.

Yet, in light of the tragic events of September 11, 2001, and the worsening economic crisis, this point of view seems strangely un-American. The simple fact remains that our whole economic system, even our way of life, depends upon the continued, sustained practice of "excessive," as some see it, American consumerism.

ONCE A CONSUMER NATION, ALWAYS A CONSUMER NATION

As long as the U.S. Department of Commerce, under the Bureau of Economic Analysis, has tracked the nation's gross domestic product

(GDP), consumer spending has been the very underpinning of the economy. Consumers' insatiable appetite to buy has contributed between 60 and 70 percent of the GDP since 1929, with only a slight downturn to about 50 percent during the war years of the 1940s. In 1929, 1930, and 1940, personal consumption as a percentage of GDP topped 70 percent, demonstrating the long-standing foundational role consumer spending has played in the American economy, as displayed in Figure 1.1.

CONSUMERS SHIFT AWAY FROM NECESSITY–DRIVEN SPENDING

Consumer spending has kept the American economy afloat throughout the twentieth century, but the way consumers spend their money has changed significantly over the past 70 years. Consumer-durable spending as a percentage of personal consumption expenditures has hovered in the range of 10 to 13 percent since 1929, with a slight peak in 1950 at 16 percent, but the share of consumer spending on nondurable goods and services has varied significantly. Nondurable spending includes such essential categories as food and clothing along with discretionary categories of gasoline, fuel oil, tobacco, toiletries, semidurable home fur-

FIGURE 1.1

Personal Consumption Expenditures as a Percentage of GDP (in billions)

YEAR	GDP	PERSONAL CONSUMPTION	PERCENT OF TOTAL ECONOMY
1929	$ 103.7	$ 77.5	74.7%
1930	91.3	70.2	76.9
1940	101.3	71.2	70.3
1950	294.3	192.7	65.5
1960	527.4	332.3	63.0
1970	1039.7	648.9	62.4
1980	2795.6	1762.9	63.1
1990	5803.2	3831.5	66.0
1995	7397.7	4975.8	67.3
1996	7816.9	5256.8	67.2
1997	8304.3	5547.4	66.8
1998	8747.0	5879.5	67.2
1999	9268.4	6282.5	67.8
2000	9817.0	6739.4	68.7
2001	10100.8	7045.4	69.8
2002	10480.8	7358.3	70.5

Source: U.S. Bureau of Economic Analysis

In the later decades of the twentieth century, essentials have captured far less of the consumers' budget.

nishings, cleaning supplies, drugs and sundries, toys, stationery, magazines, newspapers, flowers, seeds, and potted plants. Nondurable spending accounted for as much as 51 percent of personal consumption expenditures in 1950 to as little as 30 percent in 2000. One reason for the significant decline is that essentials (for example food and clothing) now cost less relative to total income. In the later decades of the twentieth century, essentials have captured far less of the consumers' budget. In 1930, food alone comprised nearly 26 percent of personal consumption expenditures, and clothes took another 11 percent. Compare that 37 percent budgeted to essentials in 1930 with consumer spending in 2000 on the same necessities, where food (14 percent) and clothing (5 percent) together accounted for only 19 percent of total expenditures. Today, after consumers budget for essentials, they have a substantial amount of money left to spend on discretionary items, as shown in Figure 1.2.

In the current economy, the services category has captured share from other categories, especially consumer nondurable spending. Services include essentials such as housing, as well as discretionary expenses, such as recreation, education, transportation, and many household operations. Various personal services such as legal, payments to financial institutions, donations to religious and welfare groups, and foreign travel are also included in the discretionary spending for services. In 1940, services made up only one-third of consumer spending, while in 2000 services rose to a startling 59 percent, an increase of 26 percentage points.

Another category of spending that most contemporary Americans would call an essential expenditure is medical care. In 2000, medical care accounted for more consumer spending, 14.8 percent, than did housing, with a 14.3 percent share. Of all spending categories, medical care has increased the most since 1930, when it represented only 3.3 percent of personal consumption expenditures.

TODAY, OVER 40 PERCENT OF CONSUMER SPENDING IS DISCRETIONARY

While one can convincingly argue that a significant share of medical care is discretionary in nature, for purposes of this exploration we consider medical care, housing, and household operations essential expenditures

FIGURE 1.2
Spending on Discretionary Items as a Percentage of All Personal Consumption Expenditures (PCE)

	1930	1940	1950	1960	1970	1980	1990	2000
Durables	10.3	11.0	15.9	13.0	13.1	12.2	12.2	12.2
Motor vehicles	3.1	3.9	7.1	5.9	5.5	4.9	5.4	5.2
Furniture	5.4	5.3	7.1	5.4	5.5	4.9	4.5	4.6
Other	1.6	1.5	1.7	1.7	2.1	2.3	2.3	2.5
Discretionary	4.7	5.4	8.8	7.6	7.6	7.2	7.7	7.7
Nondurables	48.4	6.0	51.0	46.0	41.9	39.5	32.5	29.6
Food	25.6	28.4	28.0	24.8	22.2	20.2	16.6	14.2
Clothing and shoes	11.4	10.5	10.2	8.1	7.4	6.1	5.3	4.7
Gas and oil	4.7	5.3	4.6	4.8	4.1	5.8	3.1	2.7
Other	6.7	7.9	8.2	8.3	8.3	7.4	7.4	7.9
Discretionary	11.4	13.2	12.8	13.1	12.4	13.2	10.5	10.6
Services	41.3	37.1	33.1	41.0	45.0	48.4	55.3	56.2
Housing	16.0	13.6	11.3	14.5	14.5	14.5	15.3	14.3
House operations	5.6	5.6	4.9	6.1	5.8	6.5	5.9	5.7
Transportation	3.1	2.9	3.2	3.4	3.7	3.7	3.7	4.1
Medical care	3.3	3.2	3.7	5.3	7.8	10.3	14.1	14.8
Recreation	2.4	2.4	2.0	2.1	2.3	2.4	3.2	3.8
Other	11.0	9.1	7.9	9.6	10.9	11.0	13.1	15.6
Discretionary	16.5	14.4	13.1	15.1	15.9	17.1	20.0	23.5
Total Discretionary	32.6	33.0	34.7	35.8	36.9	37.5	38.2	41.8

Source: Bureau of Economic Analysis, NIPA tables

in the services category. In the nondurable category, we categorize food and clothing as essential. Finally, among durables, we classify only spending on furniture and household equipment as essential, though, like medical care, a significant portion of spending in that category is discretionary in nature. Excluding consumer spending that is allocated to essentials, over 30 percent of consumer spending in 2000, or $2,812.5 billion, was discretionary spending. That is more than gross private domestic investment ($1,767.5 billion) and government consumption expenditures and gross investment ($1,741 billion), the other two segments that make up the national gross domestic product.

UNDERSTANDING THE DISCRETIONARY SPENDING EQUATION *OR* WHAT YOU WILL LEARN FROM READING THIS BOOK

In sum, consumers and their discretionary spending—on wants, not needs—make a surprisingly large contribution to the nation's overall economy. If consumer marketers can harness the power of Americans' need to consume, they can gain market share, build brand recognition, and increase profitability. In later chapters, we will explore the *why*s that propel consumers in their search for emotional satisfaction through the things they buy. We will also examine distinctions among four types of consumer discretionary spending, and how the consumer perceives each. The four types of discretionary spending we will study are:

1. *Utilitarian purchases.* These cover discretionary purchases that people don't necessarily need, but which they perceive as making their lives better in meaningful, measurable ways. Usually, these purchases have a practical or functional component. Consumers will often leap from what is considered an essential purchase to a more highly discretionary one, thus spending more money and gaining more emotional satisfaction from the purchase.
2. *Indulgences.* These are life's little luxuries that consumers can buy without guilt. Primarily, they bring emotional satisfaction to the consumer by being frivolous, somewhat extravagant, but not so expensive that the consumer feels remorse.
3. *Lifestyle luxuries.* These luxuries are *more* than is needed. Lifestyle luxuries have a practical aspect to their purchase, such as a car, a pen, fine china, or a watch. While they fulfill a practical need,

lifestyle luxuries are a quantum leap beyond the basic item needed to effectively serve the essential purpose.

4. *Aspirational luxuries.* Unlike lifestyle luxuries, which have a practical component, aspirational luxuries are purchased largely for the pure joy that owning them brings, such as original art, antiques and vintage collectibles, boats and yachts, and fine jewelry. As with lifestyle luxuries, aspirational luxuries usually are tied to a "brand." When consumers buy aspirational luxuries, they are making a statement about themselves—who they are, their aspirations, and what they stand for.

> If consumer marketers can harness the power of Americans' need to consume, they can gain market share, build brand recognition, and increase profitability.

Through research, we will delve into the purchase incidence for 37 different categories of discretionary purchases—what consumers look for in these purchases and what they get out of making them.

As we probe discretionary purchases, we discover that in order for consumers to buy things they don't need, they use justifiers as excuses and reasons that give them permission to buy. Some consumers and some purchases need more powerfully charged justifiers, while other consumers and purchases require little in the way of an excuse to buy something not needed. Sometimes these justifiers are fairly mundane; other times they are elaborate fantasies consumers conjure up to give them license to make the desired purchase. We have identified 14 distinct justifiers consumers combine and manipulate to give them the permission they need to buy.

We'll also explore how consumers' need for discretionary purchases impacts their shopping behavior, such as where they shop, how they research the planned purchases, and how they discover new things that will satisfy unfulfilled emotional needs.

Finally, as we build our understanding of the emotionally motivated consumer, the ultimate goal is for marketers to learn innovative ways to apply their new insights into dynamic, fresh marketing strategies. Marketers can use these insights to position their products strategically along the discretionary purchase continuum, playing to the various justifiers that consumers use to make a discretionary purchase. Throughout this book, we will bring the discussion back from the conceptual to the practical by profiling outstanding marketers and the best marketing practices that help them sell more things that people don't need, but want.

WHAT WE NEED

More Than You Ever Imagined

America is one of the wealthiest countries in the world. A typical middle-class, even lower-class, American cannot even imagine what life is like for the typical citizen of Afghanistan, Zimbabwe, or Indonesia. Our standard of living far exceeds any other developed nation. What we take for granted as an essential part of our way of life—unlimited electricity, clean running water, refrigeration, and television—is far beyond the means of a significant portion of the world's population. Worldwide, the average per capita gross national product is currently about $7,200. The United States per capita of $36,200 is five times as large, as shown in Figure 2.1. With U.S. median household income hovering around $40,000 and median net worth of $71,600, the average American's wealth is unimaginable for most of the world's inhabitants.

WHAT AMERICANS NEED TO LIVE

When talking about what we need, as opposed to what we want, it is important to account for our contemporary American standard of living. More than two-thirds of U.S. householders own their own home. They live in a median-sized home of about 1,700 square feet divided into five or six rooms. The typical home is on a one-third-acre lot, giving the typical American household some "breathing room." Almost every Amer-

FIGURE 2.1
Gross Domestic Product per Capita for Selected Countries, 2000

$36,200 and above	United States, Luxembourg
$25,000–$36,199	Austria, Belgium, Denmark, Hong Kong, Norway, Singapore, Switzerland
$20,000–$24,999	Australia, Canada, Finland, France, Germany, Ireland, Italy, Japan, Netherlands, Qatar, Sweden, United Arab Emirates, United Kingdom
$15,000–$19,999	Argentina, Bahrain, Greece, Israel, Kuwait, New Zealand, Portugal, Spain, South Korea, Taiwan
$10,000–$14,999	Chile, Czech Republic, Estonia, Hungary, Malaysia, Martinique, Slovenia
$7,200	Worldwide average
$5,000–$9,999	Algeria, Botswana, Brazil, Bulgaria, Colombia, Croatia, Guadeloupe, Iran, Lebanon, Mexico, Poland, Romania, Russia, Thailand, South Africa, Turkey, Uruguay
$1,000–$4,999	Albania, Angola, Bangladesh, Belize, Bolivia, Burma, Cambodia, Cameroon, Chad, China, Cuba, Ecuador, Egypt, Guatemala, Guyana, Haiti, Honduras, India, Indonesia, Iraq, Jamaica, Jordan, Kenya, North Korea, Kyrgyzstan, Liberia, Mongolia, Morocco, Mozambique, Namibia, Nicaragua, Pakistan, Paraguay, Peru, Philippines, Senegal, Sri Lanka, Swaziland, Syria, Tajikistan, Uganda, Ukraine, Uzbekistan, Vietnam, Yugoslavia, Zimbabwe
Under $1,000	Afghanistan, Congo Republic, Ethiopia, Madagascar, Nigeria, Rwanda, Somalia, Zambia

Source: The World Factbook, CIA, 2001

ican home (99.4 percent) has some kind of heating source and almost every home (98.5 percent) has a complete bathroom, including toilet, sink, and bathtub. Moreover, not all of the 1.5 percent of households without a complete bathroom live this way out of necessity. Some religious groups, such as the Amish (who are my neighbors in Lancaster County, Pennsylvania), choose to live without indoor plumbing and other modern conveniences.

As for the modern conveniences that grace the typical American home, a majority of American households owns a car; only 17 percent live without this symbol of American freedom. The majority also have air-conditioning in their homes. Most own a clothes

> The simple fact is the contemporary American lives so far above subsistence, we have lost touch with basic needs of life.

washer and dryer, have an automatic dishwasher, ceiling fan, microwave oven, range and oven, frost-free refrigerator, water heater, stereo equipment, color television, VCR, cordless phone, and answering machine. See Figure 2.2 for a breakdown of the American way of life.

The simple fact is the contemporary American lives so far above subsistence, we have lost touch with basic needs of life: food for nutrition, basic clothing, and shelter for warmth and protection. Many people in other countries of the world live dangerously close to subsistence and know the pangs of hunger and the chill of weather without the benefit of adequate clothing and shelter. While most Americans today enjoy a higher standard of living, it has not always been so. During the colonial period and the Civil War, among other times, Americans were also deprived, but

FIGURE 2.2
American Way of Life

Wealth:		**Cars:**	
Median net worth	$71,600	None	17%
Median household income	$38,885	1 car	48%
		2 or more cars	35%
Home ownership rate	66.8% (1999)	**Household Appliances:**	
Housing (1997):		Air conditioner:	
Median number of rooms:	5.3	Central	46.8%
If owner occupied	6.1	Room	24.8%
Median square footage	1,685	Clothes washer	77.4%
Heating equipment	99.4%	Clothes dryer	71.2%
Complete Bathrooms:		Dishwasher	50.2%
None	1.5%	Ceiling fan	60.1%
1 only	46%	Freezer	33.2%
2 or more	52%	Microwave oven	83.0%
Single units or mobile homes	74%	Oven	98.8%
Median lot size	0.33 acres	Self-cleaning oven	44.1%
Amenities (Owner Occupied):		Range	99.2%
Porch, deck, balcony, or patio	85%	Refrigerator	99.8%
Usable fireplace	42%	Frost-free refrigerator	86.8%
Separate dining room	48%	Water heater	100.0%
2 or more living/ recreation rooms	48%	Stereo equipment	68.8%
Garage/carport	73%	Color TV	98.7%
		1 only	31.8%
		2 or more	66.9%
		VCR	88.0%
		Personal computers	35.1%
		Cordless phone	61.4%
		Answering machine	58.4%

Source: U.S. Statistical Abstract, Appliances and office equipment used by households, 1997; Housing units and lot, 1999

they valued their freedom more than material goods. Americans have also faced deprivation in war and during the Depression. Generations born before World War II share cultural memories of living "without" and "in need." The generations that went before were the keepers of family traditions and passed down practical knowledge about living frugally.

However, today's baby boomers and their children are rapidly losing touch with this shared cultural memory of hardship. Boomers and younger generations know nothing about getting along before cars, indoor plumbing, and antibiotics. The generations that were born and came of age after the last World War know little about doing without, struggling to put food on the table, stretching a dollar, and delayed gratification. Spoiled the younger generations may be, but they are the consumers who express their wants, desires, and dreams in terms of needs and necessities because they have never done without.

MAJOR APPLIANCES ARE NECESSITIES OF CONTEMPORARY AMERICAN LIFE

Before moving into an exploration of the things people buy that they do not "need," we will first examine a category that most Americans view as a necessity—major household appliances. A focus group participant explains the decision-making process that she and her husband went through to decide between buying a refrigerator or an entertainment center for the new home they are building:

Our most recent purchase of something we didn't "need" was an entertainment center. We already have one, but we are building a brand-new house and we wanted something new for the house. Now that we are building, things are tight. We could have used the entertainment center we had, but we decided to buy a new one and move the old one into another room. There are other things we need for the home, like a refrigerator. The entertainment center could have been put on hold, but it was one of those things . . . we were in the right place at the right time. We went a little bit over what we needed in an entertainment center in terms of price. We upgraded the wood, so the price went up. It was an opportunistic purchase.

For this homeowner, a refrigerator is a "necessity," required for this family to maintain its way of life. With money tight and the couple strug-

> Need can wait, but want and desire drive purchases.

gling to balance the demands of building a new home while maintaining the current one, their decision to buy a luxury—a new entertainment center—rather than the necessity is inexplicable. In buying the entertainment center, they even went over their budget by ordering the center in a more expensive wood. They realize that they did not need to buy a new entertainment center, but purchasing the center gave this couple so much more pleasure and satisfaction than buying a new refrigerator. Lying under the surface of her story is a realization. The couple believes they will always have enough money to satisfy their need for the basics (e.g., a refrigerator). However, when confronted with deciding between purchasing a luxury and buying a necessity, they go for the purchase that is compelling and emotionally satisfying. Need can wait because it will always be satisfied, but want and desire drive purchases, because you never know when you will find exactly what you long for.

Major Appliance Retailers and Marketers Can Learn from People Buying Things They Don't Need

Retailers and marketers of major appliances can learn much about selling necessities from knowing more about the reasons people buy things they don't need. First, let us recognize the two reasons why people buy appliances: to replace a worn-out appliance and to equip a newly built home. Industry marketers perceive housing starts as the major opportunity because a single housing start generates sales of five to eight major appliances, whereas replacement purchases tend to be limited to a single appliance. Practical considerations, product features, and benefits are the primary drivers for sales of a particular item, but price, credit terms, and conditions also play a role. Brand is also important in the purchase decision as it carries a quality and reliability message. Consumers who have had a satisfactory experience with one brand in the past are already inclined toward the same brand in subsequent purchases.

Marketing strategist, Sergio Zyman, known for his years as brand executive for Coca-Cola, provides the best definition of marketing in his book, *The End of Marketing as We Know It*:

Marketing is how to sell more things to more people more often for more money.

Major appliance retailers, manufacturers, and marketers will sell more major appliances to more people more often for more money by turning their products from a necessity into a "desirable" that provides not just essential functionality but emotional satisfaction. The remainder of this chapter explains how they can do just that.

> Major appliance retailers, manufacturers, and marketers will sell more by turning their products from a necessity into a "desirable" that provides emotional satisfaction.

FASHION—TAKE THE ORDINARY AND MAKE IT EXTRAORDINARY

The nation's major-appliance companies tend to be run by male executives who rise from engineering, manufacturing, and other technical backgrounds. Intuitive fashion sense just does not spring naturally from the corridors of power in the major-appliance industry. With focus on product features, energy efficiency, time savings, and cost-effectiveness, the industry is left-brain dominated. Its approach to marketing: Put a chart outlining the features of the product on the front of the machine and, voila, the customer is sold. This just does not cut it with the target market for these products—women.

Women are attuned to fashion as well as performance. They want products that look good while they do their job to perfection. They take superior performance for granted. They expect every frost-free refrigerator from the lowest to the highest priced to keep their food cold and safe. However, the refrigerator that performs its basic function in style is the one that she wants to have and use in her kitchen.

Fashion takes the ordinary and makes it extraordinary. Manufacturers that produce appliances that look good can charge more for their products. As car manufacturers and fashion designers have known for years, the introduction of new styles and designs sends consumers to the store to buy the latest design. How difficult can it be for major appliance companies to incorporate a fashion or design sensibility into their new product lines? Greater profits will result when appliance manufacturers pay as much attention to the outside as they do to the inside of their products (see Figure 2.3).

FIGURE 2.3

Fashionable Appliances from Jenn-Air

JENN-AIR
Style and Performance in Kitchen Appliances for Aspirers

Within Maytag's corporate family of brands, Jenn-Air is distinguished by its 100-percent commitment to cooking and the kitchen. It is also the most exclusive, top-tier brand for Maytag, hardly a shirker when it comes to premium home brands. If Maytag is a premium brand in home appliances, how is Jenn-Air distinguished and differentiated? Susan Fisher, director of marketing for the Jenn-Air brand, explains that it all starts with design: "The Jenn-Air brand is largely defined by innovative style along with distinctive product features. Jenn-Air invented a new way of cooking with its downdraft, indoor-grilling cooktops. And convection is standard in its ovens. Jenn-Air stands for style and performance in the kitchen. While Maytag offers kitchen appliances, its Maytag brand is founded upon laundry products and its kitchen appliances are more basic than Jenn-Air. Features that are standard in Jenn-Air are often add-ons for Maytag."

The target market for Jenn-Air appliances couldn't be more distinct. Its core customers have a passion for cooking. They recognize the "badge value" of the Jenn-Air name and what it says about the owner as a cook. Buyers tend to be affluent homeowners who seek exclusivity in the brands they use in their home. A Jenn-Air kitchen is not positioned for the first-time homebuyer, but for the trade-up buyer or home remodeler. "Some 90 percent of Jenn-Air purchases involve a hammer or saw," Fisher says. "Our appliances are mainly custom-installed, so we touch a totally different consumer market than other appliance makers who specialize in simple 'plug-in' installation. When customers buy a Jenn-Air, they are often involved in a three-month, or longer, process of design, including selection of kitchen cabinets, floor and wall coverings, and so on. Dreamers and aspirers want this brand in their home."

With its position as a more exclusive brand, Jenn-Air appliances cost more, owing to their higher capital and research and development costs. While they cost more, they also deliver higher profit margins back to the company. For Maytag, Jenn-Air's style is a good investment.

With Jenn-Air's exclusive focus on cooking appliances and other kitchen appliances that support the cooking process, such as refrigerators and dishwashers, they have more specialized distribution and marketing strategies than Maytag. While some Maytag dealers also carry Jenn-Air, the brand's focus on custom installation means that designers, architects, and homebuilders often influence the purchase decision, so Jenn-Air directs marketing campaigns to these trades. While Maytag advertises almost exclusively on television, Jenn-Air devotes its advertising budget to print media, especially epicurean, home design, and shelter magazines. "When someone is designing a new house or remodeling, they tend to buy all these titles. They clip out pictures of kitchens they like and build a file. Jenn-Air wants to be in that file when it's turned over to the designer," Fisher explains. "Our customers see Jenn-Air as a central part of the kitchen they always dreamed of owning. It's a move up and a step up in quality, design, and performance."

How does Jenn-Air stay ahead of its customers' aspirations in new cooking technology?

"Jenn-Air is committed to continual research," Fisher says. "Market research for us is a continual process. We do research at every step in the process from concept development to product delivery. We are especially attuned to consumers' needs in kitchen-shopping and cooking practices. We go into their homes to study their behavior and go with them while they are shopping for appliances to observe their unarticulated needs. And there is style research—we do lots of style research."

Putting all that research to work in dreaming up new kitchen appliances for the aspirational market is a business unit composed of more women than men. "Maytag as a company has lots of women on its team," Fisher explains. "Since we are so involved with products that make women's lives better, female executives, managers, and designers bring an intuitive understanding of what the woman consumer wants and values. In the Jenn-Air business unit, women tend to predominate, not by design; they were hired as the best person for the job." Yet today's upscale appliance marketplace is becoming more attuned to men, she adds. "Interestingly when it comes to buying Jenn-Air, men tend to be more involved with this decision, largely because men are more engaged in the design-and-build process. We also see more men than ever cooking and using the kitchen, so men represent a key growth market segment for our brand," Fisher concludes.

Major-appliance manufacturers need to cross-pollinate their organizations with executives who bring training and experience in fashion and design. These kinds of people may not "fit" naturally into the existing organizational structure. There may well be a culture clash, but staffing for design expertise from outside the industry will go far to infuse major-appliance companies with fresh ideas that will transform their products from purely functional boxes into home-fashion statements.

AVOID MEDIOCRITY IN NEW PRODUCTS—IGNORE THE COMPETITION, GET CLOSE TO THE CUSTOMER

In many highly competitive industries today, corporations tend to expend considerable time, money, and human resources on competitive tracking, monitoring, and otherwise "keeping up with the Joneses." This is especially true in major appliances, where the top five manufacturers account for more than 95 percent of all core-appliance sales such as refrigerators, dishwashers, and washing machines. While these manufacturers have their eyes focused on the competition, they too frequently fall out of touch with their existing consumer markets, their potential markets, and the trends, changes, and factors that are influencing the future of the market. In too many industries, competitive analysis is the "poor-man's" substitute for market research. Companies dedicated to competitive research assume that their competitors are doing the time-consuming, hard, and costly job of consumer research. They spend their time watching the competition and the new product releases, analyzing products and features, so they can piggyback on others' efforts.

This approach to new product development is a guarantee of product mediocrity as the cycle of competitor copying competitor turns back on itself in an endless loop. I cut my teeth professionally in the field of competitive analysis and even belonged to the Society for Competitive Intelligence Professionals for a time. However, I came to realize that the end of this competitive analysis and tracking work was "me-too" marketing strategies. The simple fact is that competitive analysis work is easy. Corporate executives are highly skilled at reading balance sheets and SEC filings and deriving insight into competitive strategy and tactics. It is a realm where executives feel comfortable. They understand the inner workings of other executives' minds and thus other companies' behaviors and strategies. However, expose these same exec-

> In too many industries, competitive analysis is the "poor-man's" substitute for market research.

> Male-dominated industries selling technical (i.e., male-oriented) products to female-dominated consumer markets face a disconnect.

utives to the vagaries, conflicting information, and "hocus-pocus" of consumer market research and they are out of their element entirely. If you can't chart it, graph it, or table it, they do not want to deal with it.

Every industry that creates products for the consumer market should cross-pollinate with fashion and design experts. These industries must also invest time, money, and powerful corporate resources to understand their consumer markets better. It is not enough to bring a few consumers into a lab to test new products. They need to explore how their company's products improve customers' lives and what makes their hearts flutter when they talk about stoves, refrigerators, and washing machines. Appliance industry executives need to get beyond the left-brain-dominant product features of their appliances. They need to study how customers really decide which brand to buy, what the brand means to them, and how it reflects upon their identities and value systems. Male-dominated industries selling technical (i.e., male-oriented) products to female-dominated consumer markets face a disconnect. Taking superior features and quality for granted, women don't bring a product-and-features left-brain orientation to the store when they shop for appliances. However, if an appliance also looks good, is the right color, and is a brand that enables her to express herself, that is the one she will buy.

IF YOU SELL TO WOMEN, THEN *SELL* TO WOMEN

Retailing of major appliances is totally at odds with the way people shop, especially women. Even worse, with few exceptions, the way major appliances are sold at retail has not changed since the early 1960s when I accompanied my parents to buy a new refrigerator. I know it has not changed since the first time I shopped for a major appliance for myself in the 1980s. It's no wonder that Circuit City has gotten out of the major-appliance business and American Appliance has gone under completely. The retailing of major appliances is long overdue for an overhaul.

Recently, I was a customer for a major appliance. My dishwasher was leaking all over the kitchen floor and the repairman sent out from our local appliance store said it would cost just about as much to fix it as to buy a new one. With that suggestion, I went off to the store to buy a new dishwasher.

When you enter a major-appliance store, everything is so logically arranged. Along this wall, the refrigerators are all lined up. Over there is every variation of electric and gas stoves. Running up the middle are the washers, and on the back side of the aisle are the dryers. In one corner, stacked one on top of the other, are the dishwashers. Seemingly on every couple of items, a sale sign is prominently displayed—"$50 off" here and "Only $199" there. When I told the salesman that the repairman sent me in, he took me right over to the dishwasher display and proceeded to bore me with a recitation of each brand's features, which were all the same to me. How did I decide? I picked a quiet one, priced just under the most expensive model, that also happened to be available in black, like my last one. After we set up an appointment for delivery, I left the store knowing I had solved my dishwasher issue, and the salesman was happy to have made the sale.

The problem? This whole experience was totally wrong. I went into the store with a "need" (i.e., my dishwasher broke and I needed a new one). However, I had a significant "desire" that went undiscovered by the salesman, so the store did not profit, and I was ultimately dissatisfied. A little probing on the salesman's part would have uncovered the fact that my dishwasher was purchased, along with all my other kitchen appliances, about ten years ago when we built our house. In the life of a major appliance, ten years is a magic number. It is long enough so that the existing appliances feel "old." The homeowner can justify upgrading all the appliances in the name of energy savings, compelling new features, or getting a good deal on a whole set of new kitchen appliances. The summer before my dishwasher broke, my husband and I invested in new paint for the living room, dining room, and kitchen, and refinished the hardwood floors throughout the house. With all these upgrades, I had been thinking seriously about replacing the stove. A new side-by-side refrigerator would certainly be welcome, now that my two sons are hitting their teen years with the resulting appetites.

The simple fact: There was nothing about my major-appliance buying trip that excited me, or pulled me in to the fun of picking out a brand-new kitchen. With all the appliances lined up one after the other and arranged by type, not how I would use them in my kitchen, they all looked the same—big boxes with labels on them. In that barren setting, I could not envision what my kitchen would look like, or how I would feel cooking with brand-new appliances. While my stated need was satisfied, my desire definitely was not. It would have taken so little effort on the part of the appliance store salesman to turn my $400 purchase into a

Men may like to shop with products lined up for comparison, but women want to dream and fantasize.

$2,500 investment. Figure 2.4 is my prescription for the major-appliance retailing industry.

If I ran a major-appliance store, the first thing I would do is get rid of the row upon row of appliance boxes. I would carve out lovely little rooms to feature all the different types and styles of appliances. There would be a gourmet-style kitchen here with the latest stainless designs, and a starter kitchen there with simple cabinetry and basic appliances. There would be a top-of-the-line country kitchen with retro-appliances, and a to-die-for laundry room with a folding counter and shelves for all the soap powders and cleaning equipment. Men may like to shop with products lined up for comparison, but women want to dream and fantasize. They want to see what the appliances would be like in their own home. I would price the appliances by grouping with a nice discount on the purchase of two or three matching ones. To equip my store with these wonderful room settings, I would work out a strategic alliance with a home remodeling or cabinetry service. I would get into the business of selling not just appliance boxes, but fully-equipped, custom-designed kitchens and laundry rooms.

A store set up like this would have overcome the ineptitude of the salesman with whom I dealt. Rather than take me to the sterile dishwasher display, he would have escorted me into my "dream kitchen." It would not have taken me long to have him writing up my order for three major appliances and a new countertop to boot. I did not mention that a countertop is also on my "desire" list.

Sadly though, I do not have a wonderful new kitchen. It is entirely too much work for me today to go out and buy a new stove and refrigerator. Dealing with an appliance salesman once in a year is about as

FIGURE 2.4

Prescription for Major-Appliance Retailing

- Display appliances in room settings with matching appliances and cabinetry to encourage consumer fantasies
- Feature fewer models with better presentation to "romance" the buyer
- Offer multiple-product package pricing with financing
- Encourage one-stop remodeling by offering appliances, cabinets, countertops, and installation

much as I can handle. I do not have a clue where I can get new countertops or what kind I want, because there are so many choices today. I do not know how difficult or easy it would be to have someone come in and install them. I am too busy to undertake this

> A consumer in motion stays in motion; a consumer at rest stays at rest.

project right now. Although I'd like a new kitchen and I can afford a new kitchen, I can get by without it. After all, everything still works.

This experience illustrates a fundamental law of consumer dynamics: A consumer in motion stays in motion; a consumer at rest stays at rest. That is, it is easier to persuade a consumer who is actively in the market to buy more, than to persuade one to buy who is not participating in the marketplace. The appliance retailer's best opportunity to sell more appliances is at that moment when the consumer has overcome inertia and wants to make a purchase. Unfortunately, my retailer missed this wonderful opportunity by selling me only what I needed rather than all that I wanted. My retailer did not understand how to turn wants into needs. And, that is what the rest of this book is about.

3

IF CONSUMER SPENDING IS THE ENGINE OF THE ECONOMY, THEN DISCRETIONARY SPENDING IS THE "GAS"

As we have seen, consumer spending drives the U.S. economy. Moreover, consumers' desire for things they want, but don't need, is the lure that draws them to the stores, the mall, and now the Internet. The strong emotional gratification that consumers gain from their discretionary purchases is the reward that reinforces continued purchases of things desired, but not needed. Like Pavlov's dogs, they seek that same level of gratification repeatedly. A focus group respondent explained her experience buying things she doesn't need: "Essentials are things you need, but you also need a little 'fluff,' not all substance. Just buying essentials is boring, so you need to buy things that are frivolous to make life less boring. It makes you feel better."

What is the source of gratification? Is it achieved through the act of shopping for something not needed or gratification from the object itself? Evidence points to both as important contributors to consumer satisfaction. In planning a new purchase, a consumer often develops elaborate fantasies surrounding search for an item, finding it, and making it their own. As another focus group participant explained about the recent purchase of a car bought for pleasure, not need: "Anticipation is everything. Everything you do, you anticipate. That is the fun, and that is part of who you are. By anticipating something new, you are trying to level things out [i.e., keep your emotions level]. You go on one vacation, and before that is over, you are already planning your next vacation. You get satisfaction, and you are so thrilled you start planning the next purchase. Satisfaction sets up more anticipation. You can't wait to do it again. Anticipation is stress, healthy stress. You are still enjoying the satisfaction you got and anticipating the next time."

> In shopping, the search for a desired item encourages consumers' fantasies, allowing them to create more complex tableaus in which to act out their dreams and desires.

Another respondent adds: "You can anticipate little things, like taking a bath when you buy soap powders; buying fuzzy slippers to come home and put on after work; or going out to a really nice restaurant." In the act of consuming, these consumers act out vignettes and fantasies—sometimes small, sometimes very elaborate—that may well provide more satisfaction than the actual experience of shopping and buying the item.

In shopping, the search for a desired item encourages consumers' fantasies, allowing them to create more complex tableaus in which to act out their dreams and desires. Another recent new-car buyer explained: "The search for something adds to the anticipation. In shopping for my car, I spent time thinking about what kind of car I wanted. I had fun going to dealers, playing one against the other. I found a thrill in the search. When I finally picked the car and bought it, I almost felt a letdown. The search was over. Now that I got what I wanted, I have to pay for it." Once the purchase cycle is completed, reality sets in. Inevitably though, a new shopping fantasy will begin to brew as the consumer starts a new cycle of anticipation and searching, leading to purchase, then followed by letdown.

Some consumers gain satisfaction from developing a shopping fantasy they can act out. For others, it is the power they feel from finding something and being able to buy it. Interestingly, the consumer's feelings often may have more to do with the act of purchasing than with the object that the shopper buys. In response to the description of the thrill of the hunt, another respondent explains: "If you are an impulse shopper, you don't have any of that. There is no search, no anticipation. For me, the search can drive me crazy. I like to buy. I see something; I find it; I buy it. I like to know that I am the one who got it. For me, it's the power I feel when I buy. I am a big impulse shopper. I like to buy, not to think about it."

> The consumer's feelings often may have more to do with the act of purchasing than with the object that the shopper buys.

CONSUMERS UNDER STRESS

After the terrorist attack on September 11, 2001, the American consumer landscape changed, perhaps forever. Along with the loss of our illusion of safety from acts of war carried out on our soil, went consumer confidence and the feeling of well-being that consuming brought to Americans. Today, confronting an uncertain future, threatened by terrorist acts of horror at home, with our troops committed to military action overseas, American consumers face a crisis that our leaders warn us may extend over the next ten years.

Consumers in crisis are consumers under stress. Men and women react differently to stress. While men may seek out buddies in bars and at athletic games, women may go shopping. As we have uncovered in our research, emotional needs, not physical ones, drive a substantial amount of U.S. household spending. In the face of crisis, women who do the bulk of American households' shopping may spend more money on discretionary purchases to relieve stress and help them achieve emotional satisfaction. In our post-9/11 world, consumer marketers operating in every segment of the U.S. economy need to understand how consumers use shopping and buying things for emotional gratification and achieving psychological well-being. This emotionally driven consumption is the realm of discretionary spending.

DISCRETIONARY PRODUCT MATRIX DESCRIBES WHAT PEOPLE BUY THAT THEY DON'T NEED

Two lines or continuums can be used to define discretionary spending. The vertical continuum runs from necessities (e.g., food, clothing, and shelter) to the most extravagant purchases (i.e., things that you do not need). The horizontal continuum spans the range from physical, material comforts to emotional gratification resulting from buying something you don't need, but want. Within the matrix defined by these two continua reside the four different categories of discretionary purchases: utilitarian purchases, indulgences, lifestyle luxuries, and aspirational luxuries.

1. *Utilitarian purchases.* These are products that consumers do not strictly need but that will make their lives better in some measurable, physical way. Examples include products that help you clean better, save time, or do something you are otherwise not able to do, such as blenders, rotisserie ovens, bread machines, food proces-

sors, microwave ovens, water purifiers, and so forth. Focus is on the practical.

2. *Indulgences.* These include life's little luxuries that you can indulge in without guilt and cost pocket change to buy. Gratification is primarily emotional. Examples include candles, lotions and potions to pamper yourself in the bath, cosmetics, costume jewelry, contemporary collectibles and figurines, gourmet chocolates, fresh flowers, perfume, entertainment products, games, videos, books, and crafts and hobbies.

3. *Lifestyle luxuries.* Lifestyle luxuries offer utility and usefulness, along with the prestige, image, and superior quality conferred by the brand. Practical luxuries include automobiles (e.g., Mercedes, BMW); designer clothes (e.g., Gucci, Chanel); decorator furniture; watches (e.g., Rolex); gourmet appliances (e.g., Jenn-Air); and fine tabletop items (e.g., Reidel, Waterford, and Wedgwood).

4. *Aspirational luxuries.* Along with indulgences, aspirational luxuries satisfy primarily emotional needs. Through their purchases, consumers can express themselves, their value systems, their interests, and their passions. The satisfaction derived is primarily emotional, rather than practical, for example, when buying original art, antiques and vintage collectibles, boats and yachts, and fine jewelry.

This discretionary products matrix, shown in Figure 3.1, universally describes discretionary spending for American consumers at every income

FIGURE 3.1

Discretionary Products Matrix

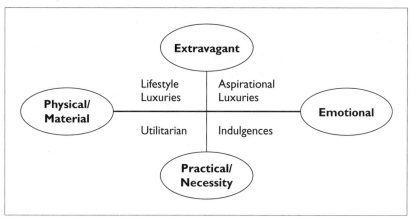

level and life stage. Yet points along the continuum are established by an individual's unique and personal value system—what one holds dear, what can easily be done without, what is affordable, and what one is willing to make sacrifices to attain. The continuum that defines what is a necessity and what is a frivolous expense is fluid, yet distinct, for each individual and different at each life stage as the person evolves and changes.

VALUES GOVERN CONSUMER SPENDING

What one person calls a lifestyle luxury another might call a utilitarian purchase. What may be an indulgence for one is an aspirational luxury for someone else. Where a particular purchase fits in the discretionary product matrix is dependent upon many variables, not the least of which are income, life stage, age, gender, and where the consumer lives. Even more individualistic is the individual's value system, passion, and identity.

An automobile purchase is highly dependent upon demographic factors. For example, if a person lives in a rural area, owning a car may be an absolute necessity, whereas for the city dweller well served by modern mass-transit systems, a car probably falls into the discretionary realm. Discretion also plays a role in what type of car to buy. Do you buy a new car or a used car? Do you buy a sedan, wagon, two-door, four-door, SUV, pickup truck, or four-wheel drive? Do you buy a Ford, Lincoln, Chevrolet, Cadillac, Honda, Lexus, Mercedes, Land Rover, or BMW? Who you are; where you live; your age, gender, and income; whether you have children; and what your friends drive all play a role in the decision that goes into purchasing a car.

Beyond demographics, a person's value system influences purchase decisions, as this respondent describes: "I don't need a Mercedes. I think a Mercedes is more than you need to get you from one place to another. It's about our belief system, which we talk about with our kids. We have tension there. On the one hand, we are embarrassed by what we have compared to some of our friends. On the other, some of my kids' friends get something and our kids come home and say, 'Why can't we get this?' That brand [Mercedes] is not me. I don't have that lifestyle. Some people do, but I don't."

A person's value system influences purchase decisions.

Let's look more closely at how a consumer's value system, her individualized judgment, and her self-identity influence her perception of her own discretionary spending.

UTILITARIAN PURCHASES ARE DISTINGUISHED BY USEFULNESS

In the matrix, utilitarian purchases are high in physical gratification and low in extravagance. These extras in life offer some materially measurable benefit or improvement to the consumer. Functionality and practicality play an essential part, usually allowing the consumer to do something that could not be done before. Implicit in the definition of the discretionary utilitarian purchase is the concept of a trade-up from the necessary to the improved, more highly functioning utilitarian item. One respondent expressed it this way: "My latest discretionary purchase was a steam vacuum cleaner. I didn't strictly need it, but I wasn't spoiling myself in buying it. It cost a good amount of money, but I will use it. And it will save in the long run because I don't have to call someone to come into my house and clean the carpets."

Consumers say they achieve a feeling of well-being from the purchase of these life-enhancing objects. Call it empowered ownership. As compared with buying a service to perform a similar function—say a carpet cleaning business to steam the carpets—consumers prefer ownership of the means or the tools (e.g., the steam vacuum) that will allow them to achieve their goal. Here is how one consumer explained her purchase decisions: "Products are easier and more convenient than services. Services require another person and are not so readily affordable. Once you do services, they are gone. Products last and last, and you don't have to depend on another person to get satisfaction from them. Product gives immediate satisfaction. And you can't really measure the quality of services. If you pay double for a haircut, do you really get double the quality? Service is less consistent."

Being able to "do it yourself" is a powerful motivator in the purchase of a utilitarian product. Suddenly you can achieve things you never could achieve before. You are more accomplished, more productive, and have more time and money to spend on other things. Your spouse, children, friends, and neighbors will admire you. You will achieve a new sense of self-fulfillment, confidence, and self-actualization. In other words, you'll be a winner.

Let's look more closely at how Ronco Inventions sells its rotisserie machine using a 30-minute infomercial. It is brilliant marketing because when you acquire the rotisserie machine, you get so much more than a machine that cooks good-tasting and healthful chicken. You become more in the know, more capable, and more resourceful—a "superior" human being.

Go beyond product features and benefits to life-transforming attributes. Create fantasies and show how the product fulfills them.

Sell More Utilitarian Products

Many products are sold solely on product features (e.g., this blender blends better than the other blender) and benefits (e.g., if you use this blender, you will be able to prepare dinner faster). For the past several decades, marketers and advertising practitioners have been banging the drum about focusing on benefits as the key to unlock consumers' wallets. However, benefits as they are presented today do not go nearly far enough. Perhaps we marketers have gotten lazy and have not pushed ourselves far enough in discovering new and creative benefits our products can provide. On the other hand, perhaps the product benefits can never go far enough, because benefits remain strongly left-brain oriented (e.g., saves time, saves money).

G*etting* **I***t* **R***ight*

RONCO INVENTIONS
Life Transformations through a Small Kitchen Appliance

Ron Popeil, founder of Ronco Inventions, has been called the "salesman of the century," and a study of his latest infomercial for the Showtime Rotisserie Grill is clear proof why. Working without an apparent script, Ron presents his Showtime Grill as a kitchen appliance described by one owner in the infomercial audience as a rotisserie that "has changed my life."

The infomercial is a tutorial in marketing and selling utilitarian products that nobody really needs. Through a simple presentation of information, supported with demonstrations and testimonials from audience members, Ron repeatedly drives home his message that owning the Showtime Grill will truly transform your life, not just the way you cook chicken. He breaks down the product-positioning message into a few essential components: easy to use, wonderful food, and high quality. His infomercial cohost reinforces the message, and his audience members, including regular people and professional chefs, underscore the same

essential message. Through this presentation, the viewer sees and believes how everyone in the audience has changed their lives through the purchase and use of the Showtime Grill. It is a magnificent job of showing how a simple kitchen appliance can transform people's lives.

The positioning strategy for the grill combines product features with product benefits. However, what sells the grill is the life-transforming value the grill bestows on the owner, not features or benefits.

According to our research, people craft fantasies—sometimes very elaborate ones—about their purchases. They know what their purchases will feel like, what they will look like, how the acquisition of particular products will transform their lives and make them better, more successful, happier, more fulfilled people. That is what the anticipation cycle

> Fantasies about how the product will fill a missing aspect of one's life fire the imagination.

that precedes buying is all about. Fantasies about how the product will fill a missing aspect of one's life fire the imagination. This builds stress—positive healthy stress—which is finally resolved in the act of purchase and initial excitement created by the acquisition. Then the cycle begins again, with new fantasies and new aspects of life that need satisfying. Figure 3.2 outlines the product positioning of the Showtime Rotisserie Grill.

A brand or product platform describing the features, benefits, and life-transforming values and experiences gives marketers and advertisers the insights needed to touch customers' hot buttons with powerful and compelling marketing messages. Ronco knows how to play to consumer fantasies. As mentioned earlier, the 30-minute infomercial for the Ronco Showtime Grill provides a tutorial in how to position a mundane small appliance that cooks chicken, the most mundane of meats, as a means to transform your life from drab, dull, and ordinary into one that is more fulfilling, rewarding, and satisfying. By spending only $99, in five easy payments, you suddenly become a better person, a better homemaker and wife, admired by your friends and family, and more fulfilled in all aspects of your life.

Eric Schulz, in his book *The Marketing Game*, makes the assumption: "Consumers are logical. If you say something that makes sense, they will believe you." WRONG! This is wishful thinking on the part of consumer-product marketing executives. On the one hand, consumers are not logical, and what they want, desire, and dream of owning is not logical. On the other hand, they need logical reasons to justify the purchase of products they don't need. But the prime motivator of desire is rooted in passion, not logic. That is why consumer marketers need to come back again and again to selling the "sizzle"—the wish fulfillment, the satisfaction of the consumer's fantasy.

I recently happened upon a Ralph Lauren commercial on television for its new Glamourous perfume. It shows actress Penelope Cruz and her date dressed in evening clothes walking in the rain to their car. As they dance and caress along the city streets, they are drenched in the rain, but clearly enjoying every minute of it. They are in public and for-

S *elling* **T** *ip*

Sell the sizzle.

mally dressed, but they act as if they are in the shower together getting ready for a night of steamy romance. The image is sexy and exciting, but I cannot escape the reality of this situation—which is a real turnoff—and

FIGURE 3.2

Showtime Rotisserie Grill Product Positioning

Features: Directly observable, physical characteristics
- Black and white
- Small size (demonstrated with comparison to toaster oven)
- Quality construction (demonstrated with hammer hit)
- Cooks all kinds of meats (e.g., chicken, turkey, ribs, pork loin, rib roast, steaks, fish, lamb)
- Under $100 retail
- Comes complete with accessories, recipes, instructional video, heating disk

Benefits: Attributes that are the result of consumers using the product
- Saves electricity (uses 1200 watts just like a hair dryer)
- Saves time (less time to cook meats; 12 minutes per pound compared with 20 minutes in oven)
- Cooks entire dinner with warming tray for two side dishes
- Best-tasting meats, crispy on outside, juicy on inside
- Fat melts out of meats to make them healthier
- Can have best-tasting meat simply and easily
- Cooks premium meats like a professional
- Easy cleanup
- Long lasting

Values and Experiences: Personal values, beliefs, feelings, and experiences that strongly motivate the consumer to buy
- "Hardworking people want to spend money on something that will last a lifetime." Grill becomes an essential part of your life conveying all its benefits (e.g., savings in energy; good, more healthful food; high quality; saved time) to the owner throughout his or her lifetime. Buy it and your life is instantly transformed.
- When you serve food from the grill, your guests will be amazed and give you "applause" (as the audience applauds Ron). They will admire you, believing you cook as well as a professional. You will be a cooking "hero."
- "This machine is my new husband." Ron's cohost makes this breathless statement that is not explained, but presented for the audience to figure out. To me it implies that this machine grills better than my husband, helps me in the kitchen more than my husband, does work for me unlike my husband, and gives unconditional support better than my husband. It's a weird statement, but it really underscores the message of life transformation through the appliance.
- Gives you a nonstress life. Easy cook-at-once meals without work; no need to be in the kitchen doing the hard work; you can be with guests. The grill does all the work for you. An audience member says, "So few products make your life more convenient." Several mentions are made of using the grill in RVs, suggesting that with this appliance you can achieve an RV-vacation lifestyle.

> The prime motivator of desire is rooted in passion, not logic.

get into the fantasy. Every rain shower that I have ever been in has given me a chill, even on the hottest summer day. Here is poor, underfed Penelope in a sleeveless evening gown walking completely unprotected in the pouring rain. Rain causes your makeup to run and your hair to become a mess, but Penelope's face is flawless and her hair, even soaking wet, looks great. Soaking wet clothes are literally a drag, but this couple is dancing around in the street. For me this ad pushes the sizzle envelope too far. A dark, dirty, smelly city street is not where I want to get caught in the rain in my evening clothes. In my fantasy, my date has an umbrella that he uses to sprint, alone, to the car, which he drives back for me.

Although the Glamourous ad failed to pull me in, water imagery is a recurring theme in advertising fantasy building. During focus groups where we studied consumers' motivations in buying things they don't need, participants were asked to clip ads and photographs from magazines that best exemplify products that transform their lives. They clipped pictures that talked deeply to them about their personal fantasies. Repeatedly, participants clipped images of water—bathtubs, whirlpools, pools, beaches, lakes—and most often these water images were linked with romance. They showed couples on a cruise ship, couples by the water, and couples in a hot tub. In addition to being linked with romance, water imagery is also evocative of purity, cleanliness, nature and natural beauty, relaxation, and adventure. Bathrooms and kitchens figure prominently in consumers' life-transforming fantasies, supporting the link between kitchen appliances and life enhancement. Bedroom pictures in ads offer consumers emotional succor. Outdoor scenes of lush backyards, mountains, valleys, and meadows promise a release from

---

S *elling* T *ip*

Fantasy branding can extend a franchise. At its root, consumer product branding is all about sparking a consumer fantasy. Branding that goes only as far as brand features and benefits will be relegated to the waste dump of consumer brands. Brands that have life and vibrancy, that really speak to the customer, do so on an emotional plane. Coke, Disney, Chanel, Calvin Klein—all truly great brands— have harnessed the left-brain power of features and benefits with the transforming magic of right-brain emotion to craft an identity, personality, and value system that consumers can really accept.

stress by returning to nature. You can sell the sizzle by presenting powerful emotional imagery that creates or extends a consumer's fantasy and the promise that the fantasy will be fulfilled by purchasing the featured product.

> Consumer product branding is all about sparking a consumer fantasy.

Even in the realm of utilitarian purchases, there is opportunity for marketers to take their products to a new level. The Rubbermaid brand comes immediately to mind as one that understands how to communicate with its target market at an emotional level, as well as on a product features and benefits level. Rubbermaid means household organization. Like "Cleanliness is next to Godliness," an organized house is the ultimate achievement for homeowners, whether their realm is the garage and basement, or the kitchen, closets, bedrooms, bathrooms, and everywhere else. Because I am not blessed with the ability to organize my home or office or anything tangible, I am a complete sucker for anything that I can buy that will turn me into an "organized" person. Buckets, baskets, shelves, drawers, and all kinds of organizers to hold things fill my house and office. The only problem for me is that once things are stored away, they are lost forever. So, I remain a disorganized, stack-them-in-a-pile type of person. However, I know in my heart that if I could only use all these wonderful Rubbermaid organizers and exercise organizational discipline, I would be transformed into a truly better, more fulfilled person who'd accomplish much more.

INDULGENCES ARE LIFE'S LITTLE LUXURIES BOUGHT WITHOUT GUILT

Offering high emotional gratification but being low on the extravagance scale, indulgences are described as "little" luxuries, something you can indulge in daily, without guilt or recrimination. One consumer, who collects, describes an indulgence this way: "Luxuries make me feel guilty. It's totally different to spend $25 to $50 on a 'Clark Gable' collector plate than to spend hundreds of dollars on a luxury. There is a difference in how much you spend." Another says: "An indulgence is something in excess of what you need, but not too much in excess." Unlike other discretionary purchases, which may demand more of a financial commitment, an indulgence is an everyday affair that involves spending only pocket change.

An indulgence pampers the individual. While it provides some physical satisfactions (e.g., features and benefits), its primary satisfaction is emotional. What kinds of products constitute an indulgence? Here are some examples taken from our research:

- "An expensive bottle of wine is an indulgence."
- "For me, candles are my indulgence."
- "Bath salts from the Dead Sea."
- "I buy lots of books. I have a friend who thinks my books are a luxury. She says, 'That's what a library card is for.' But they are my books. There is a thrill in acquiring them. I don't read all of them, but I think someday I will have time and will be able to."
- "Every week my husband buys new DVDs. He likes to say he has them."
- "I just spent $400 on plants for my front porch and the fence. I love showing off my garden."
- "I bought a bottle of perfume for $75. I'm a woman, I have to smell good."

G *etting* **I** *t* **R** *ight*

YANKEE CANDLE
Nobody holds a candle to Yankee.

Holding the number-one position in the premium candle segment of the $2.4 billion retail market for candles, Yankee Candle benefited from "exploding growth in the candle category from 1994 to 1999, but that is only part of Yankee Candle's success story," explains Craig Rydin, president and CEO of Yankee Candle.

Since its founding over 30 years ago, Yankee Candle has been able to execute a brand-building strategy that resonates with the consumers. "Consumers today are getting more 'home-centric,' and what is more central to the home than the warmth and comfort a fragranced candle represents," Rydin says. "We have built the brand around the importance of fragrance in the home." Joining Yankee Candle after serving as president of Godiva Chocolatier, Rydin is no stranger to building a brand around "affordable indulgences that give the consumer a feeling of being special."

Along with the allure, romance, and emotional appeal that Yankee's core fragranced-candle products represent, the company has built a business on a commitment to strong financial fundamentals and business execution. "Yankee manages three core channels of distribution: captive retail, traditional wholesale distribution, and consumer direct marketing through the Internet and catalogs. This gives us key advantages so that Yankee outperformed its competitive set in the very challenging macroeconomic environment it faced the fourth quarter of 2001," Rydin notes.

Key to building Yankee Candle's nationwide reputation as a premier candle brand is the company-owned chain of nearly 250 specialty retail stores. These stores, mostly mall based, are the "gold standard" for presenting the brand and the products to the consumer. "Our brand and its dominance [are] being driven by our captive-retail footprint," Rydin says. "Our strategy is not very different from many other national brands, like Godiva, that built an identity through multiple channels, especially captive retail."

The migration to company-owned-and-operated retail, while critical for the strength and continued growth of the brand, is a fairly recent development for the company. "Yankee Candle started in traditional wholesale distribution. Today we have some 13,000 stores that are our wholesale accounts," Rydin explains. "As we manage these two channels of distribution, the challenge is to present the same brand strategy in both places. We are moving toward a 'store-within-a-store' concept for our wholesale accounts. We want to present the essence of our brand consistently in our wholesale accounts as in our captive-retail stores. Communicating and building the brand is our priority."

The business of selling consumer indulgences has been good to Yankee Candle. Its business has more than quadrupled since 1996, rising from $115 million to $509 million in 2003, with significant growth tracked at the company's retail stores.

How will Yankee Candle continue its growth trajectory? "Home fragrance is what resonates with the consumer. Fragrance is the emotional bond that links Yankee Candle with our consumer and what brings them back again and again to our brand," Rydin says.

Items that exemplify the indulgence category include candles, higher-quality "lotions and potions," bath accessories, costume jewelry, collectibles, stuffed animals, toys and games, hobbies and crafts, sporting equipment, fresh flowers, gourmet foods, tabletop gifts, books, CDs, DVDs, and other entertainment products.

In the consumer's mind, indulgences, because they are not bought for functionality, always fall somewhere above utilitarian purchases, and below luxuries, which carry a heftier price tag. That's why we call indulgences "little" luxuries. They are those little purchases that give utmost gratification without guilt.

How much money people can spend without guilt varies from person to person and from item to item. For example, I feel guilty if I spend $300 on something for the home, such as a piece of furniture, a framed print (one of my weaknesses), or dinnerware (another weakness), because my husband views home-related purchases as decisions we should both make. On the other hand, I will spend $300 for a suit coat or blouse and skirt without thinking twice, not feeling guilty and never having to worry about spousal "approval." Yet I hesitate to spend $300 on a piece of jewelry, but it won't necessarily stop me if I have a "need" for it, such as buying a fabulous pin to accessorize the new $300 jacket I just bought. For another person, my $300 indulgence expenditure might be $30 or $3,000. The absolute dollar value is a function of income level and demographics, but that's not all. It is linked intimately to individual passion, value, and personal tastes for specific products. Because it is so highly individualized, consumer passion for indulgences needs to be carefully researched through psychographic analysis.

Discover the Underlying Passion That Drives Indulgence Purchases

Unlike demographic research, which focuses on quantifiable facts about consumers, such as income levels, marital status, household composition, age, and gender, psychographic studies survey motivations, drives, and passions. When you undertake a psychographic market study, you try to quantify and document the inner workings of the consumer's mind and heart. In effect, you turn the unspoken, unrealized, unconscious, imaginative right-brain drive for a product into data that you can analyze with the business executive's left-brained mentality.

> Spending is linked intimately to individual passion, value, and personal tastes for specific products.

Sounds like so much hocus-pocus? Maybe, but psychographic market research helps uncover the interior emotional life of the consumer and can ultimately make sense of it so that marketing strategies can be devised, products competitively positioned, and advertising messages persuasively crafted. Psychographic studies often start with focus groups. Selected for these groups are consumers who have an interest in, or proven history of, buying a particular product. They are usually paid a fee for two hours of their time to sit around a table and talk about themselves and their desire for the product. A professional moderator keeps a focus group from descending into chaos and getting out of "focus." The moderator asks the right questions, probes further when a particular response suggests that more lies beneath the surface, and manages dichotomous voices who try to dominate the group or get off subject. These groups generate many pages of thorough, professionally written analysis of the major findings. We call them hypotheses theories to be tested in subsequent quantitative numbers-oriented research. Just as important are verbatim quotes from consumers about what does and doesn't excite them about the product in question.

Then comes the fun part where the hypotheses from the focus groups are tested and the dominating psychographic characteristics of the consumer target market are measured and quantified. Taking the exact same phrases and wording used by the consumers, the market researcher goes to the field with a questionnaire to which hundreds, even thousands of potential consumers can respond. A battery of attitudinal statements is presented to the target market asking them to what extent they agree or disagree with the statement. With a sufficient number of respondents (usually somewhere between 200 and 2,000), the results of the attitudinal questions can be grouped and classified according to the similarities or dissimilarities of responses. Using a cluster analysis program, market researchers can segment the target market into discreet groups or clusters based upon their attitudes, motivations, feelings, and emotions about the particular product. What is the right number of clusters? There is not a right or wrong number, but cognitive research has shown that the human mind is incapable of simultaneously maintaining a list of more than nine individual items—thus our seven-digit telephone numbers. Moreover, if you are like me, you are seriously challenged with keeping a list of seven in mind at one time. In most psychographic studies I conduct, a four- to five-cluster solution is best. On a few occasions, I have found only a single cluster, which means that the target market is remarkably homogeneous in its attitude and feelings about the product. In others, I have gone to seven distinctly defined market segments.

Besides discovering the core motivations and emotions that drive different types of consumers to specific products, there are usually demographic differences among the clusters as well. These demographic differences provide marketers with measurable market segments to target through advertising-media selection.

CONSUMER MOTIVATION STUDY

To better understand why people buy things they don't need, Unity Marketing conducted a psychographic study of the typical American consumer. Using a battery of attitudinal statements centering on the emotional gratification of buying things they don't need, we asked respondents how much they agreed or disagreed with each statement. Using a cluster analysis program, five segments, or clusters, emerge when examining the attitudes and motivations that drive consumers to purchase these discretionary items, as shown in Figures 3.3 and 3.4. Figure 3.5 outlines how attitudes vary among the different segments.

Now let's look more closely at the distinguishing characteristics.

FIGURE 3.3
Discretionary Purchasers Segmentation Analysis

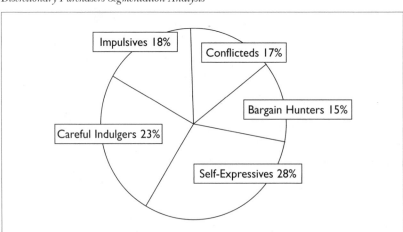

Source: Unity Marketing, 2001

FIGURE 3.4

A Quick Guide to the Five Segments of Discretionary Consumers

1. *Self-Expressives.* These consumers use their consumption as a means of self-expression, reaffirming their personal identity to themselves and declaring it symbolically to others. Their purchases satisfy their desires and fantasies. They are highly involved in purchasing goods that enrich, enhance, or improve the quality of their lives. Self-Expressives comprise the largest market segment, accounting for about 28 percent of all discretionary income consumers.

2. *Careful Indulgers.* These consumers share many similarities with Self-Expressives, but exhibit a more practical, reasoned approach to their purchases of "indulgences." They are less "driven" to make discretionary purchases and more "reasoned" in their purchases. Among all groups, these consumers rank two motivators highest: replacing an existing item and planned purchase. Unlike Self-Expressives, the Careful Indulgers gain less emotional satisfaction in making these purchases and are far less likely to make impulse purchases. Careful Indulgers are about 23 percent of all discretionary income consumers.

3. *Impulsives.* These consumers buy discretionary purchases to indulge themselves on the spur of the moment. They purchase these products for the sheer joy and pleasure the purchases bring. Their thrill is in buying products that they desire. Unlike Self-Expressives and Careful Indulgers, Impulsives are not motivated by the need to express themselves, their personalities, and value systems in the purchases they make. For them, consuming and buying is the end in itself. Impulsives represent about 18 percent of discretionary income consumers.

4. *Conflicteds.* Just as their segment name implies, these consumers feel conflicted about satisfying their desire for discretionary products. They don't see their consumer behavior as an expressive outlet, yet they desire to buy these products. However, they have mixed feelings about making such "unnecessary" purchases and so tend to feel guilty after buying or have a feeling of letdown once they make a purchase. They don't obtain the same level of pleasure or emotional enjoyment from their consumption that other segments do. Conflicteds comprise about 17 percent of the total market.

5. *Bargain Hunters.* These consumers are the least highly involved consumers of discretionary items. Compared with all the other segments, they derive the least amount of pleasure and emotional gratification from buying. They are also the least likely of all segments to make an impulse purchase, and they are the least likely to be motivated by desire to improve the quality of life. They look for bargains when they shop and tend to carefully evaluate the pluses and minuses before making a purchase decision. Bargain Hunters comprise the smallest market segment, only about 15 percent of the market.

FIGURE 3.5
Differing Attitudes among Segments

	BARGAIN HUNTER	SELF-EXPRESSIVE	CAREFUL INDULGER	IMPULSIVE	CONFLICTED
You get a feeling of personal satisfaction when you make a discretionary purchase.	Disagree	Strongly Agree	Agree	Agree	Agree
Before you make a discretionary purchase, you spend time anticipating the purchase and evaluating the pros and cons.	Agree	Agree	Agree	Disagree	Agree
You often make a discretionary purchase on the spur of the moment.	Disagree	Agree	Disagree	Agree	Agree
You make discretionary purchases because they will make your life more pleasant and satisfying.	Disagree	Strongly Agree	Agree	Agree	Agree
You get a thrill out of buying something special that you don't need but desire.	Disagree	Agree	Disagree	Agree	Neutral
You feel guilty after you make a discretionary purchase.	Disagree	Disagree	Disagree	Disagree	Neutral
After you make a discretionary purchase, you feel a letdown when you get it home.	Disagree	Disagree	Disagree	Disagree	Disagree
You express different sides of your personality with the discretionary purchases that you make.	Disagree	Strongly Agree	Agree	Agree	Agree

Statement					
The discretionary items that you purchase set you apart from your neighbors and friends and make you unique.	Disagree	Disagree	Disagree	Strongly Agree	Strongly Disagree
It is more satisfying when you have to search to find a discretionary item that is very special to buy.	Disagree	Neutral	Agree	Strongly Agree	Disagree
The discretionary items you buy for yourself and your home make your life more meaningful.	Neutral	Neutral	Agree	Agree	Strongly Disagree
The discretionary items that you buy help you fulfill your longings.	Disagree	Neutral	Neutral	Strongly Agree	Strongly Disagree
You often purchase a discretionary item because it has a symbolic meaning or links with memories of the past.	Neutral	Disagree	Disagree	Agree	Disagree
You seek instant gratification through discretionary purchases.	Disagree	Agree	Disagree	Agree	Disagree
You look for bargains and sales when purchasing discretionary items.	Agree	Agree	Agree	Agree	Agree
You spend more money on discretionary items today than you did in the early 1990s.	Disagree	Agree	Agree	Strongly Agree	Disagree
Your family, coworkers, and friends influence you in making discretionary purchases.	Neutral	Disagree	Disagree	Neutral	Disagree

Self-Expressives: Consuming as a Creative Outlet

Self-Expressives use their consumption as a means of self-expression, reaffirming their personal identity to themselves and declaring it visually to others. Their purchases satisfy their desires and fantasies. They are highly involved in purchasing goods that enrich, enhance, or improve the quality of their lives. They tend to imbue the items they buy with special meaning and may even look at some favorite items like "members of the family."

The Self-Expressive type of consumer uses shopping and personal consumption as a creative outlet. The act of consuming is highly emotional. Self-Expressives look to their discretionary purchases to satisfy their emotional needs.

Because they seek to express themselves through their consumption and the purchases they make, they are highly idiosyncratic in their purchases. That is, what turns on one self-expressive individual may be very different from what turns on another. However, some common threads emerge in the purchase patterns of these highly individualistic consumers.

They are driven by a desire to "fit in" with their aspirational group. While they are individualistic, they don't want to venture too far afield from their peer group. For example, Self-Expressives will strictly avoid painting their houses the same shade of blue as their neighbor's, yet certainly won't paint their homes a deep purple or shocking pink. Rather, they will seek to find a special shade of blue that allows them to express their individuality within the context of what is "acceptable," but not exactly like everybody else's.

With their strong emotional drive to consume, Self-Expressives respond sentimentally to items with a nostalgia appeal that takes them back to a "golden age," usually back to their youth. Any number of social trends point to this drive for nostalgia, including the collecting boom in toys, dolls, and games from the 1950s and 1960s; the explosion of online auctions, typified by eBay; and the PT Cruiser from Chrysler. Seeking out a "golden age" is a major motivator for Self-Expressives and a key to understanding their form of consumption as an outlet for personal identity and self-expression.

Demographic characteristics of Self-Expressives. This is the largest market segment. It is composed of equal shares of baby boomers, the generation born between 1946 and 1964 (38 percent), and GenXers and their younger counterparts (38 percent), all born in 1965 or later.

About one-fourth of the segment was born before 1946, making them members of the World War II and the swing generations.

While just over half of Self-Expressives are married, one-fourth are single, never married, and 10 percent are divorced.

> The Self-Expressive type of consumer uses shopping and personal consumption as a creative outlet.

Women are more highly represented than men in this segment. Compared with the other segments, the Self-Expressives are more ethnically diverse. All income levels are represented in this segment, although only about 37 percent of Self-Expressives report an income of $50,000 or more. While this consumer segment is not the most affluent, the consumers in this segment spend the highest percentage of their income on discretionary purchases (19.5 percent).

Self-Expressives agree most strongly with these statements:

- You get a feeling of personal satisfaction when you make a discretionary purchase for yourself or your household.
- You make discretionary purchases because they will make your life more pleasant and satisfying.
- You express different sides of your personality with the discretionary purchases that you make.
- The discretionary items that you purchase set you apart from your neighbors and friends and make you unique. (Boomers and older consumers don't agree, while GenXers and younger Self-Expressives do.)
- It is more satisfying when you have to search to find a discretionary item that is very special to buy.
- The discretionary items you buy for yourself and your home make your life more meaningful.
- The discretionary items you buy help you fulfill your longings.
- You spend more money on discretionary items today than you did in the early 1990s.

Most active buyers. Trend Watch: Self-Expressive consumers will continue to be the most active buying segment in the future. They deprive themselves of nothing, and while the potential impact of an economic downturn cannot be anticipated, these consumers give signs of not letting something as "insignificant" as not having money keep them from pursuing their consuming passions. Consumer product companies should target this segment by aligning their products with these youthful, self-expressive, and self-indulgent consumers.

Careful Indulgers: Thoughtful Pleasure-Buying

Careful Indulgers share many similarities with Self-Expressives, but exhibit a more practical and reasoned approach to their purchases of "indulgences." They are less "driven" to make discretionary purchases and more "reasoned" in their purchases. These consumers are more likely to make discretionary purchases due to rational motivators, such as to replace a worn-out item or to make a planned purchase. Unlike Self-Expressives, Careful Indulgers gain less emotional satisfaction in making these purchases and are far less likely to make impulse purchases.

They tend to see themselves as similar to their peers and, unlike the Self-Expressives, do not feel the need to declare their identity through their consumption. They are unlikely to ascribe special meaning to the items they buy or to animate them in their imaginations.

They enjoy the "hunt" to find a desirable item. They are not inclined toward making spur-of-the-moment decisions and impulsive purchases. If they find something they want, they are likely to go home and think about it and discuss it with their significant others before making the purchase.

Items, things, consumables do not hold the same meaning for Careful Indulgers that they do for the Self-Expressives. They look on things as things, not symbolic representations of their personality and value system.

Demographic characteristics of Careful Indulgers. Careful Indulgers are more likely to be baby boomers and have moderate household incomes under $50,000. They are more likely to be married than Self-Expressives. Women are also slightly more represented among Careful Indulgers (53 percent) than men (47 percent).

Careful Indulgers are more likely than any other segment to live in two-person households and less likely to have children living in the home. They spend, on average, about 13.4 percent of income on indulgent purchases.

While people in this segment are more reasoned in their approach to indulgence purchases, they are fairly active buyers in most categories. They tend to look at their purchases from a more practical orientation, but are hesitant to deny themselves these indulgences.

Impulsives: See It; Like It; Buy It

Impulsives buy indulgent discretionary purchases on the spur of the moment. They purchase these products for the sheer joy and pleasure the purchase brings. Their thrill is in buying products that they desire. Unlike Self-Expressives, Impulsives are not particularly motivated by the need to express themselves, their personalities, and their value systems in the purchases they make. For them, consuming and buying is the end in itself.

> Impulsives are driven much more by the need to acquire and keep acquiring new things.

As big spenders and active purchasers in the discretionary product categories, these consumers differ from the Self-Expressives mainly because they don't ascribe a higher meaning or value in their consuming behavior. Things do not become symbols of one's identity. In fact, once these indulgent consumers get their purchases home, they are likely to be lost or forgotten. These consumers are very active buyers, but driven to purchase by what strikes their fancy at the moment, not like Self-Expressives who look for more "meaning" in their purchases. While the Self-Expressives will treasure their things, the Impulsives are driven much more by the need to acquire and keep acquiring new things.

Demographic characteristics of Impulsives. Impulsives are represented equally by boomers and GenXers, at 41 percent for each group. While represented among all income levels, the Impulsives are most likely to have incomes in the $35,000 to $49,999 range.

Men are slightly more likely to be an Impulsive type of consumer. Compared with the other consumer segments, Impulsives are more likely to be single, never married. Impulsives, along with Self-Expressives, spend the highest percentage of household income on discretionary products (19.3 percent).

Impulsives agree most strongly with these statements:

- You often make a discretionary purchase on the spur of the moment.
- You spend more money on discretionary items today than you did in the early 1990s.

Conflicteds: Should I, Shouldn't I?

These consumers feel conflicted about satisfying their desire for products they don't need. They don't see their consumer behavior as an expressive outlet, yet they desire to buy these products. However, they have mixed feelings about making such "unnecessary" purchases and so they may tend to feel guilty after buying. They do not obtain the same level of pleasure or emotional satisfaction from their consumption that other segments do, largely because they suffer so much internal conflict before the purchase.

For Conflicteds, the educational aspect of their discretionary purchases is of prime importance, so they are more likely to buy computers, books, and other educationally oriented products. Perhaps owing in some small part to their feeling of conflict in their consuming behavior, they highly value stress relief and relaxation in the discretionary purchases they make.

Demographic characteristics of Conflicteds. Conflicteds are more likely than any other segment to have a household income under $35,000. Nearly half (46 percent) of Conflicteds are boomers. They spend about 12.7 percent of their income on discretionary purchases.

This is the segment with the highest incidence of women and divorced or separated individuals. Forty-six percent have children in the home, the highest of any group. With this incidence of children, it is easy to see where the "conflict" in making indulgent purchases comes from.

Bargain Hunters: Is It on Sale?

If Self-Expressives are the most highly involved consumers of discretionary items, Bargain Hunters are the least. Compared with all other segments, they derive the least amount of pleasure and emotional gratification from buying. They are also the least likely of all segments to make an impulse purchase. Of all segments, they are the least motivated by the desire to improve the quality of life. They look for bargains when they shop and tend to evaluate carefully the pluses and minuses before making a purchase decision. Buying things they do not need just doesn't turn them on.

Demographic characteristics of Bargain Hunters. Men dominate this segment, with women representing only 41 percent of the total segment. Compared with other segments, Bargain Hunters have a higher incidence of WWII and swing generation consumers (35 percent). They are not the lowest income segment. Rather, the highest distribution in this segment falls in the $50,000 to $74,999 income range. Given their older demographics, they are the segment least likely to have children in the home. They spend the lowest percentage of income on discretionary purchases (10.5 percent).

WITH INDULGENCES, MORE IS BETTER!

It is probably more than coincidence that the United States is both the world's wealthiest country and the fattest. This country is headed for a public health crisis of direst proportions with nearly 40 million Americans certifiably obese. The nation's obesity rate stood at 19.8 percent in 2000, up from a 12 percent rate in 1991. Obesity, defined as a body-mass index of 30 or more, is linked to diabetes. Further, obesity-related diseases are second only to smoking as the leading cause of premature deaths. Today more than one-half of Americans (56.4 percent) are overweight (body-mass index of at least 25), compared with 45 percent in 1991. That leaves a "slim" minority of Americans who have a healthy weight, eat a moderate diet, and get adequate exercise.

In some consumer circles, immoderation in spending is linked to immoderation in eating. After all, the same emotional needs drive many consumers to both spend too much and eat too much. There is a reason that gluttony is one of the seven deadly sins, and some American consumers are as guilty of voracious shopping as they are of gluttonous eating.

There already is enough literature available about American consumers' propensity to overspend. John De Graaf's *Affluenza: The All-Consuming Epidemic*, presented as a PBS special along with a published companion book, is one of the best and most damning. A warning: As marketers, we who want to capture a greater share of consumer spending, even overspending, need to be aware of the negative side of emotional spending and how some consumers gluttonously shop and buy.

As a "consumer in training" under the tutelage of my mother, I learned that it was better to spend money on one very-good-quality item that would last than to spend the same amount on many items of lesser quality. Thus, I have a propensity to buy classic-tailored clothes in neutral colors that I can wear for at least several seasons. However, when consumers buy indulgences, those early lessons about putting quality above quantity just don't apply. Because people buy indulgences primarily for immediate emotional gratification, fineness and high quality are not an essential issue. An indulgence isn't to be enjoyed for long or forever. Its satisfactions are transitory. Indulgences need only provide satisfaction for the moment.

Because indulgences are for the here and now, the more you buy, the better, or so the thinking goes among some consumers. That is one reason why "buy two, get one free" and "buy one get the next for half-price" offers

> Because indulgences are for the here and now, the more you buy, the better.

are so incredibly compelling for indulgence-type items. Because indulgences are often spur-of-the-moment purchases, a dynamite sale or special offer is overwhelmingly compelling to get consumers to open their wallets and buy. One focus group respondent explains it this way: "I buy clothes all the time and shoes. I love shoes and buy shoes I don't need. I am in Payless twice a week buying shoes I don't need. I spend $30 a month on shoes. I can buy more shoes at Payless than anywhere. If I see a sale—buy one, get one half off—I HAVE to go in. I'm a real bargain shopper."

The cosmetic companies have learned the drawing power of sampling as a marketing strategy that gives more to the consumer. Twice a year, cosmetic companies package their samples into gift cases and make a big deal out of their gift-with-purchase sales. How many of these cosmetic companies' regular, dedicated shoppers hold off buying until the gift-with-purchase sale? The shoppers don't need the gifts that are offered. Many times they don't even use the colors and products included. But that special free gift makes them feel like a "winner." They got something extra. They got more than they paid for. That is marketing magic and a promotional strategy that should be borrowed by many indulgence product marketers.

In other words, in marketing indulgence-type products, quality takes a back seat to quantity, given the fleeting nature of emotional enjoyment. Further, for many of these products, such as flowers, candles, bath-and-body lotions and potions, greeting cards, and collectibles, it may be hard to discern differences in quality between one product and another. That may be why some marketers that have attempted to move certain indulgence products up-market to the luxury realm have been less than successful in their attempts. For example, in today's market, while there are premium brands, no brand of true luxury candles exists. Perhaps there never will be because of the consumable nature of the product and consumers' inability to distinguish quality differences between brands.

LIFESTYLE AND ASPIRATIONAL LUXURIES LET YOU LIVE THE LIFE OF THE RICH AND FAMOUS

We define the third and fourth sectors in the discretionary product matrix as lifestyle luxuries and aspirational luxuries. Lifestyle luxuries are those luxury goods that, while they are considered a luxury, also offer a practical usefulness or utility for the consumer. Luxury cars, watches, china, furniture, and designer clothes are all lifestyle luxuries that serve a practical purpose. By comparison, aspirational luxuries, rather than providing some practical use, give primarily emotional satisfaction. Aspirational luxuries include such purchases as original art, antiques and vintage collectibles, boats and yachts, and fine jewelry. But whether the consumer is purchasing a lifestyle or aspirational luxury product, the drives and motivations are the same: They are looking for the "ultimate" in the luxury product that they buy.

So what does "luxury good" really mean? The *New Oxford American Dictionary* defines *luxury* as:

> The state of great comfort and extravagant living; an inessential, desirable item that is expensive or difficult to obtain.

A focus group respondent explained it this way: "A luxury is more than extra. It's more, more." The word *luxury* comes from the Latin "luxuria" which means "excess." Charles J. Reid, research associate in law and history at Emory University, defines luxury goods: "The operational definition of a luxury good is a good 95 percent of which is accessible to only 5 percent of the population." Jeremy Sampson, managing director of Interbrand Sampson, sees a luxury this way: "To some, it's an object of desire, sometimes aspirational, sometimes almost lust. It will be financially expensive, perhaps self-indulgent, and certainly not indispensable. It says: 'I've done it,' but that's crass. Sometimes it's a physical statement, as with a luxury car or an exquisite watch, pen, or piece of jewelery. Or as the Richemont annual report defines it: 'A luxury product is both an object and a catalyst for thought . . . the aim of a luxury brand is to awaken desire and pleasure.'"

While what is defined as a luxury good is fluid over time and may differ depending on the socioeconomic level, the best definition of a luxury good in contemporary America is "brand" and its positioning as the "best of the best." The brand identifies the product as a luxury.

Luxuries as Brands

Women's Wear Daily recently reported its fifth annual consumer survey of luxury fashion brands. The survey measured consumers' familiarity with the brand, their perception of the brand as a "luxury" brand, their purchase incidence, and what luxury fashion brand they would buy if money were no object. The top five luxury fashion brands according to *Women's*

> The word *luxury* comes from the Latin "luxuria" which means "excess."

Wear Daily are Rolex, Tiffany, Cartier, Versace, and Giorgio Armani. Lifestyle luxuries, those luxuries that offer some functional, practical use are almost always linked with a brand. In effect, the brand acts like the *Good Housekeeping* "Seal of Approval" telling us that this functionally practical product is elevated above its more ordinary competitors. A luxury Rolex watch tells time, as does a Timex, but it does it with much more style and cachet. The brand, Rolex, is the pedigree saying this watch—this brand—is better than all the rest.

Looking beyond the fashion arena, there are luxury brands in many different categories of discretionary purchases, although fashion is one of the fields where luxury brands predominate. In the decade of the 1990s, investing in luxury brands was good business, as consumers yearned for these visible status symbols that proclaimed their wealth, status, and good taste. From 1999 to 2000, the leading luxury brands averaged a growth rate reaching 17 percent (as shown in Figure 3.6), dynamic growth for any product category. After the 9/11 terrorist attack, luxury brand growth is settling down to more normal levels, as consumers shy away from purchases that are perceived as "too extravagant" in the new economy. But what is perceived as too extravagant varies from consumer to consumer, so we may well find the typical Rolex shopper trading down to a Movado, or the Louis Vuitton handbag buyer stepping back to Coach. They still are shopping in the luxury arena; they are just pulling back from the more extravagant examples.

While luxury brands face new marketing challenges in the aftermath of September 11, these brands are extremely hard to "kill off." Why? Because they have taken so many years to foster and build their reputation. Few luxury brands are created overnight. Rather, many brands go back more than a hundred years, like Cartier, founded in 1847, Tiffany dating from 1837, Rolex from 1908, Gucci from 1923. The closest we come to "instant" luxury brands is in the fashion arena. Contemporary designers, such as Donna Karan, Ralph Lauren, and Tommy Hilfiger to name a few, have crafted a luxury image through highly exclusive distribution, couture prices, fashion-forward but not jarring designs, and carefully selected licensing partnerships.

> Owners of luxury brands must walk a tight line between extending their brand too far into too many product categories and controlling it so tightly that revenue and brand-building potential are too restricted.

Licensing and its role in propagating a brand image is one of those business secrets most companies would rather keep hidden from their consuming public. Licensing is a legal agreement that allows one company to

FIGURE 3.6

Luxury Marketers Revenue 2000–2002 (in millions)

	'00	% CHG '00-'99	'01	% CHG '01-'00	'02	% CHG '01-'02
Pinault-Printemps-Redoute	$23,308.0	22.4	$24,623.9	5.6	$22,727.9	–7.7
Christian Dior	11,174.0	26.7	11,131.8	–0.4	13,798.0	24.0
LVMH	10,909.0	27.0	10,900.0	–0.1	11,313.6	3.8
Richemont**	2,792.3		3,237.5	15.9	3,358.2	3.7
Swatch	2,563.3	12.5	2,419.5	–5.6	2,446.1	1.1
Luxottica Group	2,268.9	20.2	2,731.8	20.4	2,959.9	8.3
Gucci*	2,258.5	82.7	2,285.0	1.2	2,285.0	1.2
Polo Ralph Lauren*	1,982.4	1.7	2,363.7	19.2	2,439.3	3.2
Tommy Hilfiger*	1,880.9	4.9	1,876.7	–0.2	1,876.7	0.2
Tiffany & Co*	1,668.1	14.1	1,606.5	–3.7	1,706.6	6.2
Prada/I Pellettieri d'Italia**			1,553.6	1.4	1,635.0	6.7
Hermes	1,090.9	16.8	1,086.8	–0.4	1,100.9	1.3
Waterford Wedgwood	1,021.3	15.1	902.0	–11.7		
Armani	973.6	11.6	1,126.7	15.7	1,362.5	21.0
Bulgari	636.6	17.9	678.6	6.6	810.9	19.0
Coach	548.9	8.1	616.1	12.2	719.4	16.8
Burberry Ltd.**			605.9		711.7	17.5
IT Holdings/ Ittierre	432.9	12.9	466.5	7.8	580.8	24.5
Versace	425.5	1.5	450.0	5.8		
Movado*	320.8	8.7	299.7	–6.6	300.1	1.0
Avg	3,680.9	17.9	3,548.1	4.4	4,007.4	8.4

* Fiscal year ends early in year so sales reported represent sales year
** Previous year unavailable

"borrow" the brand name, its logos, its image, and its reputation, and put it on the borrowing company's products. Owners of luxury brands must walk a tight line between extending their brand too far into too many product categories and controlling it so tightly that revenue and brand-building potential are too restricted. On the surface, licensing looks like an easy way to cash in on the value of the brand without risking anything. After all, the licensor picks up the tab and pays royalties and minimums to boot.

Over the years, companies such as Christian Dior and Oscar de la Renta have discovered the hazards of extending their brands too far. Consequently, they responded by cutting way back on their licenses. Free use of licensing inevitably cheapens the brand and threatens its exclusivity. That is why Calvin Klein recently fought its jeans' licensee, Warnaco, so hard. Calvin Klein claimed Warnaco violated its licensing agreement by distributing the Calvin Klein jeans through discount outlets. For a luxury brand, that will never do! Yet, luxury brands are remarkably resilient. They do not die easily, especially those enduring brands whose identity has been crafted over many decades, even centuries. Thus, previously overlicensed brands such as Christian Dior can pick themselves up, dust themselves off, and continue moving on in the luxury arena, even after a brief foray into the mass market. On the other hand, the more instant luxury brands, such as contemporary fashion brands, are more vulnerable to losing their cachet because they haven't forged a solid reputation based upon many years of diligent brand management.

Consumers Choose Their Luxuries

One of the common definitions of a luxury good is a product or service that only the top 5 percent of U.S. households can afford. However, the luxury business has not chalked up double-digit growth throughout the past decade by selling only to the ultra-rich. After all, the numbers speak for themselves. There are a lot more moderately affluent Americans than super-rich ones. With household incomes of $145,000 and above, the top 5 percent of U.S. households by income number only 5.3 million, while 42.6 million households boast mid-to-upper incomes of $50,000 or more.

A new egalitarianism has taken over in today's luxury market. In America, luxury products can be bought by anyone up and down the economic ladder. While the nation's ultra-rich may well limit all their personal consumption to luxury brands, the real growth in the luxury market has come from the middle and upper-middle classes reaching up to buy luxury goods. Recognizing that everyone wants a piece of the "good life," luxury marketers have started to expand their product lines by offering lower-priced goods that carry the brand name. Like Mercedes-Benz, which introduced its new C-Class of "affordable" luxury cars, other lux-

> The real growth in the luxury market has come from the middle and upper-middle classes reaching up to buy luxury goods.

ury marketers have been working on strategies to move down the price-point scale. The challenge is how to keep the exclusivity and brand image at the upper tier, while offering lower-priced models that appeal to and can be afforded by the less than ultra-rich. Early evidence is that luxury marketers have had success moving downscale to capture market share from the mid-to-upper-income consumers, while maintaining the exclusive brand cachet that results from selling to the rich.

Along with a new egalitarianism in luxury goods comes consumers' ability to choose their luxuries. Today, consumers, armed with more information than ever before, can pick the aspects of their lives they wish to luxuriate, by buying luxury brands selectively. For everything else, there is the ordinary, everyday, and commonplace. For example, one consumer may buy only the top, luxury cookware brands for her kitchen, while buying more everyday brands for bed or bath. Another might express his enthusiasm for a wine tasting hobby by buying luxury brands of wine, wine glasses, and everything else that is involved with wine tasting, while sticking to more mundane brands in kitchen appliances, bedding, and clothes.

Faith Popcorn in her book, *EVEolution*, makes the point that women don't buy brands—they "join them." I believe this applies equally to men. In fact, the way the typical consumer thinks about and interacts with brands has undergone a sea change in the past 20 years. Inundated with hundreds of thousands of new products each year and endless media advertisements, consumers use brands as a way to sift out the trash from the treasure. A consumer is much more likely to notice a commercial message linked to a brand that the consumer has experienced before than one not so advantaged. We saw a real-life example of the concept of the consumers belonging to a brand when Coca-Cola tried to introduce its New Coke formula. Consumers were outraged that the company would dare to interfere with their favorite product. The marketplace spoke: "Coke belongs to us! You may be the company that makes it, but Coke is *ours,* so don't mess with it." The passing of the Oldsmobile brand resulted in no such consumer outcry. That brand had lost its market and its connection with consumers.

More than other everyday brands, luxury brands evoke a strong and lasting image in the consumer's heart and mind. Consumers buy these brands to belong to them, to make the brand a part of themselves and their identities. For the most involved consumers, the brand confers status on the owner, but it's more than that. It becomes part of these consumers' personal identities, who they are, and what their value systems are. The passionate way consumers interact with their favorite brands is almost spiritual in nature. It goes beyond logic and reason to the depths of one's personal identity.

This high level of involvement draws certain consumers, but it may well repel others, as it did for the respondent who strenuously objected to linking her name and identity with the Mercedes brand. "To me, luxury is all about your value system. It's about your beliefs, your religious system, your personality. I don't need a Mercedes. [Owning a Mercedes] is not an example we want to set. Even if I got a great deal on a Mercedes, I would not buy it. I don't need that kind of luxury. That brand is not me. I don't have that lifestyle." This consumer was adamant and highly emotional about *not* wanting to be linked to Mercedes and what that brand stands for. Even if she found a bargain on a used Mercedes, she would never buy that car because the brand repels her.

Luxury Is to See and Be Seen

In marketing luxury products, there is clearly an aspirational component at play. Logo marks on many luxury goods are standard. Through them, the owner proclaims to the world his or her good taste and sophistication. Some consumers belong to a brand and they want the world to know about it. Fashion, cars, handbags and briefcases, jewelry, and watches are all luxury goods where brand logos are displayed. On the other hand, many classes of luxury goods are used privately and not exposed to public scrutiny. For these purchases, such as home furnishings, major appliances, and bedding, the consumer is driven to the luxury brand for personal motivations, not to see and be seen.

Juliet Schor, senior lecturer and director of women's studies at Harvard University, has published a number of books that focus on the aspirational nature of consumption. To Schor, consuming is a competitive sport that people participate in with their coworkers, family, neighbors, and friends. My research sees the primary driver for discretionary spending as the inner life of consumers and their needs and desires. In contrast, Schor's research on cosmetic consumption illustrates that for certain people under certain circumstances, the need to see and be seen is important in their choice of luxury brands.

In *The Overspent American*, Schor gives a nod to the role of emotional gratification in cosmetic purchases:

But despite its dubious effectiveness [e.g., cosmetics that promise clinical effects], women keep on buying the stuff. They shell out hundreds, even thousands, for wrinkle cream, moisturizers, eye shadows and powders, lipsticks, and facial makeup. And why? One explanation is that they are looking for affordable luxury, the thrill of buying at the expensive department store, indulging in a fantasy of beauty and sexiness, buying "hope in a bottle." Cosmetics are an escape from an otherwise all-too-drab everyday existence.

To Schor however, the primary driver is status:

Even in cosmetics—which is hardly the first product line that comes to mind as a status symbol—there's a structure of one-up-womanship.

G e t t i n g I t R i g h t

BULGARI
Its name is synonymous with luxury.

Bulgari used to be a brand known only to the rich and famous, but today it is expanding its horizons and opening its doors to well-heeled customers worldwide. Bulgari Chief Executive Francesco Trapani has moved to diversify the company's offerings beyond its core business of jewelry and watches to a range of other luxury products and services. "Today, Bulgari has a diversified product portfolio that foresees jewels and watches as the core business of the company, but that also includes perfume, scarves, ties, eyewear, and home designs. Bulgari is a luxury brand that offers products with a very distinctive style, at high prices, of outstanding quality," Trapani says.

As the company expands its realm into other luxury goods, it remains firmly grounded in the jewelry business. "Bulgari is a diversified jeweler, meaning that our core business is jewels and watches among other luxury products, but we will always remain a jeweler. We are 'The Italian Contemporary Jewellers,'" Trapani explains. Founded by Sotirio Bulgari in 1879, Bulgari's shop in via dei Condotti was renovated in 1932 when sons Giorgio and Constantino Bulgari inherited the business. Today that same shop serves as Bulgari's flagship store.

International expansion began during the 1970s when Bulgari stores were opened in New York, Geneva, Monte Carlo, and Paris. Today Bulgari's empire extends to more than 150 stores worldwide, including those in London, Milan, Munich, and St. Moritz as well as Hong Kong, Singapore, Osaka, and Tokyo. In 2002, annual sales grew 19 percent to reach $810.9 million from $678.6 million in 2001. Geographically, 14 percent of revenues are generated in Italy, with 25 percent coming from other European markets. Japan captures 21 percent of company revenues, while other Far Eastern markets comprise 17 percent. In 2002 the Americas produced 15 percent of total revenues, and the Middle East and other regions generated 8 percent of revenues. In 2002, sales growth was off in several key geographic markets, including Europe, the Americas, and the Far East. Trapani explains: "This is a difficult moment, not only because of September 11, but during the summer of 2001 business was starting to slow down because of a general economic downturn especially in the United States."

Tracking along with international expansion is Bulgari's broadening luxury product offerings. Trapani explains the diversification strategy: "Today, one can walk into a Bulgari store and buy a tie, a pair of sunglasses, or a perfume—products that cost much less than a jewel. Furthermore, there are some products within our core business, such as the B.zero1 jewelry collection or the Solotempo watch, that are entry-price products. It allows us to have a Bulgari product at an accessible price. We aim to reach all those who look for luxury products with a distinctive design of outstanding quality." In 2002, 38 percent of net revenues were derived from jewelry, with watches (38 percent), perfumes (17 percent), and accessories (5 percent) comprising the bulk of sales. The company also generates about 2 percent of sales in licensing royalties and revenues from agreements with Luxottica for eyeware and Rosenthal, part of Waterford Wedgwood PLC, in home designs.

Looking toward the future, the company foresees major opportunities from its Bulgari Hotels & Resorts joint venture with Marriott International's new Luxury Group. The plan is to open seven exclusive Bulgari five-star hotels, most of them located in big cities but also including one or two resorts. This is a category slated for significant growth as the hotels and resorts offer their clientele an opportunity to vicariously experience the Bulgari lifestyle. Trapani envisions the hotels as a key foundation for Bulgari's overall brand strategy. "The return on investment makes it a very interesting deal. While we are attracted to this joint venture for its

significant investment potential, we also see huge cross-marketing possibilities between the Bulgari stores and the hotels. The client base of the stores is very similar to the hotels. For example, I think it is reasonable to assume that a couple would buy the engagement ring at Bulgari's, do the wedding party at a Bulgari hotel, and go to our resort during their honeymoon. Furthermore, we see those seven hotels as seven public relations 'machines' for the Bulgari brand. These hotels will become a reference point for the local community, meaning that the café and restaurant will also attract the local crowd."

On the future of luxury brands, Trapani anticipates changes on the horizon. "Given the present business landscape, I foresee that only the strongest, most solid brands in the luxury business, like Bulgari, will survive. We will probably see many of the smaller brands disappear. People, though, will always be interested in luxury products."

Schor explores the status component in cosmetics by looking at brand purchasing patterns for four different cosmetic products: lipstick, eye shadow, mascara, and facial cleanser. What distinguishes each product is its relative visibility to others. For example, facial cleanser is the least socially visible product because consumers use it in private, whereas lipstick is the most visible because it is acceptable to touch up one's lipstick at the table and in public. Her research findings: Women are far more likely to buy expensive lipsticks than they are to buy expensive facial cleansers. Her research leads her to conclude that consumers buy top-end brands of visible products far more than high-quality invisible ones.

> To see and be seen plays a role in the purchase of luxury products.

> Luxury products and brands, just like all discretionary expenditures, exist on a sliding scale that is measured in the perceptions, values, and experiences of the individual consumer.

To see and be seen plays a role in the purchase of luxury products. How important it really is for each brand, each product, is highly individualistic to each consumer, but marketers are strongly advised to study the role that visibility plays in the purchasing behavior of their consumer markets. For the ultra-high-end fashion brands, the obvious display of a brand logo is considered gauche and "nouveau riche." For other brands, a visible label clearly conveys value to the consumer. How much inherent value does the Mercedes-Benz hood ornament carry in the total cost of the car? What is a Chanel bag worth without the CC? How much does the polo symbol add to the value of a Ralph Lauren oxford shirt?

Luxury Is in the Eye of the Beholder

In the final analysis, the consumer defines luxury. For one consumer, at one income level, with a passion for some aspect of his or her life—fashion, gourmet cooking, wine tasting, entertaining, home decorating—a particular item, brand, or product might be considered a luxury that is prized. For another, the same thing might be a total waste, or it may not be luxurious enough. Luxury products and brands, just like all discretionary expenditures, exist on a sliding scale that is measured in the perceptions, values, and experiences of the individual consumer. Increasingly luxury marketers are testing how far their brands can extend both up and down this consumer-defined sliding scale of values. While luxury brands must exercise great caution at the low and middle ranges of any product category, there is ample room to move along from upper-end to extravagant to luxury products, without necessarily losing brand perception and exclusivity.

4

THE 14 JUSTIFIERS THAT GIVE CONSUMERS PERMISSION TO BUY

Consumers need a reason to buy things they don't need. For products deemed necessities, like milk, coffee, bread, and meat, the need itself provides permission. For things consumers don't need (i.e., discretionary purchases), they give themselves "permission" to buy by stacking various rationally based justifiers in favor of the purchase. It is the justifiers that give consumers the illusion that they are acting rationally in purchasing, but in reality, they remain driven by personal desires and emotions.

The perceived extravagance of a particular purchase usually determines how many justifiers are needed and to what extent. For example, a homeowner who wants to replace a 15-year-old sofa that is musty smelling and stained needs fewer justifiers than does one who wants to replace a 2-year-old sofa.

In the battle for consumers' wallets, marketers need to understand how to engage them on an emotional level. They need to give customers sufficient justifiers to overcome purchase barriers. The best salespeople understand how to overcome objections to reach a sale. Unfortunately, many marketers have distanced themselves too far from the sales process. They have forgotten,

> Justifiers are the tools that marketers use to overcome objections in the store, at the mall, at the point of sale.

> When marketers really understand how their products play into the hearts and emotions of their customers, the judicious use of justifiers in marketing communications stacks the deck in the marketers' favor and gives consumers permission to buy.

or don't understand, the critical role that overcoming objections plays in the sales process.

Salespeople overcome objections interactively and in real time. Marketers must do it indirectly through marketing communications, advertisements, point-of-purchase, and the purchase offer. They must anticipate the range of objections customers may present to keep from buying. Justifiers are the tools that marketers use to overcome objections in the store, at the mall, at the point of sale. When marketers really understand how their products play into the hearts and emotions of their customers, the judicious use of justifiers in marketing communications stacks the deck in the marketers' favor and gives consumers permission to buy.

UNDERLYING MOTIVATORS

In research conducted among consumers, Unity Marketing identified an array of 14 different justifiers that consumers perceive as the underlying motivators driving their purchase of products they don't need. Pleasure, education, emotional satisfaction, entertainment, relaxation, beautify home or self, replace an existing item, planned purchase, stress relief, hobby, gift for self, and status are among the reasons consumers use to justify discretionary purchases. However, you can sum up the most important justifier for all discretionary purchases in a single overriding concept: to enhance the quality of life. One respondent described her motivation in buying discretionary items as, "products that help me be more myself." As this definition implies, people buy these products to improve and enhance the quality of their lives in all realms and aspects of their being.

For marketers of products consumers don't need, the marketing and branding challenge is to figure out how their brands and the products they are trying to sell make people's lives more meaningful, satisfying, and better. With that insight, marketers can present and reinforce the quality-of-life-enhancing message surrounding the product or brand. Quality-of-life-enhancing messages are powerful. They provide the kinetic energy that overcomes consumer objections and drives consumers to buy. When marketers do the hard work of providing the justi-

FIGURE 4.1
Justifiers for Buying Discretionary Products

Motivators and percent of consumers identifying motivator as important

Motivator	Percent
Quality of life	89%
Pleasure	84
Beautify home	83
Education	83
Relaxation	82
Entertainment	78
Planned purchase	75
Emotional satisfaction	74
Replace existing item	73
Stress relief	66
Hobby	66
Gift for self	54
Bought on impulse	39
Status	30

Source: Unity Marketing

fiers for their customers, it is amazing how this bolsters product sales. Justifiers overcome objections and compel the consumer to buy.

JUSTIFIER #1: QUALITY OF LIFE

Unity Marketing conducted a quantitative telephone survey of a statistically representative sample of 1,000 U.S. households to better understand the role of justifiers in the consumer's purchase decision. Consumers were asked about their purchase behavior in 30 different categories of discretionary and luxury products—those products people buy that they don't need. We will look at the results of the survey of product purchases in the next chapter. Here we focus on the critical role that justifiers play in motivating consumers to buy.

In the survey, we asked about the importance of 14 different justifiers for purchasing things that they don't need. Based upon their responses,

Insights into how products
enhance the quality of
life result in positioning
strategies that play back
to consumers' basic
beliefs and values.

the most important motivator driving the purchase of discretionary products was to improve the quality of life. Nearly 90 percent of those surveyed identified this as a "very important" or "somewhat important" motivator for their purchases in the 37 discretionary product categories. All other motivators, such as pleasure, beauty, entertainment, education, and stress relief, are implicit within the top motivator: to improve the quality of life.

Improving the quality of life works on different planes within the consumers' psyche. It is a deep concept that marketers need to explore for their particular products and brands. In that exploration, marketers gain tremendous insight into how shoppers perceive the products that they buy as "need fulfilling." Insights into how products enhance the quality of life result in positioning strategies that play back to consumers' basic beliefs and values.

Our research uncovered five different dimensions on which consumer products improve and enhance the quality of consumers' lives:

1. Intellectual
2. Physical
3. Spiritual
4. Emotional
5. Social

At the *intellectual* level, education and knowledge are widely recognized as a principal means for individuals to improve the quality of their life. Education may make it possible for a person to find a better job with greater opportunity for advancement. Education is a tool that enables people to deal more effectively and productively with their world. In our survey, 60 percent of respondents ranked education as a "very important" motivator in the purchase of discretionary products. Most notably, it is a prime motivator for home computer and book purchases.

Health and freedom from pain and disease are *physical* keys to enhanced quality of life. "If you have health, you have everything," is a common expression. A desire for good health drives consumption of vitamin and herbal supplements, nutritionally enhanced foods and drinks, exercise equipment, and health care. The physical component of quality of life also includes stamina and energy, comfort and safety, and freedom from physical danger. Purchases driven by this motivator include water and air filters, bottled water, home security systems, appliances, and new mattresses with special features. Following the terrorist attacks of September 11, this motivator suddenly gained new importance as the threat of death through violence or biological and chemical attacks became a real possibility.

People's *spiritual* relationship with God, or whatever name they give to a higher being, is a major source of comfort and security. Through the relationship, they have a means to deal effectively with the unknown, the loss of loved ones, and their own impending deaths. The spiritual component enables consumers to become part of the flow of history and to believe that they are not alone in dealing with the travails of life. Purchases that express spirituality include religious goods, books, and memorabilia. Some consumers may reflect their spirituality in the themes they collect such as Christmas and Easter holidays. The U.S. war on terrorism heightens the role spirituality plays in driving consumer behavior. Our enemies proclaim this as a *jihad,* a holy war of their god against ours. While we do not play into the enemy's hand by buying this spin, the simple fact is that countries, societies, and people at war and in crisis call upon God to strengthen them and give them victory. As the saying goes, "There are no atheists in fox holes," and with our world at war, we will see more and more emphasis on spirituality as a source of strength through the difficult times ahead. "God Bless America" is the motto of this first twenty-first-century war.

While we know material things cannot provide happiness, the act of buying gives many consumers deep *emotional* satisfaction. There is the buildup of anticipation in planning a discretionary purchase. One of our respondents described it this way: "You get satisfaction, and you're thrilled about where you've just been, and you plan the next one. Greater satisfaction builds more anticipation for the next time."

The emotional component includes the pleasures of love and happiness in the home, freedom from stress, and a home environment that relaxes and provides emotional security. The consumer good itself may not provide emotional satisfaction. However, it enhances and encourages such satisfaction in its acquisition and use. Examples are bath salts, candles, and beautiful home decorations.

Another respondent told us: "There is anticipation in the search for something wonderful, then stress, then ultimate satisfaction when the right purchase is made. Then you want to do it all over again." Products perceived as indulgences respond to the emotional level. In the post-9/11 world, consumers in crisis seek emotional succor and stress relief by purchasing products that promise to provide these things.

Our *social* connections and network of family, friends, and associates enhance quality of life. Our network confirms that we are not alone, that we belong. Success in the social milieu yields an enhanced quality of life and is one reason why status—that external representation of having achieved social success—is an important motivator for nearly one-third of respondents in our survey. Gift giving is another important aspect of the social component. Our society sanctions numerous gift-giving occasions, from the annual Christmas shopping spree to birthdays and formal occasions such as weddings and anniversaries. Gifting confirms our sense of belonging and yields enhanced quality of life to both the giver and the recipient. As we learn to live with the threat of terrorist attacks, the need for belonging will grow. Home party plans and other forms of direct selling, friend to friend, are perfectly suited to trends at work in our culture today. Home entertaining will also benefit from the new environment.

Demographic Distinctions

All consumers are highly driven to make discretionary purchases as a means to improve the quality of their lives, but certain consumer segments are even more responsive to this desire. This justifier motivates both genders equally. However, consumers aged 25 to 34—those who are most likely to be in the midst of career and family building—are in the age segment that rates "to improve the quality of life" as the highest driver for purchases. Black Americans also rate improving the quality of life higher than whites and Hispanics. Households with two or more individuals are more concerned than people living alone about improving the quality of their lives through consumption. Moderate-income households place a greater emphasis on quality-of-life enhancement than do lower- or higher-income households.

Finally, consumers who have completed their education, whether at the high school or college level, place a greater importance on improving the quality of life. On the other hand, those who didn't complete their education, either at the high school or college level, place less importance on quality of life. Presumably, those individuals who make the effort to complete their education at whatever level they decide is appropriate are more motivated by quality-of-life improvement.

JUSTIFIER #2: PLEASURE

Some consumers derive pleasure in anticipating, acquiring, and owning a discretionary purchase. The entire buying cycle contributes to the joy. Advertisements stimulate desire that arouses fantasies in the mind about how the product will satisfy the desire. One of our survey respondents said: "When I see commercials for beauty products, I get caught up in the fantasy. Sometimes I buy the products in those fantasy commercials, then I feel good for a while. I am satisfied for a while, then it becomes ordinary again, and I want to go out and shop for something special again."

A central part of the consumer fantasy is the buildup of anticipation leading to the purchase. The anticipation makes the ultimate satisfaction that much greater. It also enhances the shopping experience. Let us face facts. We derive pleasure in shopping at one store as opposed to another, even if we do not buy anything. Shopping at Wal-Mart is considered basic, ordinary, mundane, but shopping at stores like Bloomingdale's, Saks, or Neiman Marcus is a pleasure experience in and of itself. In the exclusive shopping venue, the illusion is that the well-dressed store clerks are there simply to satisfy the shoppers' whims. They ooh and aah when you try on something. They are honest if something does not look just right. They encourage you in the joy of shopping. In fact, the very best salespeople are so enthusiastic that they actually shop with you, rather than try to sell you something. Moreover, it is so much more fun shopping together than alone. A respondent explains: "When I am down in the dumps, shopping makes me feel better."

Pleasure as a driving force in consumer shopping is as much about the doing and experiencing (i.e., the verb), as it is in the item or product bought (i.e., the noun). No wonder that so many companies selling things that consumers don't need take control of the complete sales cycle, opening company-owned, dedicated stores to present and sell the brand. These companies recognize that consumers often derive as much pleasure from the brand in the act of acquiring a product as they do from owning it. Marketers that sell through independent retailers need to be vigilant that their brands are sold in a pleasure-focused way. Sales training and point-of-purchase marketing materials are a start, but it is clearly a challenge for a company whose products bring pleasure when the shopping experience does not.

> Pleasure as a driving force in consumer shopping is as much about the doing and experiencing (i.e., the verb), as it is in the item or product bought (i.e., the noun).

Demographic Distinctions

Pleasure is equally important for men and women as a motivator for discretionary purchases. Younger-to-middle-aged consumers, aged 18 to 54, derive the most pleasure from their discretionary purchases. Consumers in this age range are far more likely than those aged 55 or older to rate pleasure as "very important" in their consumer choices. Moderate-to-high-income households feel entitled to gain pleasure from their purchases and, therefore, are highly motivated by this factor as well. Consumers who are married or live in two-person households are more highly motivated by pleasure than singles living alone.

G *etting* I *t* R *ight*

INTIMATE BRANDS
Devoted to Sybaritic Pleasure

With its three core brands—Victoria's Secret, personal-care retailer Bath & Body Works, and White Barn Candle Company—Intimate Brands is a $5.5 billion company that markets a magic formula of sophisticated adult pleasure to its customers. It's a formula that has worked beautifully, with the company nearly doubling in sales from 1995. CEO Leslie Wexner credits Intimate Brands success to its brands. "What has been working and winning and will continue to work and win as far into the future as I can see are brands. Powerful, compelling, multichannel brands." The key to its brand magic is the company's intimate understanding of its customers and its dedication to consistently delivering on the brands' promises. Victoria's Secret targets women of all ages, body sizes, and shapes, with the promise that they can attract the passion and hold the interest of their man. While sex always sells, for women sex must come wrapped in romance. Victoria's Secret's 900 stores and its mail-order catalog are female friendly, promising sex appeal and romance in a decidedly adult, but nonpornographic, way. The catalog's voluptuous and beautiful models are nonthreatening to the female consumer because, with a touch of genius on the part of the company, the catalog uses a regular crew of models with whom the reader becomes familiar.

The company's Bath & Body Works brand works along the same lines as Victoria's Secret. Through the company's exclusive lotions and potions, a woman can entice her man with soft, caressible skin and draw him with exotic and sensual fragrances. The brands are all about pampering and indulgence, sex and romance, beauty and the power to attract. These are potent, evocative brand messages. Wexner says: "What are the characteristics of the best brands? They are always clearly defined, with a strong emotional content. It's simple. People want the brand. They buy the aspiration, the look, the attitude. All of it."

JUSTIFIER #3: BEAUTIFY THE HOME

Making a beautiful home is a priority for the majority of consumers because it is central to a person's identity. As one survey respondent explained: "I am house proud. The house is the single biggest investment you will make in your lifetime and you want it to reflect the care and love you put into it." Another says: "You want the look of your home to reflect you."

The importance of the home is magnified for women who do not work outside the home. "As a stay-at-home mom, you don't have a job that you get reassurance from, that you are worth something—that boost you get from your work. You get that feeling from your house and how it looks. You end up doing the same job over and over again. It gets tedious, but if your house doesn't look good, you aren't doing your job as a woman and mother." Another woman explains: "The house and how it looks is your responsibility. It all gets down to a reflection on yourself." For about 80 percent of those surveyed, beautifying the home is an important motivator for buying things they don't need. For these consumers, the home—how it looks and how it is decorated—is a reflection of the individual's identity, values, and self.

Cleanliness in the home is another aspect of beautifying the home. A clean home is a beautiful home. As one respondent explained: "Bathrooms are made for the SOUL. That is where I go to relax. A clean bathroom is also critical. It has to be clean and stay clean." Utilitarian products often offer cleanliness as an essential benefit. Because cleanliness is next to Godliness, the consumer connection to cleanliness is very deep, almost spiritual.

Demographic Distinctions

While men value a beautiful home, women are more highly motivated to purchase products for home beautification. The more youthful
consumers, those aged 25 to 44, are the most intensely interested in home
beautification. Households making $35,000 or more annually consider
beautifying the home a higher priority in purchasing decisions than do
those living in lower-income households where it is viewed as of little or
no importance in their purchase decisions. Single-person households
are less motivated by beautifying their home than are consumers living
in two-or-more-person households and those with children.

JUSTIFIER #4: EDUCATION

Being better educated, that is, learning something new, gaining new
insights, understanding, and skills, is an important motivator in discretionary purchases for over 80 percent of those surveyed. It is worth not-
ing that the more education Americans get, the more education they
crave. Today's American consumer is more educated than ever before.
As recently as 1980, only 16.2 percent of the adult population aged 25
and older had completed four years or more of college. By 1999, that
percentage had risen to 25.2 percent. Achieving more education will
continue to be a primary driver for important discretionary product segments, especially books, magazines, newsletters, computers and related
hardware, software, art, and even entertainment products.

Researching a new purchase—getting educated about the product
category, the available brands, and price points—comprises a part of the
anticipation cycle that gives so much pleasure to consumers. One of our
respondents explained the time-consuming process that her family went
through to select the right model and to get all the right features on a
new SUV. "We just bought a new Ford Expedition. We used the Internet
to learn about the different models, then went around to all the dealers,
looking at the different models, to see which was right for us. Then,
when we settled on the Expedition, we needed to do more research about
the model and what features we wanted. For me, the search adds to the
anticipation."

Demographic Distinctions

Women respond more strongly to education as a motivator for discretionary purchases than do men. Younger-to-middle-aged consumers, aged 25 to 54, rate education as more important than both those older than age 55, and the extremely young, aged 18 to 24. Consumers older than age 55, in particular, rate education as of little or no importance in their buying decisions. Unity Marketing predicts that the baby boomers who are just now entering their mid-50s will behave differently than the current generation of mature Americans (born prior to 1946) in terms of their desire for education. Boomers, the most educated generation in history, should continue to be ravenous consumers of products that incorporate an educational aspect. We also predict they will return to the classroom upon retirement or as their single-minded focus on career shifts. Black consumers give higher importance to education, suggesting that this market segment views education as a key to improved quality of life. In purchasing discretionary products, families with children place the highest emphasis on education.

JUSTIFIER #5: RELAXATION

Achieving a state of relaxation is a key justifier for consumers in our hectic, overscheduled world. Just as with other justifiers that stimulate purchases, relaxation is not just inherent in the product bought but in the whole shopping experience. Stores that are sensitive to the need for relaxation invite consumers to spend more time in them. Moreover, as Paco Underhill, in his book *Why We Buy: The Science of Shopping*, says, the longer shoppers spend in the store, the more they spend. Marketing relaxation products in a relaxing setting is the ticket for success.

Products that offer relaxation span a wide range including candles, home fragrance and aromatherapy products, nature and outdoor gardening, art, music, and bath lotions and potions. They tend to appeal to multiple senses just as candles illuminate, scent the room, and provide warmth. Shopping experiences that encourage relaxation also tend to be multisensory, offering an environment where scents, sounds, and lighting wrap the consumer in luxurious surroundings.

> Stores that are sensitive to the need for relaxation invite consumers to spend more time in them.

Demographic Distinctions

Relaxation is a closely related justifier to stress relief, which I will discuss later in this chapter. Relaxation is more multidimensional than stress relief and implies a broader, more life-transforming value than the stress relief justifier, which focuses on results. More than 80 percent of consumers rate relaxation an important motivator for discretionary purchases, whereas stress relief is important to only about two-thirds. While both genders are equally motivated by relaxation, women are more highly motivated by stress relief, suggesting that women need more of both relaxation and stress relief in their lives. Relaxation is more highly motivating to the middle-aged and older consumers; the prime age range for relaxation buying is 35 to 64. Blacks tend to view relaxation as a very important motivator, while whites are more likely to consider relaxation only somewhat important. Two-or-more-person households place a premium on relaxation in their discretionary purchases.

G *etting* I *t* R *ight*

LONGABERGER BASKET
Education builds loyalty.

As shoppers become more highly involved with a brand, a product, or a company, they seek out more information. Involved, passionate consumers want to learn and be educated, which results in better, more loyal consumers. The Longaberger Company, known for its handmade baskets sold exclusively through home parties hosted by the company's sales consultants, sponsors the Longaberger Homestead, near its headquarters in Newark, Ohio, dedicated to enhancing the consumers' experience of the brand.

Company founder Dave Longaberger envisioned the company facilities, which include a forest, golf course, and acres and acres of farmland, becoming an educational and entertainment destination for visitors from around the world. The Longaberger Homestead combines down-home, country-style shopping, entertainment, and dining opportunities with a tour of the manufacturing plant where people can experience, firsthand, the handcrafted traditions on which the company is founded. Visitors can even take a class where they make a basket themselves. Guests are also invited to tour the company's unique seven-story office building designed to look like one of its baskets, handles and all. Thus, Longaberger becomes far more than a company that sells baskets:

- It involves and educates potential consumers.
- It invites the consumer to become part of the Longaberger experience for a few hours or a day.
- It presents the consumer with information about why their baskets are the absolute best.
- It builds loyalty, passion, and excitement for the brand.

Longaberger has made the quantum leap from a company trying to sell products to one that becomes part of the consumer's life. Educating the consumer with its Longaberger Homestead factory tours, sales consultants' presentations, and home parties is the foundation of the company's entire marketing and brand-building program. And it has worked spectacularly.

JUSTIFIER #6: ENTERTAINMENT

Entertainment, as a powerful motivator for consumers, reduces boredom, generates excitement, provides new concepts and new ideas, and brings people together. American consumers spent $256.2 billion for recreation and entertainment in 2000, according to the U.S. Bureau of Economic Analysis. Americans have an unquenchable thirst to be entertained, with consumer spending on entertainment up nearly 50 percent from 1995.

As with so many other justifiers, entertainment is both what you buy and what you experience when you buy. "Shopping as entertainment" is a buzz phrase often heard in retailing circles. It has become so popular it has even spawned a new word: *retail-tainment*. The current trend in mall design includes combining traditional shops and anchor department stores with movie theaters, theme restaurants, museums, and other nonretail businesses. The Mall of America comes complete with an indoor amusement park featuring a full-sized Ferris wheel and roller coaster. The concept is sound. Consumers want to experience shopping in new, more dynamic ways.

Today's consumers ask more of their shopping entertainment. Not satisfied to passively

> Consumers want to experience shopping in new, more dynamic ways.

Consumers will be drawn to the next big thing in retailing that provides an entertaining respite from the drudgery of shopping.

receive entertainment, consumers seek a shopping experience that combines learning with doing to involve the complete individual. Speaking at the 2001 Urban Entertainment Development Conference sponsored by the Urban Land Institute, Mark Rivers, executive vice president of The Mills Corporation, explained that customers are drawn to shopping venues where they can participate in the excitement of entertainment. So The Mills Corporation, one of the nation's largest mall owners, worked with Vans Shoes to create skateboard parks and with Gibson Guitars to create places for people to play as well as purchase guitars. Rivers said: "The buzzword is experience. People do not want to just be entertained. They want to participate. Creating these experiences is a good way to connect with consumers."

What people buy and how they buy it has become part of a total experience. Neither part of the consuming equation can be divorced from the other. That is one reason why The Limited's Men's Express stores, which target the young male shopper, feature videos throughout the store playing music and fashion clips. Williams-Sonoma offers cooking classes, while The Home Depot will teach you how to install a sink, paint a room, or stain, clean, and even build a wood deck. The Disney Store plays Disney movies and cartoons around the clock. Big-box sporting-goods stores like Galyan's Trading Company, let the customer try out the goods before purchasing, even providing a three-story rock wall for the adventurous shopper to climb.

What's next in the one-upmanship world of retail-tainment? The sky is the limit. Be assured that consumers will be drawn to the next big thing in retailing that provides an entertaining respite from the drudgery of shopping.

G e t t i n g   I t   R i g h t

ABC CARPET & HOME
An Oasis of Luxury in the Hustle and Bustle of New York City

With the tagline "Come to your senses at ABC," the ABC Carpet & Home store in the historic Flatiron

District of New York, offers shoppers a truly one-of-a-kind shopping experience. Upon entering the doors of ABC's main building, the shopper is transported to an exotic world filled with wonderful things. The atmosphere is totally relaxing, luxurious, fascinating, and never-ever boring. ABC specializes in things for the home—rugs and carpets, furniture, antiques, home textiles, bedding, pillows, art, and collectibles. The experience is cocooning taken to extreme, spiced with objects from foreign locales and exotic places.

ABC describes its philosophy as NOT about decorating, but about collecting, "thus the process of creating one's home becomes less a makeover, and more a continual and passionate search to surround oneself with cherished belongings." The company carries out its mission in its merchandising philosophy. Its advertising describes it this way: "The ambiance of a flea market, a country antiques fair, a bustling Middle-Eastern bazaar, and a bargain-filled warehouse sale, yet with the personalized attention one finds in a boutique."

Each of the store's ten floors is thematically arranged, which offers the shopper a new shopping experience on each level. While the store is stacked and packed to the rafters with all kinds of merchandise, its atmosphere is anything but hectic. If you're feeling fatigued from wandering around such a phantasmagoria of home, you can rest and refresh in the food hall, featuring light fare, coffees and teas, pastries and other goodies. It even offers a full-course dining experience in its cafe featuring "Nuevo Latino" food. With cash registers respectfully discreet, but sales help readily available, the store lives and breathes its philosophy.

In this eclectic mix of home items from all over the world, the store encourages its customers to "trust your impulses; create your own heirlooms; value will never go out of fashion." What could be more relaxing? ABC Carpet & Home has taken away all the worry of decorating, sorry . . . collecting, for your home. It gives permission to mix an embroidered coverlet with a Ming chair. "Introduce the second piece to the first, and eventually you will have an extended family of furnishings. This is collecting, not decorating." And the shopping experience underscores the message to "relax, enjoy, explore, collect."

Demographic Distinctions

Entertainment as a justifier for purchase is rated equally by men and women. All age groups are motivated by entertainment in their discretionary purchases, but the younger group, aged 18 to 34, rank it even higher than the older consumers, aged 35 to 64, as very important in their purchase decisions. Blacks are more likely to consider entertainment a very important motivator. Consumers living in households of two or more individuals and those with children place a premium on entertainment value in their purchases. Moderate-to-high-income households are more highly motivated by entertainment, as are consumers with at least some college.

JUSTIFIER #7: PLANNED PURCHASE

Three-fourths of consumers say making a planned purchase is an important motivator for discretionary purchases. As we have seen, consumers build the anticipation of making a purchase through the planning and research phases. Once this anticipatory phase is complete, the consumer has made the decision, stacked all the justifiers in favor of the purchase, and is now ready to make the purchase. Throughout what can be an extended planning period, excitement builds to the ultimate satisfaction of the purchase. "Anticipation is stress, healthy stress," a respondent explains: "You are excited, which is healthy, positive stress." Another explains, "The fun is in the looking." The opposite of planning a purchase is buying on impulse. Planning and anticipating a purchase tends to predominate in the consuming public because only 40 percent of consumers claim that impulse is an important motivator for buying discretionary items. Shoppers who build anticipation toward a planned purchase perceive impulse shoppers as missing out on a lot of the fun in the consuming experience. As one shopper explained: "If you are an impulse shopper, you don't have any of [the fun]. There is no search, no anticipation. Sometimes the search can make you crazy, but I love it and love to buy."

> Consumers build the anticipation of making a purchase through the planning and research phases.

ETHAN ALLAN
Make it affordable through easy monthly payments.

Home-furnishings giant Ethan Allen knows that few customers wander into its company-owned stores without a plan. Furniture represents a major expenditure for most households, and consequently, it is frequently financed over time. As a vertically integrated home-furnishings company, Ethan Allen offers its exclusive brand of furniture in more than 300 company-owned stores supported by the company's own finance plan. The finance plan, introduced in 2001, was a cornerstone of the company's growth that year. The company's marketing strategy, bolstered by its finance program, encourages customers to purchase entire rooms of furniture and accessories, rather than one item at a time. It offers attractive interest rates over extended periods to make even the most expensive suite of furniture affordable to most families.

With the company's tactical marketing strategies in place, it launched a $70 million national advertising campaign to get the word out about the new affordable Ethan Allen furniture. The ad campaign, called "For Life," invites the consumer to participate in a fantasy of owning, using, and having great furniture. The ad highlights three specific products, each introduced with how important that piece of furniture is for your life. About the Horizon bed, priced at $949, it was said: "You work on it . . . You think on it . . . You play on it . . . Spend all day on it." The Tribeca sofa, for $1,349, is to "Pass the time . . . Contemplate things . . . You snooze . . . Watch TV . . . You rest on it. . . ." The spot ends with: "Ethan Allen. Furniture built for life . . . at a price you can actually live with."

This ad sends a powerful message that is perfect for our time. Your home, your furniture, your life means so much more to you now. It is the central focus of your life. Why should your furniture be an afterthought, bought quickly or cheaply? Enhance your life, add more meaning, more fulfillment, more comfort by buying the furniture you always dreamed of owning—Ethan Allen, of course, now priced so even you can afford it. This ad breaks the mold in home furnishings because it is not about style, design, quality, or workmanship. It takes all those things for granted. What it does beautifully and convincingly is communicate at the emotional level. It almost turns plain furniture into a member of your family.

It states: "You spend your life on it. Shouldn't it be the furniture you've always wanted?" What a powerful message.

This ad hit September 7, 2001, and its timing might well be fortuitous. During that awful time that followed the 9/11 tragedy, we all craved comfort, support, nurturing. This Ethan Allen ad was there to offer it through furniture. My guess: No other ad program launched during the troubled third and fourth quarter of 2001 has had such spectacular sales results.

Planning is a more important motivator for purchases that "cost" something, that is, when the consumer has to give up something to make the purchase. Consumer durable purchases—those that are financed or usually paid for by credit card—take more planning to complete. The respondent we met earlier who was buying the Ford Expedition described the decision to buy "like deciding to have a new baby." It represented a major commitment of family resources over the five-year loan period, as well as increased operating expenses. Marketers of large-ticket items that for many families, require planning and budgeting, can often plan on an extended sales cycle that may be even further delayed due to minor shifts in the economic and political winds. In this post-9/11 time, consumers can put off major purchases for a few months or even a year until their personal prospects look more encouraging. On the other hand, some consumers may be overtaken with a "you can't live forever, so get it while you can" attitude that could spark extravagant purchases that would not otherwise be made.

Demographic Distinctions

Women tend to report making a planned purchase as a more important motivator than men. By comparison, men are more highly motivated by impulse purchases. Middle-aged consumers, 35 to 54, rate a planned purchase as more important to them than consumers under the age of 24 and consumers aged 55 and older. Two-or-more-person households and those with children are most likely to make a planned discretionary purchase. Single-person households place less importance on planning in their purchase decisions. College-educated consumers tend to rate planned purchases as more important, compared with less-educated consumers. An important aspect of the planning process in anticipation of a discretionary and luxury purchase is conducting research, something that the more educated consumers are better equipped to do.

JUSTIFIER #8: EMOTIONAL SATISFACTION

Consumers buy things they don't need to achieve emotional comfort. It is the feeling of satisfaction, the gratification of having bought something desired, the happiness of purchasing something that perfectly expresses one's identity. It is the enjoyment of a beautiful home that provides safety and comfort to one's family and the challenge of being exposed to new ideas or learning new things. It is the fun of seeing the latest movie, playing the hit parade's top-selling song, or having the latest and greatest computer gadgets. It is exercising one's consuming will to buy and possess.

The art of branding is all about building an emotional connection with the consumer. While some categories are perceived as not demanding an emotional response from the consumer, no matter how mundane or low

> Consumers buy things they don't need to achieve emotional comfort.

involvement the product category, consumers usually are emotionally invested and connected with their favorite brands.

Remember the introduction of New Coke? It was so logical from a left-brain marketer's perspective, so carefully researched to find just the right combination of sweetness and tartness for today's taste. Yet cries of outrage from loyal consumers greeted New Coke. "How could you take away *my* Coke?" The brand belongs to the consumers, not the company, and they own it in a visceral, emotional way.

This level of emotional involvement is the envy of all consumer brand marketers. Any brand manager who invests in understanding the emotional links between his brand and the consumers—their needs, drives, desires, consuming fantasies, and passion—can achieve this level of emotional involvement for the brand. Few brands can span the breadth of a mass-market brand like Coke, but they can go equally as deep into their more narrow market segments by connecting with their customers on an emotional level and never letting them down.

Demographic Distinctions

Emotional satisfaction drives both men and women equally in discretionary spending. Consumers aged 25 to 54 are most influenced by emotional satisfaction in shopping. Consumers aged 65 and older are more likely than any other age group to claim that emotional satisfaction is of little or no importance when they shop. Blacks are more concerned with achieving emotional satisfaction through shopping, as compared with whites or Hispanics. Consumers living in large households of three or more individuals place a higher priority on emotional satisfaction as a reason to buy.

Getting It **R**ight

LENOX
Connecting emotionally at the most important times in people's lives.

Hidden deep in the annual report of Brown-Forman, the wine and spirits company best known for its Jack Daniel's, Southern Comfort, and Korbel Champagne brands, is a marketing success story called Lenox. The flagship brand of Brown-Forman's consumer durables segment, Lenox, along with other segment brands, including Gorham, Dansk, and Kirk Steiff in tabletop, Lenox Collections direct marketing, and Hartmann Luggage, generated $30 million in operating income in 2002 on sales of $581 million.

What accounts for the strength of the Lenox giftware brand? For starters, Lenox enjoys nearly a 40 percent share of the fine dinnerware market, thus ensuring its position as the leader in the fine china business in the U.S. Further, Lenox's brand reputation has made it the dinnerware choice of the U.S. presidents. Stan Krangel, president of Lenox Inc. boasts: "Lenox has delivered no fewer than five official sets of White House china for five presidential administrations. The world's leaders dine on Lenox." Even more impressive, each and every citizen of this country participates in Lenox as one Lenox crystal bowl is given to each president as the official inaugural gift from the people of the United States.

The Lenox brand, however, extends far beyond market share dominance and official gifts of state. Krangel explains: "Lenox is a brand consumers think of to commemorate the important celebrations in life—weddings, anniversaries, family holidays, new baby, showers, parties and entertaining, as well as more personal celebrations. Lenox serves the consumer at all these emotionally laden times of life. Lenox is a brand that people trust as a gift. For the gift giver, Lenox instills confidence in one of our most practiced rituals. For the recipient, Lenox represents appreciation of how much he or she is valued by the gift giver. Giving Lenox and owning Lenox represents American quality at its best."

With the core brand value of Lenox being "Lenox Gifts That Celebrate Life," the company targets distinctive areas in consumers' lives for their products. "Lenox's core equities are divided into four primary categories: gifts, entertaining and mealtime, home décor, and collecting. Each of these areas is driven by one form or another of celebration—the key emotional ingredient in Lenox's brand identity," Krangel says. "In essence, each of our core equities [is a form] of gift giving. Entertaining is one of the greatest gifts we share with our friends and families. Home décor and collecting are expressions and practices of self-giving. Lenox is the brand of choice for consumers' most special occasions."

The emotional connection fostered between Lenox and the consumer becomes the springboard to consumer loyalty. Lenox dinnerware patterns are designed to offer continuity at the table, as well as other giftware and decorative options. Lenox communicates with its customers through in-store support and displays, a Gold Club loyalty program, the company's Internet Web sites, and consumer catalogs. The key message Lenox sends to the consumer, according to Krangel, is: "Lenox is here to help you celebrate again and again." What could be a better marketing strategy than to link up with consumers during all of their memorable life occasions?

JUSTIFIER #9: REPLACING AN EXISTING ITEM

The desire to replace an existing item in the home is often the justifier for the purchase of a discretionary item. In fact, this often becomes the catalyst for an extended spending spree. A worn-out chair, rug, or broken television is frequently the spur that moves buyers from their homes and into the stores. Over and over in focus groups, respondents explained how the purchase of one item led to a cascade of additional spending to buy new things to complement and match the original item that started the spending spree. "We had an old chair. It cleaned up well but still looked dingy, so I went out and bought a new chair. Then when I got it home, it made the sofa and love seat look dingy, so we just replaced that. Next, I need to get new drapes, because the new furniture makes them look really bad." Another participant explains about her latest home spending spree: "We just bought four reclining chairs, including a couch with a recliner. We like to be comfortable, very comfortable. Now we need to get new things to go with [the couch]. One thing leads to another so you can justify new purchases. I've got to get a new rug. I wanted new furniture for ten years, so now it is time to do it." A new backyard patio gives another respondent a justification to continue to spend: "We just finished the patio and sidewalk, so we needed plants to complement that. Then we needed patio furniture to complement that. It's a sense of accomplishment to show off what we've done."

Part of the motivation that drives the spending spree after replacing an existing item is to extend the thrill and excitement of having something new. Another respondent explained: "I always find myself buying bigger and better kitchen appliances. The kitchen is so important to me. I bought a new coffeepot with a water filter. The first time I used it I thought it was the

> The desire to replace an existing item often becomes the catalyst for an extended spending spree.

best cup of coffee I ever made. I thought WOW! But now I just take it for granted. I just don't notice it anymore. Something new is a WOW. Improvements are amazing."

Demographic Distinctions

Women say replacing an existing item is a more important motivator for them to shop than do men. Older consumers aged 45 to 64 consider this more important when they shop, compared with younger consumers aged 18 to 44. Moderate-income households rate replacing an existing item more important in their buying decisions than do households that are more affluent. Two-person and larger households are also more likely to consider replacing an existing item as an essential motivator to purchase.

JUSTIFIER #10: STRESS RELIEF

Finding a way to relieve stress motivates three-fourths of survey respondents in their discretionary purchases. Stress relief results from the act of shopping—from the relief and satisfaction felt upon culminating an anticipated purchase and from the product itself. Stress relief is an important benefit in the marketing of aromatherapy, candles, bath products, whirlpools, hot tubs, and small personal-care appliances.

In the post-9/11, terrorist-threatened world, consumers face an emotional crisis. Threats to personal security, when combined with economic uncertainty and rising global tension, create a feeling of stress for many Americans. When people are under stress, they fall back upon past behaviors that have proven successful in the past for relieving stress. In the aftermath of September 11, some consumers turned to comfort foods. Others turned to the gym and strenuous activity for stress release or returned to old vices such as cigarettes and alcohol. Still others turned their feelings of stress into a justifier for more shopping.

When the crisis is long lasting or intensifies, stress relief will play a bigger role in shopping behavior. At the same time, consumers can cause themselves more stress by making expenditures they perceive as extravagant. Extravagance is in the eye of the beholder, but we can describe it as a purchase that a buyer cannot rationally justify. The higher the price, the harder consumers must work to find justifiers to give permission to make the purchase.

In the post-9/11 crisis, the sale of indulgence products, life's little luxuries that can be bought without guilt, will be vibrant for some time. Marketers and retailers need to be aware of new frugality taking hold in the American consumer characterized by a desire to get more perceived value for the money. Now is not the time to raise prices, but to look at ways to engineer products or find new suppliers in order to offer more indulgence value for a lower price. Promotions that focus on delivering more to the consumers, such as "two for the price of one" or "buy two get one free," are on target for today.

Consumers crave the comfort of traditions to relieve stress, so there is new demand for products that enhance and support family traditions. These include such things as Christmas and Hanukkah decorations, dinnerware for family get-togethers, kitchenware and kitchen décor, candles and fireplace or hearth products that "keep the home fires burning," and games and entertainment products that encourage high-quality family time. Back-to-basic toys give parents a chance to get down on the floor and play with their kids. Our holiday celebrations will hearken back to the past, as we try to re-create a Norman Rockwell Thanksgiving and a Victorian Christmas.

Suddenly, *Made in America* becomes a much more potent positioning statement, as buying American is now a patriotic duty. While Americans accept products manufactured in foreign countries, they will look for foreign-made goods that are produced for an American company. They also may look at labels to find out where goods are made and reject products manufactured in perceived terrorist nations, including Indonesia. Be forewarned: If your company's products are manufactured in any of these countries, be prepared to change manufacturing sources fast.

Products that convey a symbolic or inspirational meaning will be in great demand, especially flags and patriotic-themed products. Do not expect consumers to lose interest in displaying, wearing, or flying the "red white and blue" anytime soon. Inspirational themes, from God Bless America to angels, will attract more and more consumers as they seek peace in spiritual renewal. Bible sales, along with inspirational book titles, will see an upswing.

Nostalgia-themed products that recall a better, simpler time will bring comfort to consumers. Greeting cards, scrapbooks, diaries, and other products that enable personal communication will be in demand.

Inevitably, consumers seeking stress relief are going to change their shopping patterns. They may retreat to the safety of their home. When they shop, they may want to spend less time at the store. They will do more of their weekly shopping in a single shopping trip. More shopping will be done from home, with consumers turning to the Internet, mail-order catalogs, even party-based and other direct-selling businesses for their shopping needs.

Demographic Distinctions

Women are more strongly motivated than men by stress relief in their pursuit of discretionary products. Relaxation, a justifier closely aligned to stress relief, appeals more strongly than stress relief to both genders. Consumers aged 18 to 54 place a higher priority on stress relief. This justifier is not motivating to consumers aged 55 or older. Black consumers respond more strongly to stress relief in their discretionary purchases, while people living in households with two or more individuals consider it an important motivator for their purchases. Less-educated consumers feel more stress and seek relief more often in purchasing discretionary products.

JUSTIFIER #11: HOBBIES

Passion for a hobby is an important purchase justifier for two-thirds of consumers. Hobbies such as collecting, crafts, home workshops, photography, sports, and gardening drive many discretionary purchases. Collecting, for example, is a passion for over 40 percent of U.S. households, or in roughly 43 million homes. As birds of a feather flock together, so do collectors, with an average of 1.7 collectors per collecting household. That makes about 73 million Americans passionately driven to collect.

The most popular collectibles include:

- Coins, collected by an estimated 27 million Americans
- Figurines and sculpture, 20 million
- Trading cards, 18 million
- Memorabilia, 16 million
- Dolls, 16 million
- Christmas items, 15 million
- Plush/bean bag toys, 14 million

- Crystal figurines, 12 million
- Die-cast cars and models, 12 million
- Art prints and lithographs, 10 million
- Miniatures, 10 million

The typical collecting household maintains more than three separate collections. Out of the 43 million collecting households, an estimated 70 percent purchased one or more items for their collection in the past year.

The main reasons consumers collect include the joy of ownership and the thrill of the hunt. They also like the acquisition of a small luxury that brings pleasure without guilt, the achievement of special knowledge in an obscure subject area, and expression of identity, feelings, and values. As with all hobbies, the act of pursuing the hobby provides as much or more satisfaction and pleasure as that obtained in the completion of the hobby. For example, knitters and needle pointers enjoy the creation of their craft as much if not more than the actual object created. Exercisers and sports enthusiasts enjoy the playing, practicing, and working out as much or more than the toned, healthy body that is a result of their pastime. Collectors prize the search and hunt for the desired object as much or more than the new acquisition. One respondent explains his passion about collecting this way: "Don't you see? Collecting is all about the acquisition." He meant the act of acquiring (the verb), not the thing in and of itself (the noun). That is one reason why hobbyists like collectors are never finished. There is always some new challenge to pursue, some new desired object to find, something else to try.

Demographic Distinctions

Both genders are equally motivated by pursuit of a hobby in their discretionary purchases. Younger consumers aged 18 to 44 are more likely to express importance of a hobby in their discretionary purchases. While collecting tends to be more actively pursued among middle-aged consumers, aged 35 to 64, younger consumers collect icons from their youth that they can find and trade on Internet auction sites. By comparison, the oldest consumers, aged 65 and older, are more likely than any other age group to say that a hobby is of no importance at all. Three-or-more-person households rate the interests of a hobby as an important motivator for their discretionary purchases.

JUSTIFIER #12: GIFT FOR SELF

How many of us go out shopping for a gift for someone else and come home with not one gift, but two—one for the person we went shopping for and one for ourselves? Usually the personal gift bought costs more than the gift for the other person. A consumer explained how personal gifting is pursued in the course of gift shopping for someone else: "One for you and two for me." The primary gift-giving occasions are Christmas and birthdays, followed in order by Valentine's Day, weddings and anniversaries, Mother's Day, Father's Day, Easter, and other occasions, such as showers, etc. Gift spending corresponds to the relative closeness or distance in the relationship, except in the case of formal gift-giving occasions such as weddings. Thus, people spend more money on presents for children and spouses than on neighbors or work associates. In the case of formal gift-giving occasions such as weddings, consumers are far more likely to buy with an eye on status. Consequently, they will spend more on such gifts.

Nevertheless, they spend the most on themselves. One consumer explains how she picks the best for herself: "That [speaking of a less fine item] is one I would give as a gift, but this [a nicer item] is something I would keep for myself." The tendency to pick the best for yourself should not be attributed solely to selfishness. Most shoppers are far more attuned to what they like, as opposed to what someone else might like, so they are inclined to be more passionate about the gift intended for personal use.

Getting It Right

HALLMARK
The name is synonymous with gifts.

As the nation's leading greeting-card company, Hallmark's brand image is intimately tied to gift giving. With sales of $4.2 billion in 2002 and holding 55 percent of the total U.S. greeting-card market, Hallmark defines its business as that of "personal expression." Hallmark continues to extend its brand into new areas that support its core mission, including entertainment, the Binney & Smith Crayola brand, and even a corporate loyalty consulting business called Hallmark Loyalty Marketing Group. Because personal expression is a universal human need, the company maintains a global presence with operations in more than 100 countries and product offerings in more than 30 different languages. It boasts domestic distribution through 42,000 retail outlets, including 30,000 mass merchandisers, discounters, and grocery stores, and 5,700 specialty stores, the pinnacle of which is its 4,300 Hallmark Gold Crown stores.

In essence, people buy Hallmark to express emotions. Don Hall Jr., the recently named president and CEO says: "These human needs to connect, communicate, and celebrate are enduring needs, which is why I have such confidence in the future of our company." However, the way consumers express emotions is highly dependent upon the trends at work shifting and transforming the culture. Past Hallmark president Irv Hockaday explained it this way: "Hallmark doesn't look at itself so much as a greeting-card company as it does a company whose job it is to support and enhance relationships between people—parents, children, husbands, wives, friends, people in the workplace, and so on. Those needs I don't think are going to change. How our company responds to the needs is changing and will change."

To enable Hallmark to respond to the changing personal expression needs of consumers, Hallmark employs a trend expert, Marita Wesely-Clough, to head up the trend-tracking research team. Her job is to identify consumer trends as they emerge and help Hallmark prepare for the future. Wesely-Clough explains: "It's essential to stay close to consumers to know what is influencing the thoughts and feelings they want to express. We research emerging trends years ahead so that when people are comfortable reflecting new ideas and attitudes, Hallmark already has 'thought of that,' and exactly the right card is in the store."

While the company holds its "cards" close to the vest in terms of where its future lies, it does reveal it is actively investigating how it can take the "essence of the greeting card" into new arenas. John Breeder, vice president of greeting cards explains: "Hallmark also is expanding into areas that consumers give 'permission' for Hallmark to develop—where consumers trust Hallmark to provide solutions to help them communicate, connect, and celebrate."

Demographic Distinctions

Men and women are equally likely to indulge themselves in buying personal gifts. All age groups fall victim to this desire, except for the very oldest consumers, those older than age 65. Black consumers respond more highly to this tendency than other racial and ethnic groups. College graduates and those with post-graduate education are more likely than less-well-educated consumers to view giving a gift to oneself as an important motivator for discretionary purchases.

JUSTIFIER #13: IMPULSE PURCHASE

Buying on impulse is an important factor in discretionary purchases for about 40 percent of consumers. Based upon our survey, buying on impulse is about half as important as making a planned purchase. While the consumer who plans his or her purchase gains satisfaction from the emotional buildup and anticipation surrounding the upcoming purchase, the impulse shopper gains a sense of power and entitlement from making an impulse buy. One respondent explains: "I see something I like and I buy it. It's knowing that you are the one that got it. It gives me a feeling of power."

Sales are a powerful motivator for impulse purchases. Finding a good price or a bargain is the ultimate justifier for purchase because it instantly takes away any guilt associated with making an unplanned, spontaneous purchase. "I like to save money," one consumer says. "If I can save money, I'll buy it, even if it is something I was just thinking of buying, but not necessarily at that time." Another consumer explains: "When I find something on sale, I feel like a winner." Feelings of guilt are a powerful demotivator for buying something you don't need. A sale takes the guilt away. "I think if you buy something you don't need, you feel guilty, but if you find it on sale, then you feel less guilty," explains a consumer.

OUTLET SHOPPING
Brand Names at Bargain Prices

Serving the needs of impulse and value shoppers nationwide are the country's roughly 300 shopping centers that feature manufacturers' outlets. These bargain-oriented outlet malls attract consumers in search of brand-name products at a discount. Linda Humphers, editor-in-chief of *Value Retail News,* published by the International Council of Shopping Centers, explains: "From the customer's point of view, the ability to find a wide assortment of goods with well-known brand names, in a specialty store atmosphere with value pricing, is the major lure." The biggest draws in outlet shopping are the upper-tier brand names that are traditionally carried in department stores and specialty boutiques, like Ralph Lauren Polo, Liz Claiborne, and Brooks Brothers. These brand companies favor the control they get in inventory selection and brand image when they operate their own outlets. Humphers says: "Those in the outlet sector realize how much better it is to put overruns and past season's goods in an environment they control, rather than with a jobber or an off-price retailer that might jam designer goods onto broken hangers next to low-end merchandise."

Also a critical component in the outlet shopping experience is location. "Not to be underestimated is the location of many outlet centers in resorts, where time-deprived consumers can relax and take their leisure time to shop for bargains," Humphers adds.

Accounting for roughly $15 billion in annual sales, outlet shopping is still relatively small in the grand scheme of the nation's $3 trillion retail sector. Yet outlet malls exert a powerful pull on the shopper's psyche that goes beyond the right combination of price, selection, and quality. As Humphers states: "Since most of us rarely need anything we buy, outlet shoppers can justify their purchases as intelligent and sensible because they know the brands and they know what they're worth. Besides, we all like to think of ourselves as smart consumers, and smart consumers check out the outlets."

Demographic Distinctions

Men are more likely than women to buy discretionary products on impulse, thus destroying the illusion that men are the more rational shoppers. Younger consumers, especially those aged 18 to 24, are more likely to act on impulse in shopping than older consumers, especially those aged 55 or older. These more mature consumers are the most likely to rate impulse buying as of little or no importance in their purchase decisions. Consumers at lower income levels as well as those at the highest are most highly driven to make impulse purchases. Less-educated consumers also give impulse purchasing a higher priority.

JUSTIFIER #14: STATUS

Status, finally, is the least recognized justifier for discretionary purchases. In this politically correct era, less than one-third of consumers are willing to own up to status as important in making discretionary purchase decisions. Harvard University's Juliet Schor views America's preoccupation with shopping and buying as "competitive consumption." For her, buying things is all about status and class distinctions. I will not go that far, but our research clearly shows that the consumers surveyed understated status as a justifier in buying discretionary products. In focus groups, respondents describe status as feelings of envy that arise when someone else has something they desire. Consumers also express status through friends, family, neighbors, and associates whom they recognize as individuals who have "made it."

Status plays a more important role as a justifier in purchasing products that are visible to others, such as clothes, watches, cars, coats, and patio furniture. Status is of lesser importance for products that are less visible, such as mattresses, bedding, washing machines, and dryers. So the more visible the product is to the outside world, the more important, overall, the role of status in the purchase.

One consumer explained the role of status: "I collect Longaberger baskets. I must have a 100 or more. I just love them. For me, having Longaberger baskets is about making me feel good, not necessarily status. But when people come into my home and see how many baskets I have displayed, they say, 'Wow! Look at that.'" Another explains her passion for gardening as partly related to showing the garden off to her neighbors and friends: "I just spent $400 on plants, including six baskets for the front porch and more baskets for the fence. We have a huge yard and all the neighbors come to see the garden. From now until frost, there is always something new coming up. It is gorgeous. I love showing off my yard. It's not really status, but it is so cool to have people come around and see all the different plants. I like to spread my passion for gardening."

G *etting* **I** *t* **R** *ight*

TIFFANY
Status in a Robin's-Egg-Blue Box

Today's ultimate gift comes wrapped in a robin's-egg-blue box with a white ribbon. What is inside? It doesn't really matter because the package says, "It's from Tiffany's," arguably the United States' most prestigious home-grown luxury brand, which has served the carriage trade since 1837. In fact, so much of the Tiffany brand's identity is tied up in its box that the company has registered trademarks for TIFFANY BLUE BOX and the color TIFFANY BLUE.

The company's stated mission is "about things that last," reflecting its timeless delivery of superior-quality products and service. With over three-fourths of the company's sales represented by jewelry, the company also offers a broad-based mix of luxury lifestyle products, notably timepieces, sterling silver, china, crystal, stationery, fragrances, and accessories. Its reputation as a premier luxury brand has been nurtured for over 165 years, when the company opened its first retail store in downtown Manhattan. Today, about 10 percent of the company's $1.2 billion in 2002 sales are credited to Tiffany's Fifth Avenue flagship store. Besides the company's flagship store, it operates about 50 other U.S.-based retail establishments and has been undergoing worldwide expansion through over 75 international stores. Not satisfied to wait for the customer to come to them, Tiffany's also maintains an active direct-marketing program through the Internet and catalogs and mailed out 24 million catalogs in 2002. Tiffany views its brand expansively. The brand means more than simply products. It is about the experience of shopping in a wonderful environment "where exceptional products can be touched and where extraordinary service can be fully experienced," explains its 2000 annual report. While the company's hallmark is superior products and service, its strategies "have never been about fashion or luxury or excess," says the shareholders' letter from Chairman William Chaney and President/CEO Michael Kowalski. While brand identity is often thought of as a marketing concept, it also represents significant financial equity. *BusinessWeek* magazine valued the Tiffany brand at $3.48 billion in 2001, placing it among the top 75 of the world's most valuable brands. That is a lot of money riding on a simple cardboard box of robin's-egg blue.

Demographic Distinctions

Status is a gender-neutral justifier, impacting men and women equally. Younger consumers aged 18 to 34 are more likely than other age groups to say status is important in their discretionary purchasing. Black consumers view status as more important than do white or Hispanic consumers. Lower-to-moderate-income households are more involved with status as a motivator than higher-income households. Households with two or more individuals rate status as a more important motivator for their discretionary purchases.

ACTION PLAN: PUTTING JUSTIFIERS TO WORK

To move shoppers to action—that is, to buy something they don't need—consumer marketers must provide sufficient justifiers to overcome barriers to purchase and give people a reason to buy. Because consumers buy products for many different reasons, marketers need to make sure all of those reasons are reflected back to the consumer at every point of contact, including advertising and point-of-purchase. Key for any marketer is to understand how a particular product improves the quality of the consumer's life. Marketers need to define the different dimensions on which the consumer derives satisfaction from their products. Then they must communicate the new quality-of-life value proposition clearly and effectively. The 14 justifiers examined in this

> To move shoppers to action—that is, to buy something they don't need—consumer marketers must provide sufficient justifiers to overcome barriers to purchase and give people a reason to buy.

chapter all play a part in driving the consumer to action. Marketers may stimulate an impulse purchase with an attractive sales offer, capture more add-on sales as a consumer makes a major planned purchase, or offer stress relief and comfort through the product's use or the shopping experience. For discretionary and luxury purchases, consumer marketers and retailers need to stack the value equation in favor of the consumer, to break down barriers and encourage consumers to buy.

Here are some additional tips to encourage people to buy things they don't need:

- Justifiers work together to create a predisposition to buy. Consumers ultimately make the decision to buy in their hearts—at the emotional level—but they need justifiers to rationalize the purchase decision with their heads. All the rational justifiers in the world will not make consumers buy things they really do not want. Marketers need to capture the attention of the consumer, draw him or her emotionally into the product, help create personal fantasies about how life will be enhanced through ownership, and then provide rationally based justifiers that give permission to buy.

- As the consumer's purchase decision is multidimensional, so too must the justifiers be multidimensional. No single justifier works alone. Rather, they work together to encourage the consumer to buy. Marketers need to explore the comprehensive scope of how the product enhances the quality of the consumer's life. In my experience, company executives may think they know how their products enhance the quality of customers' lives, even when they have not done any research. However, rarely do they have a clue about the real emotional hot buttons that turn a desire into a need in the consumer's mind. You need to dig deeply into the consumer psyche to figure it out. It takes hard work and a commitment to consumer research. High-quality, highly intuitive consumer research is critical to uncover the full dimension of justifiers at work when consumers make a purchase decision. Focus groups, in-depth one-on-one interviews, and other qualitative research methods are useful tools to find out the real reason why consumers are drawn to the product.

Consumers ultimately make the decision to buy in their hearts—at the emotional level—but they need justifiers to rationalize the purchase decision with their heads.

- Discretionary product marketers compete against other companies and products within their class as well as across a wide range of product categories. Today's consumer can pick among many different products and services to

  > Marketers need to view the competitive landscape horizontally, as well as vertically.

  achieve stress relief, relaxation, pleasure, and so forth. Marketers must work hard to make sure the consumer picks their product, not a competitor's. They need to view the competitive landscape horizontally, as well as vertically. With such stiff competition, no company that wants to grow and succeed can ignore the need to engage their consumers on an emotional level, to turn wants into needs, and win their hearts through effective marketing and communication.

- Justifiers are even more important when marketing to women. Women as a rule are more frugal than men are. They are less willing to spend money on themselves, and when they do, they spend less money than men do. It takes more effort on the part of marketers to get women to open their pocketbooks and buy products they don't need. Therefore, in the marketing of products that appeal mainly to women, marketers need to work even harder in stacking the justifier equation in the consumer's favor. Women need more permission to buy, and justifiers are the secret.

- The cascade effect offers opportunity for add-on purchases. One purchase often leads to another as the consumer uses the original purchase as a justifier for a cascade of additional purchases. Marketers and retailers can put this cascade effect to good use to spur additional sales. Opportunities abound to offer items in groupings, special-offer packages, and suites. Make these deals even more attractive by offering special-discount pricing to give the consumer one more reason to buy today. Look at ways to engineer products in order to offer more indulgence value for a lower price. Promotions that focus on delivering more to the consumers, such as "two for the price of one" or "buy two get one free," are on target for today.

  > Women need more permission to buy, and justifiers are the secret.

5

WHAT THINGS PEOPLE BUY
THAT THEY DON'T NEED

Now that we have explored why people buy things they don't need, let us look more closely at exactly what categories of discretionary products they are buying. In 2000, 2001, and 2003, Unity Marketing conducted a nationwide survey of 1,000 U.S. households representing a statistical sample of the country's population, thus providing statistically reliable and projectable information. These surveys were also conducted at the same time in the year, during the third quarter, to provide reliable trend information. But what's really special about this survey data is it provides a snapshot of the consumer market in the last week of August 2001, just about a week before the 9/11 tragedy and resulting consumer turmoil.

A period of two years spans the previous survey and the final survey conducted during the fall of 2003, a period of tremendous political and economic upheaval at home and abroad. These ensuing two years give us some needed distance and perspective with which to evaluate the real impact of September 11 and its aftermath on the consumers' psyche. Personally I believe September 11 will prove to be a defining moment for all Americans alive at the time, but especially among the generation of younger Americans. It will be a turning point in the course of economic and political history in this country and the world. This twenty-first century is a very different kind of world than the post-war years from 1950 to 1999. It is my hope that September 11 and its aftermath will never reach the comparable cost in American lives and resources as World War II. But its impact on the soul of America and Americans, I believe, will be just as profound. Why? It's the CNN effect. World War II was fought at a distance and viewed in carefully edited movie reels of black & white. Soldiers like my father fought and fully experienced that war; everybody else just saw shadows. But we all lived and experienced September 11 together, thanks to 24/7 cable news. It was virtual reality at its most real.

> September 11 will prove to be a defining moment for all Americans alive at the time, but especially among the generation of younger Americans.

In this marketing research survey of consumer purchases within 37 different categories of products most people describe as extras and things we simply don't need, we can begin to see and measure how September 11 and its aftermath have influenced and changed the consumer's mind-set and thus their shopping behavior. In the 2003 survey, we added a few additional categories, most notably apparel and clothing as well as window curtains and coverings and musical instruments, that were either intentionally omitted or overlooked in the previous survey. In 2003, we continue to exclude from our discussion discretionary consumables, or food and drink people buy that they don't need, because so much of the food we consume is extra and unnecessary. My apologies in advance to the candy, cookie, cake, and snack producers, as well as the beer, wine, and distilled spirits industry.

AFTER RISING IN 2001, CONSUMER PURCHASES RETREATED A NOTCH IN 2003

Long before the Internet, omnibus telephone surveys, and mall intercepts, Benjamin Disraeli said, "There are three kinds of lies: lies, damn lies, and statistics." So let's just forget about the worst of the three, statistics, and talk a little about the limitations of consumer surveys.

Consumers are notoriously fickle and what they remember buying one day may be different than what they remember buying the next. So when analyzing the results of this or any other consumer survey, we must recognize that the resulting data is only as good as the answers that go into it. In other words, no survey will ever give you the REAL answer, only an approximation of reality within the scope and limitations of the survey methodology and sample that is used.

There are ways to gather really precise and accurate consumer purchase data that involves large panels of consumers willing to record their

The consumers have taken a step back in their purchase of most discretionary products after September 11.

purchases daily or weekly in consumer diaries. And those types of surveys cost bucket loads of money. That isn't what we have here. Rather, we asked a similar group of people during a similar time of year about their purchases of various consumer products using the same wording and the same telephone fielding company and methodology. The result we trust is a similar result that allows for general comparisons from year to year. Any survey, even those most precisely conducted, has a margin of error, which means the real answer is somewhere within a range of 2 or 3 or 5 percentage points above or below the stated result. So we also must consider those margins of error when we look at the purchase incidence data that follows.

Given those limitations, one could argue that most of the ups and downs noted year after year in these surveys of consumer purchase incidence of discretionary products falls within the margin of error and so in reality are meaningless. But my researcher's highly refined sense of the data says that this is not so. We see a notable upward trend in the purchase incidence of just about every discretionary product category from 2000 to 2001, just prior to September 11. In 2003, on the other hand, the overall direction is downward, with many categories falling back to pre-2001 levels or even lower in some instances. While my reason tells me most of these ups and downs can be attributed to margin of error, my intuition says otherwise.

The consumers have taken a step back in their purchase of most discretionary products after September 11. These changes are meaningful to every consumer retailer and marketer in the country. If we compare the average percentage point change in purchase incidence from 2000 to 2001 and 2001 to 2003 for comparable categories, we find the average change in purchase incidence is positive 10 points for 2001, while it is negative 2 points in 2003. The only product categories that posted meaningful positive increases in 2003 over 2001 were sporting goods, exercise equipment, and supplies in the entertainment, recreation, and hobbies category, and aromatherapy, Christmas and other seasonal decorations, art, prints, and lithographs, and wall décor in home. Everything else either remained the same as in 2001 or declined. See Figure 5.1 for the results in each category.

As we stand back and assess these differences, there are two things that have been brewing in the culture that change what we buy. Everything about shopping and the way we shop has undergone titanic changes since the early 1990s. And the cocooning trend that has dominated our consumer culture has come to an end only to be replaced by the new

FIGURE 5.1

Discretionary Product Purchase Incidence

	2000	2001	2003
Entertainment, Recreation, and Hobbies			
Audio equipment and stereo systems	31%	35%	26%
Books, magazines, and newsletters	68	78	74
Computers and software for home use	40	50	47
Crafts, sewing, knitting, and needlework supplies	33	39	29
Musical instruments*			10
Pet accessories	35	42	41
Photography equipment and supplies	38	51	43
Prerecorded video, music, DVD, etc.	66	79	62
Sporting goods, exercise equipment, and supplies	36	43	48
Toys, games, and dolls	45	54	50
TVs, radios, VCRs, DVD players, etc.	38	46	38
Home and Home Décor			
Aromatherapy and scented household products	39	42	49
Arts, prints, and lithographs	21	27	42
Baskets, boxes, vases, pots, and decorative holders*			42
Candles and candle accessories	54	65	62
Christmas decorations and other seasonal decorations		55	61
Collectibles	31	34	36
Figurines and sculpture	20	19	22
Florals and greenery for indoor use	38	43	41
Flowers, seeds, shrubs, and trees for outdoor landscaping	50	59	56
Furniture and occasional furniture	35	41	41
Garden equipment and decorative items for garden and patio	41	47	42
Greeting cards and personal stationery		72	83
Home textiles and rugs	51	60	52
Kitchenware and accessories	46	58	56
Lamps and lighting accessories	24	33	30
Picture frames	40	52	48
Tabletop china, crystal, silver, sterling flatware, and other dinnerware	16	26	16
Wall décor, such as sconces, mirrors, shelves, and tapestries	22	25	38
Window coverings, blinds, curtains, and other window treatments*			37
Personal Luxuries			
Fashion accessories such as handbags, wallets, belts, shoes, etc.*			63
Infant's and children's clothing and apparel*			36
Jewelry and watches	40	48	46
Men's clothing and apparel*			55
Personal care products that are more "special" or "exclusive" than everyday brands	50	71	64
Teen and tween clothing and apparel*			24
Women's clothing and apparel*			65

New categories added in 2003

connecting trend with paradigm shifting impacts on the consumer culture. Let's look more closely at each of these trends.

SHOPPING: SO MANY STORES, SO LITTLE TIME

Virtually everything about shopping has changed. From the early 1990s until the present, the number and range of our shopping choices have exploded. Just look around your town. Where there used to be a couple of shopping areas clumped together in defined shopping districts, today there are minimalls, strip centers, and freestanding stores on almost every corner. Shopping options are everywhere and continue to grow and expand.

Even while stores and shopping centers are multiplying exponentially, our ability to shop from the comfort and convenience of home has also mushroomed. Just about any consumer good you can think of can be purchased over the telephone or via the Internet. A review of retail sales by type of store in 1992 and 2002 provides insight about the winners and losers in retail shopping. Total percentage change in retail over the period was 77 percent, from $1,275 billion in 1992 to $2,257 billion in 2002. An index based upon the average percentage change shows how much faster or slower the particular type of store's results were compared to the average, as shown in Figure 5.2.

Among the biggest winners from 1992 to 2002 were nonstore retailers, which includes the Internet, direct mail, mail order catalog, and television shopping. The nonstore retailing segment more than doubled revenues during the previous ten years and grew 80 percent faster than the retail average (e.g., index of 180). Furnishing and electronics stores also were big gainers, growing 34 percent faster than the average, along with building and garden retailers, up 32 percent more than average, and health and personal care, increasing 44 percent more than average. But the fastest growing retail segment were the other general merchandisers, warehouse clubs, and all the other general merchandise stores (Wal-Mart, Costco, Sam's Club, and all the rest), which increased by 2.5 times faster than the retail average.

So how are consumers responding to such far-reaching changes going on in the retail marketplace? Because shoppers are shopping less and less out of need, and more and more out of desire, and they have more and more choices in where and how they shop, the mental checklist they use to decide where to

> Virtually everything about shopping has changed.

FIGURE 5.2

Total Retail Trade in Millions

Retail Sales by Type of Store, 1992–2002
in billions, excludes motor vehicles, gasoline, and food service

	1992	2002	% CHG '92-'02	INDEX
Furnishings and electronics	$ 97.8	$ 198.6	103.1	134
Building and garden	160.2	323.1	101.7	132
Food and beverage	371.5	508.5	36.9	48
Health and personal care	90.8	191.6	111.0	144
Clothing and accessories	120.3	178.6	48.5	63
Sporting goods and hobby/books	49.3	81.5	65.3	85
General merchandise total	248.0	476.1	92.0	119
Department store	177.1	217.9	23.0	30
Other general	70.9	258.3	264.3	343
Miscellaneous stores	55.8	105	88.2	114
Nonstore	81.3	194	138.6	180
Total retail trade	1,275.0	2,257.1	77.0	100

Source: Census Bureau

go for their particular shopping objective has fundamentally changed. Going shopping is no longer a question of what product do I need and where am I likely to find it. Rather because consumers can find the product—any product—they need in so many new and different places, the shopping equation is reduced to one thing: What kind of shopping experience do I desire? Shopping today has shifted at its very core; shopping is no longer about the thing, but about the experience.

And the experiences they want in shopping have expanded and diversified as much as the particular shopping choices have. Do I want a luxury shopping experience, where I am pampered and waited on? Do I want a discount shopping experience, where I get the experiential thrill of finding something great for less? Do I want an efficient shopping experience? Do I want a convenient shopping experience? Do I want a fast shopping experience? Do I want a browsing, leisurely shopping experience?

For me as a shopper—and I think I am pretty representative of many women my age who work and have a family to care for—the shopping experience I want 90 percent of the time is one that is efficient, easy, simple, and fast. I am not a discount, coupon-clipping shopper. That takes too much time and effort. I am always willing to trade off more money for less

Shopping is no longer about the thing, but about the experience.

> Thus, we have three different shoppers with three different priorities and they all end up at the same place: a discount department store.

hassle. But with the Super Wal-Mart store five miles from my house, I don't have to do that. I can get my groceries cheap at the same time I maximize efficiency. I know people who won't shop at Wal-Mart on principle. For me, principles be damned, I have so little time in which to shop I want it as quick and painless as possible.

Other women, so many of whom I see in focus groups, are driven to buy things at the lowest price. Their mental arithmetic is very different from mine. They are willing to trade off time for savings and will drive an extra half-hour to save a few dollars. And where do they shop? They shop at the same Wal-Mart store where I shop.

Other women are just born to shop, and I see lots of them in the luxury focus groups I do. They live and breathe to shop. They spend their spare time browsing the stores, seeing who has what and at what price. While they can pay full price, they measure their success at the shopping game through the amount of money they save. They are the type who will take their weekly shopping list and go from butcher to baker getting the very best of everything. Then they will go to Wal-Mart or Costco to get everything else. Thus, we have three different shoppers with three different priorities and they all end up at the same place: a discount department store.

In terms of the 37 product categories researched here (see Figure 5.3), discount department stores are the most widely chosen shopping source for 18, or about half, of these products. For the remaining 19 product categories where discount department stores are not number one, discount department stores are the second most popular source in 15 categories. In other words, for 90 percent of all the discretionary products researched here, discount department stores are either the number one or number two shopping source.

While more and more consumers turn to discount department stores to shop for life's extras, the Internet is becoming more important for many consumers. For these shoppers the Internet delivers a shopping experience that they crave. Out of the 37 product categories researched in this book, there are 7 where more than two out of ten shoppers are likely to buy through the Internet. The high-incidence Internet product categories include: books, magazines, and newsletters (32 percent); computers and software for home use (30 percent); women's clothing and apparel (29 percent); collectibles (28 percent); musical instruments (24 percent); prerecorded video, music, DVD (23 percent); and teen and tween apparel (21 percent). Among the Internet's key experiential advan-

FIGURE 5.3

Where People Buy Things They Don't Need

	SOURCE #1	SOURCE #2	SOURCE #3
Entertainment, Recreation, and Hobbies			
Audio equipment and stereo systems	Electronics/ Appliance	Discount Department Store	Nonstore
Books, magazines, and newsletters	Sport/Hobby/ Book/Music Store	Discount Department Store	Nonstore
Computers and software for home use	Electronics/ Appliance Store	Discount Department Store	Nonstore
Crafts, sewing, knitting, and needlework supplies	Discount Department Store	Sport/Hobby/ Book/Music Store	Other Specialty Store
Musical instruments	Sport/Hobby/ Book/Music Store	Other Specialty Store	Nonstore
Pet accessories	Discount Department Store	Other Specialty Store	Food and Beverage Store
Photography equipment and supplies	Discount Department Store	Electronics/ Appliance Store	Nonstore
Prerecorded video, music, DVD, etc.	Discount Department Store	Electronics/ Appliance Store	Sport/Hobby/ Book/Music Store
Sporting goods, exercise equipment, and supplies	Sport/Hobby/ Book/Music Store	Discount Department Store	Traditional Department Store
Toys, games, and dolls	Discount Department Store	Other Specialty Store	Traditional Department Store
TVs, radios, VCRs, DVD players, etc.	Discount Department Store	Electronics/ Appliance Store	Traditional Department Store
Home and Home Décor			
Aromatherapy and scented household products	Discount Department Store	Traditional Department Store	Other Specialty Store
Arts, prints, and lithographs	Furniture and Home Furnishings Store	Discount Department Store	Other Specialty Store

(continued)

FIGURE 5.3

Where People Buy Things They Don't Need, continued

	SOURCE # 1	SOURCE #2	SOURCE #3
Baskets, boxes, vases, pots, and decorative holders	Discount Department Store	Traditional Department Store	Home Improvement Store
Candles and candle accessories	Discount Department Store	Other Specialty Store	Furniture and Home Furnishings Store
Christmas decorations and other seasonal decorations	Discount Department Store	Traditional Department Store	Other Specialty Store
Collectibles	Other Specialty Store	Nonstore	Discount Department Store
Figurines and sculpture	Other Specialty Store	Traditional Department Store	Discount Department Store
Florals and greenery for indoor use	Home Improvement Store	Discount Department Store	Other Specialty Store
Flowers, seeds, shrubs, and trees for outdoor landscaping	Home Improvement Store	Discount Department Store	Other Specialty Store
Furniture and occasional furniture	Furniture and Home Furnishings Store	Discount Department Store	Traditional Department Store
Garden equipment and decorative items for garden and patio	Home Improvement Store	Discount Department Store	Traditional Department Store
Greeting cards and personal stationery	Discount Department Store	Food and Beverage Store	Other Specialty Store
Home textiles and rugs	Discount Department Store	Traditional Department Store	Furniture and Home Furnishings Store
Kitchenware and accessories	Discount Department Store	Traditional Department Store	Other Specialty Store
Lamps and lighting accessories	Discount Department Store	Traditional Department Store	Furniture and Home Furnishings Store
Picture frames	Discount Department Store	Traditional Department Store	Other Specialty Store
Tabletop china, crystal, silver, sterling flatware, and other dinnerware	Traditional Department Store	Discount Department Store	Other Specialty Store

FIGURE 5.3

Where People Buy Things They Don't Need, continued

	SOURCE #1	SOURCE #2	SOURCE #3
Wall décor, such as sconces, mirrors, shelves, and tapestries	Furniture and Home Furnishings Store	Discount Department Store	Other Specialty Store
Window coverings, blinds, curtains, and other window treatments	Discount Department Store	Traditional Department Store	Home Improvement Store
Personal Luxuries			
Fashion accessories, such as handbags, wallets, belts, shoes, etc.	Traditional Department Store	Discount Department Store	Clothing Store
Infant's and children's clothing and apparel	Discount Department Store	Traditional Department Store	Clothing Store
Jewelry and watches	Traditional Department Store	Clothing Store	Discount Department Store
Men's clothing and apparel	Traditional Department Store	Discount Department Store	Clothing Store
Personal care products that are more "special" or "exclusive" than everyday brands	Discount Department Store	Health/Drug Store	Traditional Department Store
Teen and tweens clothing and apparel	Traditional Department Store	Discount Department Store	Clothing Store
Women's clothing and apparel	Traditional Department Store	Discount Department Store	Clothing Store

tages are the convenience of shopping at home and the ability to easily compare prices. While many consumers remain concerned about sharing their credit card numbers over the Internet, shoppers are increasingly shopping across media. For example, they might comparison shop online then go to the store to make the actual purchase. Or they might visit stores to touch-and-feel specific branded items, then go home to get the best price online. Figure 5.4 lists the percentage of items not purchased in traditional retail stores.

Among the Internet's key experiential advantages are the convenience of shopping at home and the ability to easily compare prices.

FIGURE 5.4

Where People Buy Things They Don't Need

	NONSTORE
Entertainment, Recreation, and Hobbies	
Audio equipment and stereo systems	13%
Books, magazines, and newsletters	32
Computers and software for home use	30
Crafts, sewing, knitting, and needlework supplies	15
Musical instruments	24
Pet accessories	8
Photography equipment and supplies	15
Prerecorded video, music, DVD, etc.	23
Sporting goods, exercise equipment, and supplies	13
Toys, games, and dolls	15
TVs, radios, VCRs, DVD players, etc.	7
Home and Home Décor	
Aromatherapy and scented household products	12
Arts, prints, and lithographs	8
Baskets, boxes, vases, pots, and decorative holders	13
Candles and candle accessories	13
Christmas decorations and other seasonal decorations	11
Collectibles	28
Figurines and sculpture	18
Florals and greenery for indoor use	5
Flowers, seeds, shrubs, and trees for outdoor landscaping	6
Furniture and occasional furniture	7
Garden equipment and decorative items for garden and patio	7
Greeting cards and personal stationery	15
Home textiles and rugs	9
Kitchenware and accessories	10
Lamps and lighting accessories	10
Picture frames	6
Tabletop china, crystal, silver, sterling flatware, and other dinnerware	12
Wall décor, such as sconces, mirrors, shelves, and tapestries	8
Window coverings, blinds, curtains, and other window treatments	7
Personal Luxuries	
Fashion accessories, such as handbags, wallets, belts, shoes, etc.	17
Infant and children's clothing and apparel	14
Jewelry and watches	17
Men's clothing and apparel	18
Personal care products that are more "special" or "exclusive" than everyday brands	11
Teen and tweens clothing and apparel	21
Women's clothing and apparel	29

Shopping today has fundamentally changed. It is no longer about the thing, but the experience. Every shopper has different experiential expectations and to make it even more confounding they have different experiential expectations at different times and under different circumstances. Store-based retailers are like spiders spinning a web trying to trap shoppers and draw them into their store. Too many retailers make the mistake of thinking that the primary snare to draw the shopper in is the things they sell. Sometimes that may work, but less and less so. Rather they need to spin a web of experience, communicate the experience, and use that as the primary draw to attract shoppers into the store.

G *e t t i n g* **I** *t* **R** *i g h t*

BUILD-A-BEAR
It's all about the experience.

Back in 1997 during the heady days of the Beanie Babies phenomenon, Maxine Clark figured there had to be some creative retailing opportunity based upon the universal attraction between kids and bears—teddy bears, that is. While Maxine had an impressive retailing résumé including being named one of the "30 Most Powerful People in Discount Store Retailing" by *Discount Store News* in 1995 and serving more than 25 years with the May Department Stores Company, most recently as president of May's Payless Shoe Store chain, she knew she couldn't go it alone in the new business venture she was conceiving. So she looked around and got the very best toy consultant she could find, her ten-year-old friend Katie. Together in one night they created a business plan and Build-A-Bear Workshop was born.

For Maxine the road to Build-A-Bear started in her own childhood. "Back when I was growing up, going shopping was a really 'big thing.' There were no malls, so when you went shopping, you got dressed up and went downtown. There was magic in the shopping experience back then and I wanted to re-create that feeling for kids today," Maxine says.

Since its founding, Build-A-Bear has grown to 151 stores in the United States, including four locations in Canada. The industry has taken notice by naming Build-A-Bear Workshop the International 2001 Retail Innovator of the Year. With sales expected to be $200 million in 2003, the

The bears are free; you only pay for the fun of creating them.

company has just opened its first international shop in England with plans to franchise the concept overseas in Korea, Japan, and France, among other countries. Explaining the growth strategy, Maxine says: "Ours is a really unique retailing concept that appeals to the 'kid' in all of us. People love teddy bears and they also love the bear-making process.

"We've taken the plush business to the next dimension. We designed personalization and customization of our bears into the core of our business concept. That makes it very hard for other people to imitate or copy us," she explains.

In today's discount-driven shopping environment, Build-A-Bear has mastered the price/value equation. "Our basic bear costs between $10 [and] $25, and that price hasn't changed since we first opened. That includes the unstuffed animal 'skins,' the stuffing that you select the thickness of, the heart you put into the bear with a wish, the birth certificate where the child names his or her bear, and the 'cub condo' box that is used to transport the bear to its new home. The only thing[s] a la carte are the clothes, shoes, and accessories that we call 'bearphernalia,'" Maxine says.

So the price is right, but in reality you really aren't buying the bears at all, as one of Maxine's customers pointed out: "The bears are free; you only pay for the fun of creating them." Thus the experience building a bear is like the price of an admission ticket to Disney World, and what you "really" pay for. The teddy bear you create in the Build-A-Bear store becomes a tactile reminder that connects you with the memories of a special day. "Kids are wonderfully creative and parents and grandparents happily pay for the experience of their kids creating something really special and meaningful to them. We want our stores to be truly fun places for children and their parents. I think we have done that by all the letters I read. It's a priority for me to stay in touch with the customers by reading and responding to their mail and e-mail," Maxine explains.

One of the secrets of Maxine's success in Build-A-Bear Workshop is she has kept the company firmly 'kid-centric.' She holds the opinions of kids as so fundamental to her company's mission that she has recruited an advisory board made up of 20 children ages 6 to 14. "Our Cub Advisory Board personally reviews all the animals, clothes, and new products. They keep us focused on their priorities and issues. We don't do anything without getting their input," Maxine says.

Maxine's got big, bold plans for the Build-A-Bear Workshop that extend far beyond the store concept. "Very early in my career I discovered the power of licensing, where one plus one equals ten, not just two. It's about taking something wonderful and extending it even further than you ever expected," she says.

For starters, they have teamed up with Evergreen Concepts, a Los Angeles, California–based licensing management firm to license books, calendars, greeting cards, and gift products featuring Build-A-Bear characters. They have a unique licensing arrangement with shoe retailer Skechers to cobrand a line of bear shoes. They also have just announced a deal with Hasbro to take a line of unique-sized stuffed animals, clothes, and accessories to major toy retailers, thus extending their offerings beyond their current chain of stores. Hasbro will also develop other products that extend the Build-A-Bear Workshop brand and associate them with Hasbro's iconic brands as well.

Maxine concludes, "For me this business has never been about the money. I love the industry and love the creativity that children demand. It's been a business driven solely from the heart." She proves that day in and day out in the charity efforts and good works that the company does. For example, they invited shoppers into their California stores to build a bear for the kids who lost their homes in the recent wildfires. "We try to make a difference in people's lives," she explains. And it shows in the company's success and Maxine's continued passion for the brand that she and her team of kid consultants have created.

END OF COCOONING:
NEW AGE OF CONNECTING

The concept of cocooning, a trend identified by Faith Popcorn back in the 1980s and which has dominated our thinking about the consumer culture ever since, has finally come to an end. As a culture, Americans en masse have emerged from the cocoon that kept us inwardly focused and house-bound for the past 20 years. During that time, consumers spent their energy and resources filling up their emotional empty spaces with things. We collected and we consumed until every nook and cranny of our homes were chock-a-block full of stuff. Our homes were literally bursting at the seams, so we had to buy even bigger homes with more square footage to hold all our stuff.

But today an entirely new sensibility is taking over. A new downscale, downsize, and anti-clutter approach is being reflected all throughout the culture. Martha Stewart who was so instrumental in helping us fully realize the cocooning lifestyle has taken a fall. *Real Simple* magazine, the magazine about simplifying your life, is Time Inc.'s runaway best-seller, while the rest of the shelter magazine category is struggling to remain afloat as advertisers abandon ship due to declining subscriber bases. TLC's *Clean Sweep* and HGTV's *Mission: Organization* teach us how to take control of our lives and get rid of the clutter.

Even TLC's enormously popular *While You Were Out* and *Trading Spaces* are not about the materialistic cocooning lifestyle, rather they reflect a new do-it-yourself approach to home decorating that is about doing more with less, not about gathering more stuff, collecting more things, or filling up all the empty spaces. Architect Sarah Susanka's surprise best-selling book, *The Not-So-Big House,* has given rise to a whole series of books based upon the original concept of living big in smaller spaces.

In focus groups with consumers whenever the home comes up, and it always does, so does a discussion about how much participants hate clutter and how they strive for an uncluttered, peaceful home environment. Just because the cocooning trend has come to an end, it doesn't mean consumers aren't going to buy things for their homes. But it does signal an entirely new nonmaterialistic sensibility that is driven by a need to express real values, meaning, and experience and not by a need to have and have more.

Consumers today are like butterflies that have emerged from the cocoon. They are turning away from the overt materialism that was characteristic of the cocooning trend. With a "been there, done that" attitude, consumers have had their fill of feathering the nest and are now directing their energy beyond the home and into the outside world. The key trend word today is *connecting* and the marketers and retailers must turn their focus to connecting with the consumers' new needs and passions.

The connecting trend is about finding ways to link up and forge meaningful relationships in our social sphere. It is reflected in new linkages through media, travel, and electronic networks, as well as a desire to know our neighbors, get involved with our communities, to be better parents, better employees, better neighbors, better citizens, and better friends. It's about becoming a part of something bigger than one's own narrowly defined inner landscape. Through connecting we search for true meaning and an expres-

> Consumers today are like butterflies that have emerged from the cocoon. They are turning away from the overt materialism that was characteristic of the cocooning trend.

sion of essential values about who we are and what we hold most dear. We all know in our heart that things won't bring happiness and through connecting we are seeking beyond mindless consumerism to find ultimate meaning.

> We all know in our heart that things won't bring happiness and through connecting we are seeking beyond mindless consumerism to find ultimate meaning.

As Americans break out of the cocoon, they are assuming an active role in the social milieu by taking leadership in the social, political, and cultural landscapes that define their identity in relation to the outside world. At the local level people are becoming more involved with the schools, neighborhood watch programs, fire and emergency services, and church activities. This extends to the national arena where ordinary people are banding together to form interest groups that can take their grievances and concerns about injustice to the courts, our elected representatives, and to the media where Fox News's Bill O'Reilly promises to look out for you.

Connecting is all about creating meaningful relationships with others, near and far. We recognize today in a way that we couldn't really grasp before this period of global upheaval since September 11, that we are incredibly blessed to be Americans and to have all the material and social wealth and personal freedoms that we do. We are learning about our place in history and how for generations that came before, from the Founding Fathers to the soldiers now facing hostilities in Iraq, that our enormous blessings carry with them great responsibilities. In 2002, Americans directed $202 billion toward social giving, a 17.2 percent increase over $172.3 billion in personal giving in 2000. We want to give back to the society that has given us so much. We want to leave the world a better place for future generations. Thus, connecting links us with the past and the present, and into the future.

Consumers seek to connect by establishing a new equilibrium between the roles they play in their inner and external worlds. It is about connecting through both having and getting and giving and sharing. We see this played out with many of our cultural icons, like Bill Gates and Ted Turner. Both are extremely wealthy individuals with all the material riches and both are dedicating a significant portion of their wealth to endowments and charities that they believe will make the world a better place when they are gone.

> Connecting links us with the past and the present, and into the future.

Connecting brings values to the fore and a search for deeper meaning. And while we

The key marketing challenge for the future is to establish a true, meaningful, and lasting connection with the customer and prospective customer.

still want material goods and while we will still buy, connecting is ultimately a desire for a richer, deeper, more meaningful experience, rather than about more and more things. Figure 5.5 details personal consumption expenditures for 2000, 2001, and 2002.

The new connecting trend brings new challenges to product marketers and retailers. As consumers make new choices in the stores where they shop, the brands that they select, and the product categories they purchase, consumer marketers and retailers are discovering that their connection with the consumer is growing more and more tenuous. Today, connecting why people buy your product or shop in your store with how to reach them and where to reach them takes on new meaning. The key marketing challenge for the future is to establish a true, meaningful, and lasting connection with the customer and prospective customer.

Because connecting means a shift of focus from the concrete thing to the emotional experience, businesses that sell to the consumer need

FIGURE 5.5

Personal Consumption Expenditures in Millions

	2000	2001	2002	CHG '00-'02	SOM '02
Total personal consumption expenditures	$6,739.4	$7,045.4	$7,385.3	9.6%	100%
Food and tobacco	1,003.7	1,047.8	1,094.8	9.1	14.8
Clothing, accessories, and jewelry	397.0	396.8	405.5	2.1	5.5
Personal care	93.4	94.3	97.2	4.1	1.3
Housing	1,006.5	1,073.7	1,144.6	13.7	15.5
Household operation	719.3	738.4	748.3	4.0	10.1
Medical care	1,218.3	1,322.8	1,436.6	17.9	19.5
Personal business	539.1	539	564	4.6	7.6
Transportation	853.4	874	876.7	2.7	11.9
Recreation	585.7	603.4	633.9	8.2	8.6
Education and research	163.8	176.3	187.9	14.7	2.5
Religious and welfare activities	172.3	186.1	202	17.2	2.7
Foreign travel and other, net	−13	−7.2	−6.3	−51.5	−0.1

Source: Bureau of Economic Analysis

to connect with the consumer on this new emotional, experiential plane. Here are ways to achieve just that:

- *Talk less and listen more.* Today virtually all commercial communication is one-way (i.e., through advertisements the marketer tells the consumer what they want them to know). But that doesn't forge a connection. Rather it results in consumers turning off to an avalanche of meaningless, irrelevant ads. Marketers must establish new ways of creating meaningful two-way dialogue with their consumers. The success of eBay is that their entire corporate culture is based upon the premise of listening more to the consumer. Anything else won't do in today's connecting world.

- *Give more value, rather than take more money.* All businesses are in the business of making a profit, and consumers do not begrudge businesses a fair and reasonable profit. But they resent companies that are greedy and don't provide a good value for a fair price. Consumers today are driven by an experiential passion for bargain hunting because marketers and retailers have trained them to expect sales and discounts. There is another way, and that is to give the consumers more meaningful value in the products you offer and the shopping experiences you deliver. Women's fashion marketer, Chico's FAS, fully embraces the concept of connecting with the customer by giving more value and their reward is written every quarter on their rising balance sheet.

- *Become involved with the customer, rather than waiting for the customer to get involved with you.* Marketers today have a totally backwards view of customer loyalty. They believe customer loyalty is something that the customer does for them, whereas in truly connecting with the customer, marketers discover that customer loyalty is something that they give to their customers. Southwest Airlines thrives by reaching out to their target customer and staying loyal to their customers' needs: dependable fast service at the lowest possible cost.

- *Connect with the consumers' community.* No man is an island and consumers are connecting more and more within their social, political, and cultural landscapes. Connecting with the consumer today also means connecting with the community in which they live. One of the secrets of Wal-Mart's phenomenal success is that, despite their enormous size, each local Wal-Mart store reaches out to become a hub of the local community, for example, by supporting local schools and fraternal organizations in fundraising.

- *Create your business for your customers' needs.* Ultimately marketers and retailers need to turn themselves around 180° and look at their business, their products, and their services totally from their customers' point of view. Connecting means you place their needs, desires, priorities, and concerns first.

WHAT IS TO COME

The following chapters in Part II provide details about consumer purchases of 37 discretionary/luxury product categories. They are divided into three broad categories: entertainment, recreation, and hobby products; home and home decorating products; and personal luxuries, such as jewelry, apparel, and personal care.

These sections are designed for readers' grazing and skimming, rather than for careful reading page after page. They provide basic reference material about the size and growth of the market segment, as well as a summary of consumer research into each of the 37 product categories.

Yet while I advise skimming coming sections, it is important to recognize that competition for what people buy has suddenly gone horizontal rather than vertical. In business we are trained to think of our competitors within a narrow band of vertically defined categories, so a candle company competes with other candle companies, a traditional department store competes with other traditional department stores. But companies and retailers today compete horizontally across many different industries and product categories for the only true measure of success: the consumers' discretionary dollar. That means companies that sell home products compete with apparel companies and entertainment companies. Retailers that sell clothes compete with home retailers and entertainment retailers for their sales. Everyone everywhere is competing with everybody else for a limited resource—the consumers' discretionary spending. Today marketing and retailing executives must learn how to function in this immeasurably more complex competitive environment.

In this new horizontally oriented competitive landscape, companies will achieve success only in so far as they tap into the hearts, minds, and desires of their target market. The consumers' discretionary pocketbook has never been larger. Consumers will ultimately decide the fate of companies that don't hearken to their needs and

> Connecting means you place the consumer's needs, desires, priorities, and concerns first.

desires. Therefore, the coming discussion of the 37 different products takes on important implications for all marketers and retailers who seek to really connect with their consumer. Every consumer product company

These sections are designed for readers' grazing and skimming.

ultimately is in the consumer satisfaction business and the coming sections will help everyone understand the depth and scope of consumers' desires more completely.

Chapter

6

WHAT PEOPLE BUY
Personal Luxuries

OVERVIEW

The business of looking good is a major contributor to the U.S. economy. The market for clothes, jewelry, and fashion accessories and fashion services, such as dry cleaning, totaled $405.5 billion in 2002, while consumer expenditure on personal care articles including cosmetics and spending on beauty parlors, barbershops, and health clubs reached $97.2 billion. While food, clothing, and shelter are thought to be basic necessities of life, the reality is most clothing purchases are driven by fashion (i.e., a luxury desire) not need. For most Americans today, our closets are full and we simply don't need to shop for clothes. Because we don't need any more new clothes, we tend to look for justifiers that give us permission to buy, such as needing a new outfit for a special occasion, or finding something really great on sale. Clothing is no longer part of the basic necessities of life. For most of us, clothes and fashion are luxuries that make our lives more pleasurable, more fulfilling, more exciting, more rewarding, and more fun.

While most consumers recognize the importance of dressing right for every occasion and presenting a good self-image when out in society and at work, many of us are simply not willing to devote the time, energy, and money that dressing more stylishly or fashionably requires. Just over

40 percent of personal luxury shoppers agree with the statement: I would like to dress more stylishly, but I don't have the time and/or money that it takes to achieve it. Dressing fashionably is sort of like taking vitamins. We all know it is good for you and we should do it, but only the most passionate minority makes it a point to take vitamins every day.

> Clothes and fashion are luxuries that make our lives more pleasurable, more fulfilling, more exciting, more rewarding, and more fun.

So most Americans are satisfied with their fashion and style sense, even if they know it is not quite up to par. Being unwilling to invest the effort necessary to dress better, we tend to think that everybody else spends more time, money, and effort to look better than we do.

REALITY TV RESCUES FASHION FLUBS WITH TLC'S *WHAT NOT TO WEAR*

Thanks to 24/7 cable television, for every human failing there is a reality television show that is guaranteed to solve your problems, or at least offer suggestions and advice to the clueless. So too for the fashion-challenged. The BBC was first on the scene with its *What Not to Wear* show hosted by Susannah Constantine and Trinny Woodall. After doing stints in fashion reporting, the two got together for a Granada Television show about shopping and wrote the book *Ready 2 Dress*. The "fashion emergency" concept was snapped up by the BBC and thus an international phenomenon was born. TLC adapted the original concept for the U.S. market with two very American style gurus, Stacy London and Clinton Kelly, as cohosts. The premise of both the American and British shows is the same: fashion victims (i.e., those who only know what not to wear) are nominated by friends to get a complete fashion, hair, and makeup makeover. The subjects come into the studio toting their entire bad wardrobe, which is critiqued, not gently but with ruthless, brutal honesty. With 99 percent of their wardrobes left on the trash heap of bad style, they are given a Visa card preprogrammed with a generous cash allowance, style rules of what kinds of clothes to buy, then sent off on a two-day shopping extravaganza in New York City. The first one to spend $5,000 on clothes that follow the rules wins. But old habits die hard, so a favorite feature of every show is the second day rescue when Stacy and Clinton pop up to personally pull their charges away from their old preferences in clothes and guide them toward fashions that work. By the end of the show, Cinderella is transformed into a princess and all is right with the world, until next week when another victim takes the cure. Everyone in my house knows not to disturb me on Friday nights between 10:00 and 11:00 when I get my weekly fashion fix.

OVERVIEW: PERSONAL LUXURIES PURCHASE INCIDENCE

Many of the product categories included in this year's survey of personal luxuries are new. All clothing and apparel was intentionally left out of previous years' surveys with the idea that clothing was a necessity and survey respondents would have a hard time distinguishing their necessity-based purchases from their emotional-based ones. This year, though, I threw caution to the wind and included apparel for many reasons, the most important of which is that women's apparel is the number one thing that I personally buy that I definitely don't need.

Women's apparel is the most widely purchased personal luxury based upon this survey, with 65 percent of consumers reporting a discretionary, desire-based purchase in the category (see Figure 6.1). Personal care products that are more "special" or "exclusive" than everyday brands are second most widely bought, with 64 percent purchase incidence. Next follows fashion accessories, such as handbags, shoes, wallets, scarves, and all the rest, bought by 63 percent of shoppers. Only 14 percent of the consumers surveyed made no discretionary purchases of personal luxuries.

So who are these people that deny themselves the pleasure of personal luxury shopping? They are mostly male, with some 20 percent of men surveyed doing without any of these items out of desire, as opposed

FIGURE 6.1
Personal Luxuries Purchase Incidence (percentage)

	2000	2001	2003
Women's clothing and apparel			65
Personal care products	50	71	64
Fashion accessories			63
Men's clothing			55
Jewelry and watches	40	48	46
Infant and children's clothing			36
Teen and tween clothing			24
None			14

to only 8 percent of women. They also are more likely to be 65 years and above, with 26 percent of the mature consumers not buying. The low-income households do without, as 17 percent of the under $25,000 households do not buy. Some 21 percent of single people and those with no children are also more likely not to buy.

The rest of this chapter is devoted to profiling the markets for personal luxuries, including fashion accessories, jewelry and/or watches, infant and children's clothing, teen and tween clothing, men's clothing, women's clothing, and personal care products.

WHAT PEOPLE BUY: FASHION ACCESSORIES, SUCH AS HANDBAGS, WALLETS, BELTS, SHOES, ETC.

Nearly two-thirds of U.S. households purchased fashion accessories, such as handbags, wallets, belts, shoes, etc. A new category added to this year's survey, fashion accessories are an important discretionary purchase for many consumers.

Industry Snapshot

Personal consumption of fashion accessories totaled $53.2 billion, according to statistics compiled by the U.S. Bureau of Economic Analysis. Sales rose about 2.8 percent from 2000 to 2002, with strongest growth generated in the shoe category (see figure 6.2). Sales of luggage for men and women, which includes wallets, handbags, and other accessories, as well as travel luggage, declined as consumers cut back on travel in the post-9/11 landscape.

Coach, with sales of $950 million, is a major player in the U.S. fashion accessories business. The company specializes in leather-crafted accessories and gifts for women and men including handbags, business cases, luggage and travel accessories, wallets, outerwear, and gloves. They also have added scarves and fine jewelry to their mix as well as watches, footwear, and furniture through licensing partnerships. Thus Coach is building a lifestyle brand that will serve many facets of their customers' lives. As they extend their brand into new categories, they also are expanding their distribution strategy to meet different segments of the market in the places where they choose to shop. They currently operate over 200 Coach full-priced stores, and maintain branded Coach boutiques in leading department stores and specialty retailer locations.

FIGURE 6.2

Fashion Accessories Industry Snapshot

	2000	2002	% CHG '00-'02
Total Personal Consumption in millions	$51,703	$53,155	2.8
Shoes	47,026	49,096	4.4
Luggage for women	3,434	2,980	-13.2
Luggage for men	1,243	1,079	-13.2

Source: Bureau of Economic Analysis

They have dedicated Coach outlets scattered throughout the country in off-price fashion outlet malls, as well as an online store. The company is being rewarded for their expansive approach with net sales rising 32 percent in fiscal 2003.

Retail Overview

Three types of stores dominate where consumers shop for fashion accessories. Department stores with their strong emphasis on fashion are shopped by 60 percent of accessories buyers, followed by discount department stores, chosen by half of the shoppers. Specialty clothing stores, including shoe and jewelry stores, were used by 46 percent of shoppers in the past year. (Note: This does not add up to 100 percent due to shoppers' shopping in multiple stores over the course of the year.) An important emerging source for fashion accessories are non-store retailers, notably the Internet, television shopping channels, and mail order catalogs. Some 17 percent of accessories shoppers used these outlets to make purchases.

Purchase Drivers

The "fashionistas" would have us all carefully buy new fashion accessories—shoes, handbags, scarves, and the rest—to coordinate with each of our outfits. But in reality few consumers have the luxury of paying such careful attention to their fashion accessories. Only 45 percent of female fashion consumers agreed with the statement: "I have a wardrobe of classic clothing styles and designs that I update regularly by buying new fashion accessories and accents." The young aged 18 to 24 and the affluent with incomes of $75,000 or more are the consumers most likely to pay special attention to their fashion accessories. Not too many others are willing to pony up $1,500 for the latest Louis Vuitton Dhanura yoga bag to carry around their yoga outfits and mats in style. For most everybody else, the basic accessories, purchased as needed, will do.

Demographic Variables

It's no surprise that women are the primary buyers of fashion accessories. Some 71 percent of women, as compared with 56 percent of men, bought fashion accessories in the past year. The young consumers aged 18 to 34 have the highest purchase incidence, though purchases remain fairly strong through age 65, after which it drops sharply. Consumers living the in the Northeast, including the major cities New York, Boston, Philadelphia, Baltimore, and Washington D.C, are the biggest consumers of fashion accessories, as compared with shoppers living in the south, west, or north central regions. All ethnicities buy accessories at the same pace.

Rising income is correlated with purchase incidence and starts to rise at the middle-income $35,000 level. The most affluent consumers, with incomes of $75,000 and above, purchase at the most active rate of all. This is not a category linked to household size or presence of children, though the more educated consumers tend to buy more.

Key demographics of fashion accessories buyers.

- Women take the lead, though men also buy.
- Younger consumers, under age 34, buy more but incidence remains high through age 64.
- Rising income impacts buying, with most affluent buying more.
- Consumers living in the Northeast buy more.
- More educated consumers buy more.

WHAT PEOPLE BUY: INFANT AND CHILDREN'S CLOTHING AND APPAREL

Just over one-third of households (36 percent) bought infant and children's wear in the past year. This is a category of purchase that is perceived more as a necessity than one that is discretionary. After all, babies grow fast and they need clothes, rather than fashion.

Industry Snapshot

Americans spent $11 billion on clothing for infants, about 4.1 percent more than they spent in 2000 (see Figure 6.3). With the industry's fortunes linked directly to birth rates, prospects are good for the category over the next ten years or so as the millennial generation, 71 million strong and almost as big as the baby boomers, marries and has children, thus starting another baby boomlet, this one being the grandchildren of the baby boomers.

New statistics about the age of first-time mothers also bode well for the baby clothing business. Today the average first time mother is older than she's ever been, just a little older than 25 years, a significant increase since 1970 when the average age was 21.5 years. Older, more mature mothers have more financial security and thus more money to spend on their newborns. Another positive sign for the baby and children's industry comes out of the same study: Birth rates among the most mature mothers, aged 35 to 44, are at their highest levels in three decades.

Retail Overview

Shoppers turn first to discount department stores to buy infant and children's clothes, as two-thirds of buyers said they shopped in these stores. Next comes traditional department stores, a source for infant and children's clothing among 60 percent of shoppers. Clothing specialty stores follow third, used by 41 percent of kids clothing shoppers in the past year.

Rising acceptance of discounters' private label brands in children's clothing is an important reason why shoppers turn to these outlets. According to NPD Group, private label clothing brands account for 36 percent of the total apparel market. For retailers like Target, their private label infants' business is a platform on which they construct the entire baby department.

FIGURE 6.3

Infant's Clothing Industry Snapshot

	2000	2002	% CHG '00-'02
Total Personal Consumption in millions	$10,617	$11,050	4.1

Source: Bureau of Economic Analysis

FIGURE 6.4

Infant and Children's Apparel Market Share Leaders

	2002 SALES
Kids R Us	$1.9 billion
The Children's Place Retail Stores Inc.	587 million
Too Inc.	545 million
The Gymboree Corp.	448 million
OshKosh B'Gosh Inc.	222 million
The William Carter Co.	207 million

Source: *The 2002 Directory of Apparel Specialty Stores*

Key specialty competitors in kids clothing include The Children's Place with nearly 650 stores targeting kids clothing and accessories from infant to age 12; GapKids and BabyGap, the chain of Gap stores just for kids spun off by the apparel giant; Gymboree, with 580 stores for infant through age 7, who then graduate to the company's Zutopia tween chain; Carter's, a leading brand in infant apparel, with 160 outlet stores, as well as branded boutiques in department stores; and OshKosh B'-Gosh, which operates 150 outlets and specialty stores as well as distributes through 4,600 stores nationwide. (See Figure 6.4.)

The children's apparel market is losing a major player as Toys R Us closes its 146 freestanding Kids R Us chain locations. At the same time, they will continue to operate their 180 Babies R Us stores, which target the infant and toddler market. Babies, rather than Kids, has proven a more successful concept for the company. They also announced that about 15 of the Kids R Us stores may be converted to Babies R Us stores.

Purchase Drivers

Being tied to birthrates, the infant clothing market is destined to grow over the next ten years. With this new generation being the grand-babies of the baby boomers, they will be blessed with the most active, healthy, and affluent grandparents of any generation that has come before. Wealthy boomer grandparents will lend support to their own offspring in caring for the next generation by getting back into the market for baby clothes among other things. This will mean new opportunity at the luxury end of the market. With over 30 franchised specialty boutiques located in only the most exclusive shopping centers nationwide, Jacadi Paris offers a very exclusive line of children's clothing and nursery accessories at ultra exclusive prices. Many luxury brands, such as Burberry's and Ralph Lauren, are also getting into the business of out-fitting kids, as is Saks Fifth Avenue, which now stocks Ralph's baby line along with Burberry's, Best of Chums, and Petite Bateau.

Demographic Variables

Women take the lead in buying infant and children's clothing. Some 42 percent of women, as compared with 30 percent of men, report making these purchases in the past year. The peak age for buying kids clothing is 25 to 34 years, while the age ranges that bracket those years (i.e., ages 18 to 24 and 35 to 44) also have high purchase incidence. There is another small bump in purchase incidence found among consumers 55 to 64, a prime age for grandparenting.

Affluence links with purchase incidence of children's clothing, with the highest income households, $75,000 and above, having the highest purchase incidence. And, of course, the presence of children in the home is tied directly to purchase incidence, 54 percent among households with children as compared with 25 percent among households with none. For these households with no kids, gifting is the primary reason behind purchase.

Key demographics for buyers of infant and children's clothing and apparel.

- Women take the lead, though men also buy.
- Peak buying years are ages 25 to 34, with elevated incidence among ages 18 to 24, 35 to 44, and 55 to 64.
- The most affluent buy more.
- Households with children are the primary buyers.

WHAT PEOPLE BUY: JEWELRY AND WATCHES

After advancing from 40 percent in 2000 to 48 percent in 2001, household purchase incidence of jewelry and watches remained about even in 2003. Some 46 percent of households bought jewelry and/or watches in the past year. Contributing to the growth in the jewelry market is the expanding availability of jewelry sold at discount prices. In 2002, Wal-Mart was the nation's largest jewelry retailer, with over $2 billion in jewelry sales. Zale Corporation, number two in the retail jewelry market—with their Zales, Gordon's, and Bailey Banks and Biddle brands among others—is getting into the discounting business in a serious way. They have a chain of 100 Zales outlet stores that sell jewelry 20 to 70 percent off traditional retail prices.

Industry Snapshot

Total sales of jewelry and watches were $51 billion in 2002, up 0.8 percent over 2000's sales of $50.6 billion, according to statistics collected by the Bureau of Economic Analysis (see Figure 6.5). The past two years have been full of turmoil for jewelry and watches, the epitome of luxury products. Retail sales of jewelry and watches actually declined in 2001 only to recover in 2002. Because of the economic slowdown following September 11, consumers were challenged to justify making purchases in what most consider an extravagant category. On the other hand, mass market jewelry, especially costume jewelry that gives maximum style at a minimal price, and fine jewelry bought at discounts of 50 percent off and more helped keep consumers in the market during the slow time. After all, jewelry provides an emotional lift that people need in times of stress and trouble.

Retail Overview

Shoppers are turning away from traditional jewelry stores, used by 39 percent for jewelry purchases last year, as they seek out and find nice jewelry sensibly priced in a wide range of retail outlets, including traditional department stores, used by 48 percent of jewelry shoppers in the past year; discount department stores, used by 38 percent of shoppers; and nonstore retailers including Internet, mail-order, and television shopping, a source for 17 percent of jewelry shoppers. The U.S. Census

FIGURE 6.5
Jewelry and Watches Industry Snapshot

	2000	2002	% CHG '00-'02
Total Personal Consumption in millions	$50,568	$50,978	0.8

Source: Bureau of Economic Analysis

Bureau's retail census reports that traditional jewelry store sales totaled $25.1 billion in 2002, 1 percent less than jewelry store sales in 2000 of $25.3 billion. That means that market growth in the jewelry business has come about through increased sales in all other retail channels of distribution.

Direct to consumer channels are increasingly capturing a greater and greater share of the jewelry business. Television shopping giants QVC, with estimated jewelry sales of $950 million, HSN, with jewelry sales of about $415 million, and Shop NBC, which boasts category sales of $300 million, all rank in the top 20 national jewelry retailers, according to *National Jeweler* magazine (see Figure 6.6). Numerous pure-play Internet jewelers are cropping up too, notably Bluenile.com, which specializes in diamonds, and ashford.com, which focuses on fine jewelry for less. Not to be left behind in cyberspace, most of the name brand retailers, including Tiffany's, Zales, Fortunoffs, and Ross Simons, have implemented "bricks-and-clicks" strategies to ensure that their brand names come up when jewelry shoppers google to find their next jewelry piece.

Purchase Drivers

Jewelry is a favorite indulgence item for women and an important fashion accessory. Jewelry, especially fine jewelry, is also a favored gift item for men to give on ceremonial occasions such as weddings and anniversaries, as well as birthdays, Christmas, Valentine's Day, and Mother's Day. Moreover, women are prone to give themselves a gift of jewelry when they need a boost, as one woman clarifies: "I bought a bracelet for myself on my birthday. I spent $5,000 at Neiman-Marcus buying a bracelet that I always wanted. For my birthday, my husband took me out to dinner at a restaurant not far from where I bought the bracelet. He thought [dinner out] was all I was getting. But I felt I deserved [the bracelet] now."

With rings given to celebrate marriage, jewelry carries a more symbolic meaning than many other discretionary items as one young respondent explains: "I like to shop for jewelry. There are so many things connected with jewelry, like Christmas and the birth of a child. It is symbolic and meaningful to someone. I have lots of nice jewelry that I will pass down to my daughters." Another respondent explained that, often, it is the symbolic meaning of a jewelry item that drives its purchase: "I was in Toronto and found an emerald ring in an antique shop. I had to buy it. It took me back. It was nostalgic, fulfilling a desire I have had for 20 years to own a ring like that. I will always associate that ring with Toronto. At the time, I was making memories, as well as enjoying them."

FIGURE 6.6

Jewelry and Watches Market Share Leaders

	2002 SALES
Wal-Mart	$2.3 billion
Zale Corporation	2.1 billion
Sterling	1.6 billion
JCPenney	1.0 billion
Sears	1.0 billion
Finlay Fine Jeweler	953 million
QVC	950 million
Tiffany & Co.	786 million
Helzberg Diamond Shops	500 million
Kmart	500 million
Fred Meyer Jewelers	450 million
Target	450 million
Home Shopping Network	415 million
Friedman's	411 million
Macy's East	400 million
Whitehall Jewelers	338 million
Costco	325 million
Macy's West	300 million
Shop NBC	300 million

Source: *National Jeweler* Magazine

Demographic Variables

With a purchase incidence of 51 percent, women are just slightly more likely than men (41 percent) to have purchased jewelry and/or watches in 2003. While the highest purchase incidence of jewelry is found among households with consumers aged 18 to 24, jewelry is actively purchased at all age levels under age 65. Even the seniors have a purchase incidence of 37 percent, which is less of a drop off than found in many other discretionary categories.

While households at all income levels buy jewelry, those at the highest level, $50,000 and above, report the highest purchase incidence (52 percent among $50,000 to $75,000, and 59 percent for $75,000 and above). Two-person households, as opposed to those with children or more members, buy jewelry the most.

Key demographics for buyers of jewelry and watches.

- Women buy slightly more than men.
- High-income households of $50,000-plus buy more.

- Younger households aged 18 to 24 are the most active buyers, but buying remains strong through age 65.
- Two-person households buy more.

WHAT PEOPLE BUY: MEN'S CLOTHING AND APPAREL

Over half of U.S. households (55 percent) purchased men's clothing out of desire, not strictly out of need, in the past year. While men's desire-based purchases of clothing are less than women's, which totaled 65 percent in 2003, it still represents a significant discretionary purchase category for the majority of households in America.

Industry Snapshot

Personal consumption of men's and boys' clothing totaled $93.7 billion in 2002, up about 1 percent over the 2000 total of $92.8 billion (see Figure 6.7). Brooks Brothers is both a leading manufacturer and retailer of men's apparel. The company's heritage stretches back nearly 200 years. Brooks Brothers is famous for the custom-made topcoat they provided Abraham Lincoln on his second inauguration. He is also said to have worn a Brooks Brothers suit that fateful night he attended a play at Ford's Theater. But they are not satisfied to rest on their laurels. Having been recently acquired by Retail Brand Alliance, the parent company of Casual Corner, Brooks Brothers is defining classic American style for a new generation of shoppers. They operate about 160 stores in the United States and bring American style to shoppers in Japan, Hong Kong, Taiwan, and Italy through 90 locations.

FIGURE 6.7

Men's and Boys' Clothing and Apparel Industry Snapshot

	2000	2002	% CHG '00-'02
Total Personal Consumption in millions	$92,750	$93,656	1.0

Source: Bureau of Economic Analysis

FIGURE 6.8

Men's Apparel Market Share Leaders

	2002 SALES
The Men's Wearhouse	$1.3 billion
Brooks Brothers	661 million
Structure	569 million
Casual Male	380 million
Jos. A. Banks	206 million
Today's Man	168 million
S & K Famous Brands	168 million
Bachrach Clothing Inc.	106 million
After Hours Formalwear Inc.	84 million
Salant Corporation	77 million
Rochester Big & Tall	60 million

Source: *2002 Directory of Apparel Specialty Stores*

Retail Overview

Most men's apparel shoppers turn to traditional department stores to fill their closets. Some 65 percent of men's buyers shopped in traditional department stores. Discount department stores also serve as an important source for more casual clothing, with 56 percent of shoppers. Specialty clothing stores round out the top three sources for men's apparel, used by 50 percent of shoppers in the past year.

The biggest name in specialty menswear retailing is Men's Wearhouse (see Figure 6.8). With sales of $1.3 billion, Men's Wearhouse operates about 500 stores located mostly in free-standing malls. They are positioned as a discount retailer by offering their tailored suits at 20 to 30 percent discount over competitors' prices. Like Brooks Brothers, they are vertically integrated and so they design and manufacture the clothes that they sell.

Another important retail name in men's fashion is Structure. Structure was founded by The Limited as the male version of their Express chain, which targets youthful female shoppers. With nearly 300 stores, The Limited changed the name of the chain to Men's Express in a repositioning strategy. Today, The Limited operates both the men's and women's fashion business under the $2 billion Express division. Meanwhile, they sold rights to the Structure brand to Sears in September 2003, which will be introducing new Structure men's apparel into the Sears stores in 2004.

Purchase Drivers

The business of men's apparel has been hit by a double-whammy that hurt the business. First, businesses everywhere adopted the new casual dress trend, then economic lethargy befell retail after September 11. For the past ten years or so, professional men traded in their three-piece suits for polo shirts and khakis. Because they could work in casual clothes, they didn't feel compelled to buy suits, formal shirts, and other "buttoned-down" looks for work. But that trend is beginning to reverse, perhaps in part due to the flagging economy. If everyone else is dressed in chinos, a man in a beautifully tailored charcoal gray suit commands attention and respect. Dressing for success is a simple though expensive way to gain stature in a challenging, competitive business environment.

A new research study by Dr. Jeffrey Magee, a Tulsa, Oklahoma–based psychologist, provides factual proof that casual dress isn't good for work or the worker. In a study of productivity among 500 firms, he reports that casual dress leads people to take their work more casually, and as a result it suffers. He says, "When people are dressed more casual, they take a more relaxed view towards their work and their workplace." The study found that more than 50 percent of executives and 70 percent of employees feel how one dresses influences their daily behavior. Organizations that adopted business casual dress codes reported decreased productivity and an increase in tardiness, absenteeism, and sexual harassment lawsuits. "The more casual and more relaxed the dress policy is, the more work productivity declines," argues Magee. "People are more inclined to socialize in this atmosphere. . . . The workplace becomes less valuable as employees take its legitimacy for [a place of work] less seriously."

Retail leader Men's Wearhouse has embraced the new dress-for-success ethic. The company notes that both Lehman Brothers and Bank of America have announced a return to business dress. To help confused workers learn the new rules for business dress, they employ in-store Wardrobe Consultants in their 500 Men's Wearhouse stores to offer expert advice on what to wear and not to wear to work.

Demographic Variables

While men buy more men's clothing, purchased by 59 percent of men in 2003, women buy nearly as much, bought by 50 percent of women.

In my home, for example, I am behind virtually every single men's clothing purchase that is made. With three men to dress—my husband and two teenage sons—there is a lot of market potential in my house, but all marketing efforts better be directed toward me or nothing is going to be bought, guaranteed. The prime market for men's apparel is households under age 45, though purchase incidence remains high with purchases among about half of households through age 64, at which point it drops sharply.

The most affluent households with incomes of $75,000 and above are the most active buying menswear, though middle-income households from $35,000 and above all maintain fairly active purchases in the category. Households with two or more members and those with children spend more buying men's clothing. And higher educational attainment links with higher purchase incidence.

Key demographics for buyers of men's clothing and apparel.

- Men buy slightly more than women, but women buy lots too.
- Middle-to-high-income households buy more.
- Younger households aged 18 to 34 are the most active, but buying remains strong through age 65.
- Two-person and larger and households with children buy more.
- Purchase incidence is linked to rising educational attainment.

WHAT PEOPLE BUY: PERSONAL-CARE PRODUCTS THAT ARE MORE "SPECIAL" OR "EXCLUSIVE" THAN EVERYDAY BRANDS

Nearly two-thirds of Americans said they purchased personal-care products that are more "special" or "exclusive" than everyday brands in 2003, down slightly from the 71 percent that did the same in 2001. These "special" personal-care products include cosmetics, soaps, lotions, and hair care. This category ranked as the second most frequently purchased personal discretionary product, after only women's clothing and apparel. Purchase incidence in this category rose from 2000 when only half of households bought these products, suggesting that American consumers are looking for more highly specialized personal-care products and turning away from the everyday brands.

Industry Snapshot

According to the Bureau of Economic Analysis, the government agency that charts the U.S. economy for government policy making as well as calculates the gross national product, the total personal-care market, including "mass" and "class" brands, fell to $54.3 billion in 2002, down 1.3 percent from 2000 (see Figure 6.9). But while the macro view is down, the luxury or prestige category of makeup and skincare grew 2.8 and 2.6 percent, respectively, in 2002, according to the NPD Group. Focusing exclusively on the $7.3 billion market for prestige cosmetics, they report the $2.8 billion fragrance category declined 3.5 percent from the previous year, while the $2.5 billion makeup and $1.9 billion skincare categories rose. Anti-aging skincare regimes are expected to continue to grow as baby boomers turn to nonsurgical treatments to halt the inevitable progress of time and gravity. For these boomers, price is no object, with many of the best-selling department store skincare brands, such as Lancome, Estee Lauder, Chanel, Shiseido, and La Prairie, selling at $70 a bottle and up.

Destined to bring changes to the prestige cosmetics and skincare business is the recent announcement that department store exclusive brand Estee Lauder is developing a new line of cosmetics for discounter Kohl's. While the new line won't be available until 2005 and it reportedly won't be released under the Estee Lauder brand name, it's an important move by an industry leader as they finally admit that their target customer (i.e., affluent middle-aged women who can afford to pay full price) shop at discount stores.

FIGURE 6.9

Personal-Care Industry Snapshot

	2000	2002	% CHG '00-'02
Total Personal Consumptions in millions	$55,016	$54,320	−1.3
Soap	4,630	4,971	7.4
Cosmetics and perfume	15,573	15,146	−2.7
Other personal hygiene	34,814	34,203	−1.8

Source: Bureau of Economic Analysis

Retail Overview

When they shop for personal-care items—even those that are more "special" than everyday brands—consumers turn first to discount department stores, where 51 percent of shoppers reported buying these items in the past year. Specialty health, personal care, and drug stores are the second most widely used source, with 44 percent of shoppers. With about one-third of shoppers, traditional department stores follow.

The business of cosmetics is the ultimate in experiential marketing. While companies and retailers are in the business of selling cosmetics (i.e., a thing), consumers are actually buying beauty (i.e., an experience). As Charles Revson, founder of Revlon, said, "In our factories we make cosmetics; in our stores, we sell hope." While department stores have dominated the traditional cosmetics business, consumers changing shopping patterns are playing havoc with "business as usual" in the cosmetics world. Direct-sales giant Avon has tried to break in to retail through partnerships with Sears and J.C. Penney, with no success. J.C. Penney is so turned off by the cosmetics business that it has banished all color cosmetics from their stores. While traditional department store retailers reel, new specialty retailers, such as Sephora, Victoria's Secret, Bath and Body Works, and Ulta, get into the premium beauty business with a vengeance.

Nonstore retailers are also finding a willing audience to buy beauty products online. Along with such pioneers as beauty.com and efforts by established brands to gain a toehold in cyberspace, such as Estee Lauder's entire family of brands, including Bobbi Brown, Clinque, Estee Lauder, M.A.C., Aveda, and Origins, San Francisco–based reflect.com has done all the name brands one better over the Internet. Backed by an investment—and the marketing muscle—of Proctor and Gamble, reflect.com offers truly customized beauty care and cosmetics formulations online. Customers answer a series of questions to help the cosmetics mavens at reflect.com determine your skin care needs and color preferences. After the de rigor credit card transmission, you receive your very own personalized cosmetics at your door in a week or two.

Being somewhat of a cosmetics enthusiast myself, I was so intrigued by the concept of customized cosmetics online that I gave reflect.com a trial run for foundation, a particularly problematic cosmetics purchase for me. Even cosmetics sales consultants who have my face right in front of them can't seem to get a satisfactory foundation match with my sun-damaged skin, so I didn't hold too much hope for reflect.com to get it right over the Internet. But we only went through one nearly painless iteration of a poor color match (i.e., you don't send your returns back, you simply throw them away and they send you a new formulation) before they actually did the job. Now I am a religious believer in their system and rely upon reflect.com exclusively for foundation and mascara, another category I am particular about.

Purchase Drivers

Signs are positive for continued growth in this product category as people crave products like cosmetics and lotions and potions that pamper and indulge them. Consumers have a voracious appetite for the latest and most scientifically advanced personal-care and cosmetics products. Among the trends that have propelled growth in the personal-care and cosmetics industry is a search by aging baby boomers for cosmetics and beauty regimens that reverse the ravages of time. Changing fashion in makeup colors for the youthful consumer and the demand for more product lines featuring natural, "healthy" ingredients are other trends that have had a positive impact.

Men are emerging as a strong new market for cosmetics, and skincare and hair care treatments. The popularity of Bravo's reality series *Queer Eye for the Straight Guy* and the official coining of the term *metrosexual* as the descriptor of the contemporary man who is concerned about his appearance have given men new justification for taking a little extra time and spending a little more money on their clothes and grooming.

But the personal care category is still mainly a female province. Drawn like a moth to a flame, women cannot seem to get enough of this product category. One consumer explained her passion for perfumes this way: "I could wear a different perfume every day of the year. I have so much perfume, but every time I smell a new fragrance I like, I have to buy it. I am addicted to scents." Another says, "I really go for bath gels and salts. It is a pleasure and a stress reducer. For me this isn't a reward. I am *entitled* to have the nice 'stuff.' If we don't take care of ourselves, who is going to? Even with taking care of a large family, I have to have my hour in the bath."

Demographic Variables

The reported purchase incidence of special personal-care products is higher for women (73 percent) than for men (54 percent), but men are beginning to purchase more of these products for their own use.

While the youngest consumers are the most active purchasers, consumers through age 54 purchase at a higher incidence than the average. After age 55, purchase incidence drops. People of all racial and ethnic groups purchase special personal-care products. The most active purchasers are consumers living in the most affluent households, $75,000 and above, though consumers living in households at all income levels are still fairly active buying special personal-care products. Household size correlates with increased purchase incidence in the category, with two-or-more person households buying more.

Key demographics for buyers of special personal-care products.

- Purchase incidence is highest under age 34, but remains strong through age 54.
- Middle-to-upper-income households buy more, with most affluent buying significantly more.
- All races and ethnic groups buy equally.
- Two-or-more-person households buy more.
- Females buy more, but male share is growing.

WHAT PEOPLE BUY: TEEN AND TWEEN CLOTHING AND APPAREL

Teen (ages 13 to 17) and tween (ages 7 to 12) clothing is the lowest purchase incidence category included in the personal luxuries survey. Only about one-fourth of households, 24 percent, purchased teen and tween clothing in the past year.

Industry Snapshot

The niche teen and tween market is getting lots of attention in marketing circles as marketers come to realize that these young people exert a powerful influence on family purchasing across a whole range of product categories including clothing, electronics, travel, sports, food and drinks, and entertainment. While the government lumps statistics on teen and tween clothing purchases into the broad men's and women's clothing categories, the NPD Group, which tracks apparel purchases more closely, estimated the market for teen clothing to be $20.9 billion in 2002, while tweens spent about $10.1 billion on clothes.

Retail Overview

Traditional department stores (63 percent), discount department stores (56 percent), and clothing specialty stores (55 percent) take the lead in stores where consumers shop for teen and tween clothing. Non-store retailers, including the Internet and mail order, are also particularly important outlets for teen clothing, with 21 percent of purchasers using this source in the past year.

Because teens have very definite and different style preferences than adults and they generally require a different fit in their clothes, many specialty retailers have emerged to target the unique needs of this market niche. The Gap's Old Navy brand of 840 stores does an outstanding job of hitting the sweet spot of the teen market, even while their advertising tries to draw in a more adult crowd thus jeopardizing their unique competitive strength with young people, who definitely don't want to wear the same brand as their parents. Hot Topic, with 400 mall-based stores, offers kids apparel and accessories with a contemporary culture edge and an emphasis on licensed goods. Limited Too, a chain of 400 stores for tweens is a Limited spinoff. Pacific Sunwear targets the surf and skateboarding set, while Aeropostale, American Eagle Outfitters, Tommy Hilfiger, J. Crew, Gap, Urban Outfitters, and H&M all offer their own unique looks for the teen set.

But the biggest name in teen and tween apparel is Abercrombie & Fitch, a $1.6 billion company that operates 700 stores in total under their flagship Abercrombie & Fitch brand, and Hollister Company stores, which is a lower-priced chain focused on 14- to 18-year-olds. While the company's flagship brand officially targets college-aged kids, their appeal has been directed toward the underaged teen and tween market. As a multichannel marketer, Abercrombie & Fitch has traditionally pushed the decency envelope in their skin-revealing catalogs, but it never got them into serious trouble until the Christmas 2003 A&F Quarterly edition. The catalog featured male and female models in "pictures hotter than a backyard barbeque," according to the company. It was considered too racy for the company's real target market (i.e., kids and teens buying with mom and dad's credit card). With family values groups from one coast to the other calling for a company boycott, they took heart and recalled the December 2003 issue, thus creating an after-market feeding frenzy on eBay for the "forbidden" catalog.

Purchase Drivers

There are any number of reasons the teen and tween market is appealing to retailers and apparel marketers. Their bodies are growing and changing, thus creating a dependable repeat business as kids outgrow their old clothes. Their tastes and styles are also changing at a split-second pace, which predisposes this market to be continually on the prowl for the next trend look. The teen market is expected to grow 37 percent faster than the total U.S. population through 2008, thus based upon sheer numbers alone they are an attractive niche market to target for the future.

Demographic Variables

In teen and tween apparel purchasing, women take the lead, with 29 percent of women, as compared with 18 percent of men, saying they made a purchase in the past year. The prime age for purchasing teen and tween apparel is between 35 and 54 years, the age of the parents of the teen generation. Middle-to-upper-income households, $35,000 and above, are more active buyers of teen apparel, as are households with children and three or more members living in the home.

Key demographics for buyers of teen and tween apparel.

- Women buy more.
- Buying peaks in ages 35 to 54.
- Middle-to-upper-income households buy more.
- Presence of children and three or more household members leads to greater incidence.

WHAT PEOPLE BUY: WOMEN'S CLOTHING AND APPAREL

Women's clothing and apparel comprise the number one most purchased category among the personal luxuries tracked. Nearly two-thirds (65 percent) of consumer households reported buying women's clothing and apparel that wasn't strictly needed, but bought out of desire. While women's clothing may be considered a necessity, women's fashion is strictly a luxury business and one that most women, young and old, rich or poor, reed thin or those with generous proportions, indulge in at one time or another.

Industry Snapshot

With sales of women's and girls' clothing topping $146.6 billion, women spend one-and-a-half times more money on apparel than men and boys do. Overall sales of women's clothing increased a modest 2.8 percent from 2000 to 2002 (see Figure 6.10). This is an intensely competitive industry with apparel and designer brands competing at retail against their peers, as well as with the private label fashions increasingly offered by traditional and discount department stores. Numerous marketers have found success targeting specific niche markets within the fashion business, such as Chico's FAS for the baby boomer; Lane Bryant for the plus-sized crowd; Talbots for the country-club set; Dress Barn, TJ Maxx, and Ross for the bargain shopper; and Ann Taylor for the young, urban professional type.

Retail Overview

Women are changing the way they shop for clothes. They have traditionally relied upon the department store for their fashions, but today more women, even fashionable women, are looking to discount stores for clothes, maybe not for work or evening attire, but there really isn't that much difference in T-shirts, after all. With women shopping for clothes in discounters, department store and boutique-only designers, like Isaac Mizrahi who is now delivering "Luxury for Every Woman Everywhere" though his affiliation with Target, are following. Curiosity drove me to Target to get a firsthand look and feel of the Mizrahi line. While I don't think they have really got "it" yet with the line, I also think it holds promise if they go with a slightly more luxurious feel to the fabrics

FIGURE 6.10

Women's and Girls' Clothing and Apparel Industry Snapshot

	2000	2002	% CHG '00-'02
Total Personal Consumption in millions	$142,642	$146,574	2.8

Source: Bureau of Economic Analysis

and better in-store signage that makes the line pop. But even if I didn't buy any clothes, I also didn't leave Target empty handed, which is their ultimate goal after all.

While traditional department stores still hold the lead, used by 69 percent of shoppers in the past year, discount department stores are only a few points behind with 62 percent of shoppers. Next come specialty clothing retailers, used by 54 percent of women's clothing shoppers, followed by nonstore retailers with 29 percent of shoppers.

A personal favorite of mine, both as an admiring marketer and avid consumer, is Chico's FAS. I have a closet overflowing with dress-for-success business suits, jackets, skirts, and blouses that I wear for client meetings, speaking engagements, television appearances, and other need-to-dress events. But in my day-to-day life I work in a small casual office where it's just me and my assistant and I go for comfort and ease. Chico's clothes give me the feel of gym clothes and sweat suits with a look that I am not embarrassed to wear to the store or at the mall or on a plane. I don't know how they do it, but they make a pair of jeans that even I find comfortable to wear.

But it's as a marketer where my real appreciation for Chico's FAS shows. They operate 400 stores nationwide and have an active catalog and Internet marketing arm. Their styles are easy-wear for women of a certain age and proportion and their prices are affordable, especially on sale, which they have often to keep the stock in the store fresh. They have a loyalty program called Chico's Passport Club, which offers members an automatic 5 percent discount off all purchases along with other benefits. They don't insult the customer by charging for membership

FIGURE 6.11

Women's Clothing and Apparel Market Share Leaders

	2002 SALES IN BILLIONS
The TJX Companies	$8.2
Gap	7.6
Nordstrom Inc.	5.5
Footlocker	4.2
Old Navy	3.9
Victoria's Secret	3.3
Ross Stores, Inc.	2.7
Saks Fifth Avenue Enterprises	2.7
Burlington Coat Factory Warehouse Corp.	2.4
Banana Republic	2.2

Source: *The 2002 Directory of Apparel Specialty Stores*

into the "club," rather you earn yourself in after you spend $500 at Chico's, and once you are in, you are in for life. They are savvy multi-channel marketers. Every month Passport members and prospective members, said to number over 2.5 million, receive a catalog that includes two coupons: one (the lesser value of the two) that can be redeemed online, by mail, or in the store, and another (the more valuable one) that can *only* be redeemed in the store. Thus, they use mail order to drive shoppers into the store, where they know they will drop a whole lot more money than if they order online or by telephone. In the local strip mall where I shop, I have often seen the Chico's store packed with shoppers lined up at the cash register, while the Ann Taylor Loft store next door and the Talbot's shop a few doors down are virtually empty. Chico's FAS is definitely doing something right.

Purchase Drivers

Most women are active purchasers of both fashion (i.e., luxury) and clothes (i.e., necessities). In my previous edition of this book, I intentionally left out apparel as one of those things that people buy but don't need, figuring it would be hard to determine what was a need-based versus desire-driven clothing purchase. And I may have been right because consumers couldn't really determine what is a discretionary or luxury purchase and what is needs driven.

In a recent discussion with affluent, luxury consumers, they shared that fashion was a necessity in their lives. One well-dressed woman said: "Fashion is a requirement for those who are high up in their successes and are upper class." Another said: "I buy a brand because I know that the brand fits me well and I can depend upon the cut. It isn't so much a luxury as a necessity. I know Liz Claiborne fits me in this size." These women must dress appropriately to their stage in life, their social level, and their position in society. As a result, they go for classic looks that are well made and high quality, and eschew trendy fashions and styles that are here today and gone tomorrow. One woman said she buys fashion fads, but only in the knockoff brands: "I like to buy expensive clothes. They are better made, fit better, and will have a place in my wardrobe for a long time. Every once in a while I buy a fashion trend, but I go for the knockoffs then. I will not pay luxury price for a fad, but only a classic."

While they need fashionable clothes and are willing to spend generously to look good, the word *fashion* is a hot button for many of the affluent women I researched. These more mature women, most of whom range in age from 35 to 64, say the fashion industry views them as the "forgotten" women because they are over 30 and not fashion-model size. A middle-aged affluent shopper said: "I feel we are forgotten in this age bracket. None of those advertisements speak to me because they are made for the younger generation." Another affluent woman explained: "Fashion is so trendy and unrealistic. Most of us aren't built the way we used to be built, so we don't wear as much of the trendy things because they don't look good on us." And another forgotten woman speaks: "Fashion is a turn off. I have a personal issue with many of the designers displaying skinny little women. All the models are 20 years old and I feel like the forgotten woman."

This argument resonates with American women everywhere at every income level. The simple fact is only a small fraction of the female population is a model or movie-star size 2, 4, or 6. The most popular women's dress size today is a 14, as more than 60 percent of the population is classified officially as "overweight."

If size 14 is the norm today, why are women who fit the norm made to feel abnormal when they shop for clothes? Here is what one luxury shopper said: "They never have nice stylish clothing for ladies of plus sizes (sizes 12 and up). I don't understand why retailers don't carry that and why retailers put the plus sizes next to the junior sizes. It just makes me feel horrible to shop and have to walk by the juniors to get to my size. I'm still young enough not to want to look like my mother. Just because your body changed doesn't mean your style has to."

Viewed solely through a marketer's lens, maybe designers, marketers, and retailers feel they can afford to alienate the forgotten low-income women, but how can they possibly disenfranchise the upper-income, middle-aged woman who has the means and the motive to spend a sizeable share of her considerable budget on clothes? The fashion business needs to gain a new marketing focus and meet the needs of the real American woman: "There are certain designers I like, but they are not the most expensive ones either. It's probably not fashionable, since I don't have the body of those younger models. I think it is very offending that they are targeting the younger market for fashion and leaving us older working women out."

Some of these affluent women mentioned they had gained weight since their youth, others were too short to fit into normal-sized clothes. Here is what one member of the jet-set shared about fashion: "That [apparel] is one of my weaknesses. It is so much fun to go shopping for clothes. I like going over to Paris and seeing what is there, then coming back here and trying to find the same look at TJ Maxx or Marshall's."

140   *Why People Buy Things They Don't Need*

These women want to look fashionable, but feel they cannot partici-pate in the fashion market because there is too little product that targets their needs. In effect, fashion manufacturers are out of touch with their market and the needs of their market. The fashion designers spend all their energy designing fashions that look good on the fashion runway, and too little time on understanding and designing for the needs of the real women that are their market. Thus they are opting for publicity and public relations instead of the discipline of marketing in their businesses.

Demographic Variables

It's no surprise that women (80 percent of all women) buy more women's apparel than men (47 percent of men). While the younger consumers, aged 18 to 44, have the highest overall purchase incidence, shoppers aged 45 to 64 still buy women's apparel actively. Purchase in-cidence drops sharply after age 65. All regions and ethnicities buy women's apparel.

This category skews toward a more affluent market, with incomes of $50,000 and more. The highest-income households, $75,000 and above, are the most active, making the comments of the affluent women shop-pers above even more poignant. Educational levels link with purchase, so the more educated consumers buy at a higher incidence. The pres-ence of children in the home and living in a two-person-or-larger house-hold also correlate with higher purchase incidence of women's apparel.

Key demographics for buyers of women's apparel and clothing.

- Women are the most active buyers.
- Incidence rises with income and education, with the most affluent being the most active.
- Younger consumers, under age 45, buy more though incidence stays vibrant through age 64.
- Two-or-more-person households and those with children buy more.

7

WHAT PEOPLE BUY

Entertainment, Recreation, and Hobbies

OVERVIEW

Americans spend a prodigious amount of money on entertainment, recreation, and hobbies. In terms of the national economy, consumer spending on recreational and entertainment products and services in total was $633.9 billion in 2002, or 8.6 percent of the nation's $7.385 trillion consumer economy. That includes $35.3 billion spent on admissions to sports, movies, entertainment, and other amusements, as well as consumer product purchases, which are the focus of this book and include everything from books, magazines, and newspapers to sporting equipment, toys, video, audio, DVD hardware and software, and craft supplies among others.

Americans spend more on recreation and entertainment than clothing, accessories, and jewelry, which totaled $405.5 billion in 2002. And spending on recreation is 85 percent of what we spend on household operations, which amounted to $748.3 billion in 2002 and includes such essentials as furniture, furnishings, utilities, telephone, and services.

Placed into a global content, Americans spend about the same amount of money on

> Americans spend about the same amount of money on entertainment and recreation as the entire GNP of Canada.

entertainment and recreation as the entire GNP of Canada, Australia, or Spain. Further, our expenditures in this area are about half of the size of the GNP of the United Kingdom.

NEW LEISURE ERA PREDICTED

With expenditures on entertainment so vast, it is easy to see why futurist Graham T.T. Molitor believes that a new era of leisure is dawning when the leisure industry will become the largest provider of employment in the country and will account for the biggest share of gross domestic product. Trends in the culture today, notably shorter workweeks, more holidays, longer vacations, earlier retirement, longer life spans, faster transportation, smaller families, and more labor-saving devices, are converging that will allow people to spend as much as 50 percent of their lifetimes on entertainment, sports, travel, and other leisure activities.

Molitor, president of Public Policy Forecasting, Inc., vice president of the World Future Society, and editor of *Encyclopedia of the Future,* says our current economic era of knowledge and information is passing and that a new leisure time era will emerge shortly. "The current Information Age has relatively few remaining years of dominance—possibly as few as 20," predicts Molitor. He expects a leisure-time era to emerge by 2015 and dominate the world economy until 2100.

"Leisure-oriented businesses—everything from bars to video stores to opera houses—will account for 50 percent of the U.S. gross national product shortly after 2015." He predicts that entertainment conglomerates, such as Disney's ABC, will be in the forefront of this growing sector. The industries that will grow in the leisure era include hospitality, recreation, entertainment, travel and tourism, gambling, and all manner of diversionary experiences and pastimes.

ENTERTAINMENT SPENDING REFLECTS
DRIVE FOR SELF-ACTUALIZATION

Americans are confused about leisure time, what it is, how to use it, and whether they really deserve it. While Europeans without guilt enjoy their annual August vacation season when virtually everyone takes holiday, it is unthinkable that Americans could ever free themselves for such an extravagant month-long vacation. Perhaps owing to the founding fathers' "Puritan work ethic," Americans find it hard to simply relax, enjoy, and recreate.

> We want to accomplish "something" that is measurable and meaningful when we recreate.

Bringing a uniquely American achievement orientation to our leisure time, we want to accomplish "something" that is measurable and meaningful when we recreate. Futurists Watts Wacker and Jim Taylor call this the "paradox of leisure," which is the blurring between work and play. For example, if you play golf with a customer, is it work or leisure and how can you tell the difference? Today with so much of business activity directed toward leisure and entertainment, we tend to define ourselves by our favorite recreational passion or pursuit, rather than through our job or work.

For goal-oriented Americans, in particular the hard-driving affluent, luxury consumers, achieving greater self-actualization is the objective for leisure time. So they spend their free time away from work responsibilities—along with serious amounts of money—pursuing leisure to self-actualize. From yoga class to spa vacations, adventure travel to gourmet cooking classes, Americans are pursuing rest and relaxation with a vengeance.

Psychologist Abraham Maslow defined the concept of *self-actualization* as the pinnacle of the hierarchy of human needs, to be satisfied only after the basic needs for food, clothing, and shelter. According to Maslow, self-actualization refers to "man's desire for fulfillment . . . to become everything that one is capable of becoming."

For the typical American, especially the affluent whose physical needs are completely satisfied and who have everything one could want or need, what's next? That is the ultimate challenge for marketers today. Our society is so wealthy, that even the poorest in our society partake in luxury. Where else in the world would you find those at the bottom of the income ladder owning cars, color television sets, VCRs/DVD players, air-conditioning, and other luxurious "necessities" of twenty-first-century life?

Marketers and retailers that sell entertainment and recreation products primarily serve consumers' self-actualization needs, for these products have no practical purpose other than providing emotional satisfaction. But to ensure the greatest long-term success, entertainment and recreation marketers need to connect with the consumers' inner emotional lives and create new products and services to meet those needs. For today's consumer with an excess of things, achieving self-actualization, as defined by Abraham Maslow's hierarchy of needs, is the ultimate expression of their most compelling personal desire.

> Americans are pursuing rest and relaxation with a vengeance.

OVERVIEW: ENTERTAINMENT, RECREATION, AND HOBBIES PRODUCT PURCHASE INCIDENCE

Consumer purchases of entertainment products are highly depend-ent upon what properties are hot at the moment. Because they are far more faddish than other categories of products, like food and other con-sumables, we would expect to find significant ups and downs in pur-chase incidence of specific products from year to year—and we do!

For example, our 2003 purchase incidence survey was conducted while the latest Harry Potter book was on the best-seller list. As a result, books, magazines, and newsletters took over the top slot from prere-corded videos as the most purchased entertainment product category. On the other hand, in 2001, the last time the survey was conducted, pre-recorded videos, music, and CDs were ranked number one. In 2003, purchase incidence of prerecorded media dropped sharply, from 79 per-cent in 2001 to 66 percent in 2003. This decline is an important issue for the record companies who claim that pirating of music from the Internet is the primary cause for lost revenue and decreased consumer purchase.

Among the 11 entertainment product categories included in the purchase incidence survey shown in Figure 7.1, only one product cate-gory shows significant growth in purchase incidence in 2003 over 2001 levels and that is sporting goods, up from 43 percent in 2001 to 48 per-cent in 2003. All the others are either about even or slightly behind pur-chase incidence in the 2001 sales year.

Let's take a closer look at each entertainment, recreation, and hobby product category through the rest of this chapter.

FIGURE 7.1

Entertainment Purchase Incidence

	2000	2001	2003
Books, magazines, and newsletters	68%	78%	74%
Prerecorded videos, music, DVDs, etc.	66	79	62
Toys, games, and dolls	45	54	50
Sporting goods and exercise equipment	36	43	48
Computers and software for home use	40	50	47
Photography equipment and supplies	38	51	43
Pet accessories	35	42	41
Televisions, radios, VCRs, DVD players, etc.	38	46	38
Crafts, sewing, knitting, and needlework supplies	33	39	29
Audio equipment and stereo systems	31	35	26
Musical instruments			10

WHAT PEOPLE BUY: AUDIO EQUIPMENT AND STEREO SYSTEMS

About one-fourth (26 percent) of consumer households purchased audio equipment or stereo systems in 2003, as compared with just about one-third in the previous study years of 2001 and 2000 (see Figure 7.2). This represents a slight downward shift in purchase incidence in the audio equipment category.

Industry Snapshot

Consumers continue to invest some of their discretionary budgets to update their home entertainment systems, including the audio equipment that enhances their music listening experience. Since 2000, personal consumption of audio equipment rose 7.7 percent to reach $25.9 billion in 2002. This product category appeals both to the youth market, especially young men who buy audio equipment not just for their home but also portable equipment to carry their favorite music wherever they venture, as well as the aging baby boomers, who are replacing their analog music libraries of "oldies" with new digital recordings of their favorite rock 'n' roll classics. This migration to digital has led to investment in new sound systems and the proliferation of surround-sound home-entertainment systems that antiquate yesterday's two-speaker systems.

The Bose Company, founded in 1964 by Dr. Amar Bose, an electrical engineering professor at MIT, has made reproducing the sound quality of live music in a little box their goal. Through extensive research in the fields of speaker design and psychoacoustics—the human perception of sound—the company aims to deliver to the listener a sound experience that captures the emotional impact of live music. With sales in excess of $1.3 billion, the company surely must be delivering what they promise. In the years to come, consumer demand for better quality and more authentic sound technology will keep this market vibrant.

FIGURE 7.2

Audio Equipment Industry Snapshot

	2000	2002	% CHG '00-'02
Total Personal Consumption in millions	$24,037	$25,898	7.7

Source: Bureau of Economic Analysis

Retailer Overview

In Unity Marketing's latest survey, electronics and appliance stores, such as Best Buy, Circuit City, and others, are the shopping choice for the majority of audio system buyers. Some 63 percent of buyers used these kinds of stores for audio equipment purchases in the past year.

The next most popular source for these items are discount department stores, including warehouse clubs, used by 29 percent of shoppers, followed next by nonstore retailers, including mail order and Internet, frequented by 13 percent of audio shoppers.

According to Roper, there are over 30,000 audio and electronics stores in the U.S. Best Buy, with over 500 stores, and Circuit City, with more than 600, are the market share leaders at retail (see Figure 7.3). While Best Buy offers major home appliances along with a wide selection of electronics and computers, Circuit City has stopped selling major appliances in favor of the more profitable and faster-moving electronics.

Purchase Drivers

Consumers accent their life with music, using it to set a tone or a mood in the home. As they spend time in their homes, consumers see a need for high-quality audio equipment to bring the sounds of life into the home. One respondent explains: "My husband has been studying classical music and composers for the last couple of years. While we have a portable CD player, [it] became less adequate as his interest in music grew. So this year we bought a complete home-entertainment system

FIGURE 7.3
Electronic Stores Market Share Leaders

	EST. 2002 SALES
Best Buy Company (550 stores)	$19.6 billion
Circuit City Stores (629 stores)	12.8 billion
RadioShack (7,173 stores)	4.6 billion
Fry's Electronics (22 stores)	2 billion
Bose Corp. (100 stores)	1.3 billion
PC Richard & Son (43 stores)	925 million
Good Guys (79 stores)	820 million
Tweeter Home Entertainment (170 stores)	796 million

Source: 2002 *Directory of Computer & Home Electronics Retailers* by *Chain Store Guide*

that has surround sound. It even plays DVDs, so we had to get a new flat-screen television, too, to get the most from the system."

Demographic Variables

Men are the prime purchasers of audio sound equipment in the household. Some 30 percent of men reported their households bought such equipment in 2003, compared with only 22 percent of women, suggesting that more men than women are bringing new equipment into the home. This is a youth market, with purchase incidence highest among the youngest households, aged 18 to 24. Purchase incidence remains strong, however, through age 54, when it drops to 13 percent; after age 64 purchase incidence continues to decline.

A key question for audio retailers and marketers is now that the leading edge of the baby boom generation is over age 55, will this generation's continued aging signal a declining interest in music, as has been found among previous generations? Or will boomers continue to have a steady appetite for music and audio systems like they did when they were young?

This is a category more favored by the affluent households, with purchase incidence highest among households with incomes of $50,000 and above. The presence of children under age 18 in the home relates positively to increased purchase incidence of audio equipment.

Key demographics of audio equipment and stereo system buyers.

- This is a male-dominated market.
- Upper-income households buy more.
- Households with children buy more.
- Younger households aged 18 to 34 buy more, with a sharp drop after age 55.

WHAT PEOPLE BUY: BOOKS, MAGAZINES, AND NEWSLETTERS

In 2003, the category of books, magazines, and newsletters took over the number one position from prerecorded media as the most purchased entertainment and recreation product. About three-fourths of adult consumers purchased books, magazines, or newsletters in the past year, dropping from 78 percent in 2001.

Industry Snapshot

Personal consumption of books and maps totaled $35.8 billion in 2002, up 6.3 percent over sales of $33.7 billion in 2000, according to the Bureau of Economic Analysis (see Figure 7.4). Consumer sales of magazines, newspapers, and sheet music declined in the same period, down from $35 billion in 2000 to $34.2 billion in 2002. While the rising educational level among the population provides a favorable environment for reading material, the sales of magazines and newspapers, in particular, are seeing an erosion of their subscriber base as more consumers turn to the convenience of the Internet for research, current events, and other personal information.

New trends in book retailing support sales growth in the category. The big bookstore chains, Barnes & Noble and Borders, have taken the concept of the small, private bookseller and completely overhauled it. They have introduced category-killer bookstores on a nationwide scale. They offer coffee, tea, and treats in a cafe setting, provide comfortable chairs so you can read as well as shop, and have expanded into music and DVDs in a more adult-friendly environment than the typical youth-oriented "record" store.

The Internet, too, is a powerful retailer of books, with Amazon.com leading innovation in the category, and barnesandnoble.com following behind. The online merchants offer access to both in-print and out-of-print titles, including a growing list of used and secondhand titles. Amazon.com reported total corporate sales of $3.9 billion in 2002, with books making up the largest share of sales. Barnesandnoble.com is a far distant second in the online book market, with 2002 sales of $422.8 million.

Retail Overview

Not surprising, the most frequent source for books, magazines, and newsletters is the category of stores that includes book stores (sporting goods, hobby, book, and music stores). Some 46 percent of consumers visited these stores in the past year to buy books.

The next most popular destination is discount department stores, visited by 40 percent for book purchases. The third most popular source for books is nonstore retailers, including the Internet and Web sites such as Amazon.com. Some 32 percent of consumers made a purchase of reading materials through a nonstore retailer, which also includes catalogs and TV retailing.

FIGURE 7.4

Books, Magazines, and Newsletters Industry Snapshot

	2000	2002	% CHG '00-'02
Total Personal Consumption in millions	$68,702	$69,932	1.8
Books and maps	33,654	35,772	6.3
Magazines, newspapers, sheet music	35,048	34,160	−2.5

Source: Bureau of Economic Analysis

No other retail source comes close to the top three shopping sources, although 18 percent pick up reading material in food and beverage stores.

At retail, national bookstore chains are the market share leaders (see Figure 7.5), with many independent bookstores being forced to close as they can't effectively compete with the national book chains and the Internet. Mass merchants and discounters, such as Wal-Mart, also sell books with an emphasis on best-sellers and specialty titles that target their shoppers' tastes. While traditional mail-order book clubs have been on the decline for years, the Christian specialty retail market is growing by offering a careful selection of spiritual and religious titles. The Christian Booksellers Association estimates that Christian booksellers have a total market of $2.5 billion in book sales.

Purchase Drivers

Consumers are motivated to buy books by many of the same reasons they purchase movie videos and DVDs. These include convenience, sav-

FIGURE 7.5

Book Store Market Share Leaders

	EST. 2002 SALES
Barnes & Noble (1,321 stores)	$5.3 billion
Borders Group (1,246 stores)	3.5 billion
Follett Higher Education Group (680 stores)	1.5 billion
Books-a-Million (203 stores)	443 million
Nebraska Book Company (110 stores)	339 million
Family Christian Stores (350 stores)	323 million
LifeWay Christian Stores (115 stores)	205 million

Source: 2002 *Directory of General Merchandise Stores by Chain Store Guide*

ing time by not having to return books to the library, and for personal and kids' entertainment. One consumer explains: "For me I always have to have something to read. I read a lot and buy books everywhere. My friends ask me about using the library, but the library doesn't fit my schedule. I get a sense of desperation if I don't have a book to read."

A unique emotional equation is at work in the motivation to purchase books. Consumers are more personally and emotionally involved with their books than they are with videos and music. Part of a book's appeal may be that it is "low-tech"—one reason why so many industry pundits see little threat to the book publishing industry from e-books. Another factor may be simple nostalgia because we all grew up reading books, holding books, and striving to understand what was in books. For some consumers, this early exposure to reading never took off, but for others, books have become a very real and essential part of their lives. This emotional attachment to books is what makes them so collectible. In describing her library, a focus group respondent said: "My husband and I love books and buy lots of books. Our house is full of bookshelves. I have a friend who thinks this is a luxury. She says 'that is what libraries are for.' We go to the library, but I still buy books. They are *my* books. It's about the pleasure of re-reading old 'friends.'" Another respondent wishes for a library to store all of her books. "I would love to have a library to keep all my books. Having a house with as many books as I have without a library is a challenge. I love books. I don't read every one, but I think in maybe a year or two I will get to them. I wish I had time to read all of them."

For most households, books and magazines are a personal indulgence, representing a small luxury that they can buy without guilt. For those with an inclination to buy books, the library is not a viable alternative. Consumers with a passion for books want to have a personal relationship with them and that requires ownership.

Demographic Variables

Three-fourths of American households bought books, magazines, and newsletters in the past year. Demographically, women are slightly more likely to buy in this category, as are Caucasian consumers. From young to old, households between the ages of 18 to 64 have a high purchase incidence for books, magazines, and newsletters. Purchase incidence of these items also correlates with higher incomes. Households with incomes of $35,000 or more are the most active book buyers, as are those with higher educational levels. As educational attainment rises, so too does the household's purchase incidence for books. Larger households of three or more individuals also buy books more actively.

Key demographics of buyers of books, magazines, and newsletters.

- Females buy more.
- Highest incidence among ages 18 to 54.
- Middle-to-upper-income households buy more.
- Those with higher education buy more.

WHAT PEOPLE BUY: COMPUTERS AND SOFTWARE FOR HOME USE

The purchase of computers, hardware, and software for household use, rather than for use in a home office, rose from 40 percent in 2000 to 47 percent in 2003. Today consumers generally are upgrading their older home computer models with the latest technology as the price for computers has fallen below $1,000 for a fully equipped model. Householders also are adding new software and hardware accessories to handle photograph files, music recordings, and household records. Seemingly, the appetite for the latest computer technology is unquenchable.

Industry Snapshot

Personal consumption of computers, peripherals, and software peaked in 2000 when sales reached $43.8 billion, according to statistics compiled by the Bureau of Economic Analysis (see Figure 7.6). After dipping in 2001 to $42 billion, personal consumption of home computers, related equipment, and software rose back in 2002 to $44.2 billion, up slightly from results in 2000. Now that the majority of American homes already have a home computer, and the computer systems they own are not becoming obsolete as fast as they did back in the 1990s, further growth in the sales of home computers, peripherals, and software is going to be hard to come by.

In order to move the home computer market off its current plateau, manufacturers must feed the consuming public's desire for new technology and upgrades, as well as convince the nation's 49 percent of households that do not yet have a computer to go out and buy one. Today, the

FIGURE 7.6

Computers and Software Industry Snapshot

	2000	2002	% CHG '00-'02
Total Personal Consumption in millions	$43,834	$44,162	0.7
Computers and peripherals	33,514	33,721	0.6
Software	10,320	10,441	1.2

Source: Bureau of Economic Analysis

upgrade market is very different from the new computer market. The market for new home computers targets a lower-income demographic because far more lower-income households have no computers. On the other hand, the market for computer upgrades is toward the upper-middle and affluent consumers. According to the latest government census, nearly nine out of ten family households with incomes of $75,000 or more have at least one computer and about eight in ten have at least one household member using the Internet at home. Among households with incomes below $25,000 a year, only three in ten have a computer and about two in ten have Internet access.

The desire to purchase a home computer and equip it with Internet access is particularly strong among households with school-aged children. Having children in the home is a key demographic associated with buying and/or upgrading home computers. Two-thirds of households with school-aged children have a computer and about 53 percent have Internet access.

Retail Overview

As the price of computers declines and their ease of use increases, computers, computer peripherals, and software can be found at a growing range of retail outlets, from local Wal-Mart stores, office supply stores, such as Office Depot and Staples, specialty computer stores, such as Gateway and CompUSA, home appliance centers, such as Best Buy and Circuit City, and even local video, game, and books stores. Online and direct marketing retailers, such as Dell and Gateway, are also an important retail resource for this category of goods.

When consumers seek computers and software for home use, they look to electronics and appliance stores first (see Figure 7.7). Some 57

FIGURE 7.7

Computer Stores Market Share Leaders

	EST. 2002 SALES
CompUSA (224 stores)	$7.96 billion
CDW Computer Centers (2 stores)	4.3 billion
Gateway (300 stores)	4.2 billion
Micro Electronics (18 stores)	1.5 billion
PC Warehouse (87 stores)	480 million

Source: 2002 *Directory of Computer & Consumer Electronics Retailers by Chain Store Guide*

percent have made purchases of home computers and software at these stores in the past year. Next are the discount department stores, visited by 31 percent of computer and software consumers. The discount stores are a surprisingly important place for consumers to buy computers. Because they offer little in the way of customer service, being strictly cash-and-carry type outlets, their appearance as the number two most important source for consumers to buy home computers suggests that the computer shoppers in 2003 are confident about their ability to un-pack the box and get the computer working on their own without any special assistance or store support. It also demonstrates the role of price in leading shoppers into the store to buy.

Nonstore retailers are also an important place that shoppers turn to buy computers. Some 30 percent of consumers have made a purchase through a nonstore outlet, including the Internet, television shopping, and mail-order catalogs in the past year. Demographically, the older con-sumers, aged 55 to 64 years, are the most likely to choose nonstore re-tailers in making their home computer purchase. This suggests they feel more confident and comfortable buying these items from home, rather than in the store face-to-face with a store clerk.

Increasing convergence of electronic technology is a key trend in the electronics sector as a whole. Computers, traditionally thought of as work tools, are converging with entertainment electronics, notably tele-visions, home theatre systems, gaming systems, and audio equipment. The rapid growth of the Internet and its worldwide communications ca-pability is linking consumers even more closely with their computers and extending the computer's potential as a multifunctional home ap-pliance. Due to this convergence, retailers will find many opportunities in this marketplace to serve new and emerging consumer needs for state-of-the-art electronic tools.

Purchase Drivers

The need to upgrade an existing home computer is a key driver for new computer buying. As one recent computer purchaser explained: "We just bought a computer. We already had one, but it was about 300 years old in computer years. We needed a faster computer. Now with the new computer, if I wanted to work at home, I could." Another consumer purchased a second home computer with the plan that this machine will last for a few more years. "We just bought a computer. This was our second computer. I could have lived with the old computer, but I wanted a new one. I hope we don't have to upgrade it anytime soon, so we got all the bells and whistles. We even added surround-sound speakers."

In buying new computers, consumers are looking for expanded functionality—the ability to do something with the computer they never could do before, positioning computers squarely as a utilitarian discretionary purchase. As one respondent put it: "We just bought a new laptop computer. We didn't strictly need it, since we have three others at home already. But we needed the laptop because of changes at my work. I have to drag things back and forth for work so the laptop is a real convenience."

Often, the educational needs of children justify computer purchases. In our research, one parent told us: "A basic computer is almost a necessity today, especially for the kids who have to do research on the Internet and write papers. The educational component of the computer is very important. Your kids have to keep up."

Once the computer is in the home, consumers often want to upgrade their machines to add capabilities and functionality. Another respondent said: "We added a CD burner to our computer so we can pick and choose the songs we listen to. The reason I purchased the CD burner is because we recently suffered a number of deaths in my immediate family. It made us realize that life is too short. You should have fun. If something gives you pleasure, then you should enjoy it. We deserve it, and it makes you a better person and a more pleasant person to be around. Music is important to our family, and now we can do custom mixing, so we enjoy life more."

Demographic Variables

Men take the lead in household computer purchases, with 50 percent of men reporting the purchase of a computer, software, or hardware for home use, as opposed to 44 percent of women. Youthful households, especially those aged 55 or younger, are more likely to have purchased a computer or related equipment in the past year. However, 38 percent of households headed by persons aged 55 to 64 bought a computer in the past year, suggesting that the perceived need for a computer is spreading in the mature market as well.

Middle-to-upper-income households are far more likely to have bought a computer, with purchase incidence exceeding 60 percent for households with incomes greater than $50,000. A computer purchase is also strongly linked to the presence of children in the home; 58 percent of households with children, compared with only 40 percent of those without, reported buying a computer and related equipment in 2003. Households with "some college" and those with more educational attainment are much more likely to purchase computers.

Key demographics of buyers of computer hardware and software for home use.

- Buyers are more likely men.
- The presence of children favors purchase.
- More educated households buy more.
- Households under age 55 buy more, with the strongest purchase among households 25 to 44 years of age.
- Households with income levels of $50,000 and above buy more.

WHAT PEOPLE BUY: CRAFTS, SEWING, KNITTING, OR NEEDLEWORK SUPPLIES

Craft supplies were purchased by 29 percent of households in 2003, down some 10 percentage points from reported purchase incidence in 2001 of 39 percent of households. A hobby for some, cheap "therapy" for others, crafting is enjoyed by over half of U.S. households, according to research conducted by the Hobby Industry Association. Susan Brandt, director of communications at the Hobby Industry Association, explains that interest in crafts rose in the aftermath of September 11: "We are an industry people go to in times of trouble. They take solace in staying busy and doing things with their hands."

Industry Snapshot

Do-it-yourself has taken on a whole new meaning today. As the cost of basic necessities, such as food, clothing, and shelter, fall, saving money through crafting is no longer the prime motivator for consumers to craft. Rather consumers turn to crafting today to express creativity and find personal fulfillment in the creative process. Trendsetting home decorating shows, such as *Trading Spaces* and *While You Were Out* on The Learning Channel and *Christopher Lowell Show* on The Discovery Channel, as well as the daily programming from HGTV, have taught consumers new ways to have fun and connect with family and friends while doing it yourself.

Driven by consumer interest in crafting hobbies, the growth in the crafting industry has been dynamic, according to statistics compiled by the Hobby Industry Association. The total market for craft and hobby supplies reached $29 billion in 2002, up about 13 percent over sales in 2001. The sales of general crafts ($12.5 billion) and needlecrafts ($8.4 billion) account for nearly three-fourths of industry sales in 2002. The other segments of the craft market, painting and finishing ($4.9 million) and floral crafts ($3.2 million) are much smaller by comparison.

Retail Overview

Discount department stores take the lead in stores where people shop for crafts, sewing, knitting, and needlework supplies. Some 49 percent of craft-buying shoppers have made purchases of their supplies at discount department stores, while 37 percent visited specialty hobby stores when shopping for crafts. Other specialty stores are also a favored place for buying craft supplies. This class of stores, a category that includes such stores as gift stores, office supply stores, and stationers, attracted 29 percent of the crafts, sewing, knitting, and needlework consumers in the past year, putting it in a strong third place.

Nonstore retailers, including Internet, mail order, direct sales, and television shopping, was used by 15 percent of crafts buyers, with those 35 years and older being more likely than the younger consumers to use these outlets.

While discount department stores may take the lead in craft supplies, when consumers really want to appease their passion for crafting they turn to the specialty craft stores. Michaels Stores is the nation's largest specialty crafts retailer, with nearly 800 craft stores in operation (see Figure 7.8). The chain generated $2.5 billion in revenues in 2002. Michaels

FIGURE 7.8
Craft Store Market Share Leaders

	EST. 2002 SALES
Michaels Stores (920 stores)	$2.5 billion
Jo-Ann Stores (920 stores)	1.6 billion
Hobby Lobby (272 stores)	905 million
Hancock Fabrics (430 stores)	412 million
A.C. Moore Arts & Crafts (70 stores)	393 million

Source: 2002 *Directory of Discount and General Merchandise Stores by Chain Store*

Stores' growth has become legendary, rising from a chain of only 16 stores in the mid-1980s. Today, the Michaels Stores company also operates a chain of 150-plus art and framing stores under the Aaron Brothers brand. Michaels Stores also offers custom picture framing as part of their service mix.

Keeping an eye on emerging trends in the crafting business, Michaels has identified a significant opportunity in the scrapbooking crafts market, a hobby that appeals to both the traditional crafts market (i.e., middle-aged women tied to traditional paper and scissors) as well as the youth and teen enthusiasts who are incorporating computer technology into the hobby. It has launched a new chain called ReCollections just for the scrapbooking audience and plans to open as many as 10 new ReCollections stores in its first year of operation. What accounts for Michaels steady growth? By keeping focused on its mission—to help people express themselves creatively—and tracking the evolving interests of its customers, the company has found a formula for success that taps deep-seated longings in people everywhere.

Purchase Drivers

Crafting provides a creative outlet that many consumers need, especially in today's complex, technology-driven society. A respondent explained: "If you have a creative nature, you have to do something. For some, it is art, or acting, or writing, but for me it is crafts. I have to have an outlet, something to do with my hands." Crafting relieves stress for some, as another consumer says: "It takes the place of me going to a therapist."

The Hobby Industry Association reports that scrapbooking and memory crafts are the most popular crafting activities being participated in by 38 percent of crafters. Interest in scrapbooking has exploded in the past several years, rising from a participation rate of 11 percent in 2000 to be the leading crafts activity today. Through scrapbooking crafters are connecting with their past, present, and future. By creating a scrapbook, one is collecting and sharing memories and emotions with family and friends. The scrapbooking passion also crosses age barriers, with tweens, teens, and young adults creating personal scrapbooks right alongside of their mothers and grandmothers.

After scrapbooking, the next most popular crafts include general crafts (35 percent), followed by needle crafts (28 percent), and painting/drawing (25 percent).

Demographic Variables

Crafting is a female-dominated activity with women reporting much higher purchase incidence for their household (41 percent) than men (16 percent). While men strictly speaking "craft," they tend to use different terms than women to describe their crafting activities. For example, a man might putter around his home workshop doing woodworking, but he perceives those activities as "work" rather than crafting, though his wife might beg to differ.

This activity tends to skew older, with consumers aged 45 to 64 years having the highest overall purchase incidence. As with most categories, purchase incidence drops sharply at age 65. Whites participate in craft purchasing more than blacks. Middle-to-upper-income households ($35,000 or more) buy more crafts than do lower-income families. Households with children tend to buy more craft supplies than do those without children.

Key demographics of buyers of crafts, sewing, knitting, and needlework supplies.

- This is a female-oriented market.
- Households with incomes of $35,000 or more buy more.
- Mature households between ages 45 and 64 buy more.
- Households with children buy more.

WHAT PEOPLE BUY: MUSICAL INSTRUMENTS

While only 10 percent of households purchased a musical instrument, this category enjoys the most rapid sales growth of any of the other product categories in the entertainment and recreational products market-place. So while this is a narrow niche market, it offers significant growth prospects in the future, both for the purchase of new instruments and add-on purchases, such as accessories and sheet music.

Industry Snapshot

More Americans than ever are making music, according to a new poll by the Gallup Organization. In the majority of American house-holds (54 percent), at least one member plays a musical instrument. Be-cause birds of a feather flock together, households with one musician are twice as likely to have other members who also play an instrument. Pianos, played by 34 percent of musicians, and guitars (22 percent) lead the list of favored instruments, with drums (6 percent), flutes (5 per-cent), clarinets (4 percent), saxophones (4 percent), keyboards (4 per-cent), trumpets (3 percent), and violins (3 percent) rounding out the most popular instruments.

Playing an instrument is not just kids' stuff anymore, with adults aged 35 to 50 (i.e., baby boomers) being the most active age group mu-sically. Some 42 percent of amateur musicians are middle-aged Ameri-cans, while kids aged 5 to 17 make up 31 percent, and young adults aged 18 to 34, account for 27 percent of the musically inclined.

Given their commitment to music and musical training, Americans are purchasing musical instruments at the highest levels since 1978. In 2002, retail sales of musical instruments reached $5.1 billion, up a dra-matic 17.2 percent over sales in 2000 of $4.3 billion (see Figure 7.9). The future of the musical instrument market looks bright throughout the decade as more and more affluent baby boomers trade in their older in-struments for luxury models and higher-end instruments they now can afford to buy.

FIGURE 7.9

Musical Instruments Industry Snapshot

	2000	2002	% CHG '00-'02
Total Personal Consumption in millions	$4,344	$5,089	17.2

Source: Bureau of Economic Analysis

Retail Overview

Not surprising, music stores lead as the source where people are most likely to buy musical instruments. About one-third of consumers in the past year bought their musical instruments in music stores. The next most frequently used sources are other types of specialty stores, used by 27 percent to purchase musical instruments, and nonstore retailers, such as the Internet, mail-order catalogs, or television shopping, favored by 24 percent of buyers.

Riding the wave of musical enthusiasm is market share leader Guitar Center. This nationwide retailer, which just broke the $1 billion sales mark in 2002, operates 108 Guitar Center stores. It specializes in gear for rock and pop musicians, such as guitars, amplifiers, percussion instruments, keyboards, and professional audio and recording equipment. It also services school music programs with its American Music division of 20 stores that target teachers and band directors with band instruments for sale or rent. It is a multichannel retailer with its Musician's Friend direct response brand.

No other national retailer comes close to matching Guitar Center. Sam Ash, with about 30 stores and sales of $350 million, lags far behind in sales volume. As a result, musical instrument retailing in America remains largely a mom-and-pop business.

Purchase Drivers

My household is one of the 10 percent across the country that purchased musical instruments in the past year. I believe we are fairly typical of the musical instrument buying household today composed of baby boomer generation parents and two millennial generation teenagers. Both my husband and I were "musicians" of sorts in the late '60s. I played piano for years and my husband was the lead guitarist in his own rock 'n' roll band. Once in college, though, we both lost touch with our music, only to return 25 years later with a renewed passion to play as our children began their own exploration of music.

Today, I take piano lessons every week and plan on upgrading our current instrument to a baby grand piano as soon as we expand our house, because we don't have room for one right now. My husband bought a fairly expensive guitar within the past couple of years and now takes weekly lessons also to learn blues-style finger picking. And my oldest son just got a new electric guitar and amplifier—one of our musical instrument purchases this year—though he doesn't take lessons yet.

But our youngest son is the family's true musician. He started with piano lessons several years before I did and inspired me to return to playing. This past year he became intrigued with the accordion, so we bought him a 60-button accordion appropriate for his size—another of our purchases this year. He is teaching himself the accordion and so far so good, but he has been complaining that he is having trouble with the finer points of the bellows and I expect we will add accordion lessons to his schedule next year.

He is also interested in getting a drum set and has picked out the one he wants for Christmas this year. Having told him he is not likely to get drums this year, he says he'll settle for a bass guitar. With his talent and widespread interests in all kinds of instruments, I see him as a budding young Paul McCartney, and have plans for him to help pay for college by performing his music live. He's likely to do just that.

Demographic Variables

Men are more likely to purchase musical instruments than women, with male purchase incidence at 13 percent, compared to female incidence at 8 percent. Two age groups are the most active purchasers of musical instruments: the most youthful adult households, aged 18 to 24, and middle-aged households, aged 35 to 44. The only other demographic factor that strongly influences the likelihood to purchase musical instruments is the presence of children in the home. Households with children under age 18 have a reported purchase incidence of 16 percent, compared to households with no children at 7 percent.

Key demographics of buyers of musical instruments.

- Men are more likely to buy than women.
- Two age groups dominate: those aged 18 to 24 and 35 to 44
- Households with children are more active buyers.

WHAT PEOPLE BUY: PET ACCESSORIES

Consumers are buying more for their pets, with the purchase incidence of pet accessories rising to 41 percent of U.S. households in 2003 from 35 percent in 2000. In the most recent study done of pet ownership by the American Veterinary Medical Association, nearly 60 percent of U.S. households (58.9 million) owned one or more companion animals, as they are called in the study. American households keep 59 million cats and nearly 53 million dogs. Consumers are more likely to have multiple cats than dogs, so there are 4.2 million more households that own dogs.

Industry Snapshot

Between the beginning of the twentieth century and this century, a paradigm shift occurred in how Americans relate to their cats, dogs, and other pets. Back in 1900 when America was a far more agrarian country, people were in many ways dependent on animals to maintain their standard of living. At that time, animals "paid their way" in services rendered to the turn-of-the-century household. Horses were still the primary means of personal transportation. Dogs were kept to guard the land or help with herding or hunting. Cats did duty protecting grains and feed from vermin.

But today, our relationship with animals, especially pets like dogs and cats, has undergone a radical transformation. Pets today no longer are expected to perform services in exchange for their room and board. Rather, they are valued as companions and friends. They have become full-fledged members of the family. In a recent survey among pet owners, over 90 percent agreed with the statement: "Your pet is considered part of the family."

With this transformation of the relationship with our pets, Americans are lavishing more attention, emotional affection, and spending on their four-legged "family" members. Given their new status as family members, Americans spent $42.2 billion on their pets in 2002 (see Figure 7.10).

FIGURE 7.10
Pet Accessories Industry Snapshot

	2000	2002	% CHG '00-'02
Total Personal Consumption in millions	$37,711	$42,149	11.8
Pet food	21,315	23,588	10.7
Veterinarians and other pet services	16,396	18,561	13.2

Source: Bureau of Economic Analysis

Retail Overview

When it comes to shopping for their pets, consumers visit two types of stores in nearly equal numbers to buy accessories and pet items. Half of the consumers visit discount department stores to shop for pet accessories, and nearly half (49 percent) visit other specialty stores, a category that includes pet specialty stores. No other category of store comes close to these two in terms of shoppers' preferences, although food and beverage stores rank third, used by 16 percent of shoppers to buy pet accessories.

Today more and more retailers are targeting the pet business as a growth market. Some 7,500 shops in the United States specialize in selling pets, while more than 9,300 stores classify themselves as pet food and supply stores. Many of the nation's 50,000 veterinarians also service their patrons' pet supply needs. Wal-Mart, Target, Kmart, and the rest of the nation's nearly 35,000 mass merchants, department stores, and warehouse clubs also provide pet supplies. Wal-Mart is estimated to generate $2 billion out of their pet supply department alone. But the most significant change in pet accessories retailing today is the emergence of national big-box retailing giants PETsMART and PETCO, whose strip mall stores in affluent areas target the needs of enthusiastic pet owners.

PETsMART is the market share leader in pet supplies, with nearly 600 stores in the United States and Canada (see Figure 7.11). Pets are allowed in the stores with their owners to browse the 12,000 products available in each large-format store ranging from 19,000 to 26,000 square feet. Their current growth plan calls for adding 60 more stores in 2003. PETsMART's target market is the large group of pet owners they define as "pet parents." Pet parents are passionately committed to their pets and consider their pets family members. To meet the pet parents' needs, PETsMART focuses on providing a one-stop shopping destination that offers Total Lifetime Care™ for pets in an easy-to-shop, full-service spe-

FIGURE 7.11
Pet Accessories Market Share Leaders

	2002 SALES
PETsMART (about 600 stores)	$2.5 billion
PETCO (about 600 stores)	1.3 billion

Source: Unity Marketing's Pet Report

cialty environment. They also sell through direct marketing channels including two branded catalogs, on the Internet at PETsMART.com, and through a Web site dedicated to equine products. PETsMART sells both national brands and the company's private labels. Many of the stores offer services such as grooming and obedience training. Veterinary care is also available in 300 PETsMART stores through a strategic relationship with Banfield, The Pet Hospital™.

Trailing PETsMart is number two PETCO Animal Supplies, which operates 600 stores in 40 states. While the competition in pet supplies is hot and heavy, there is little discernable difference in the shopping experience offered by the two market share leaders.

Purchase Drivers

There has been a fundamental shift in consumer psychology that has impacted the purchase of pet accessories. Today's pet-owning households tend to look at their pets as members of the family, rather than simply animals. With this shift in the way that people view their relationship with their pets, they are spending more money buying "gourmet" pet foods, toys, beds and carriers, and other accessories for their pets. A respondent explains: "We have a dog and a cat. They are like members of the family."

Pets are often treated as surrogate children, given toys, and taken on play or adventure outings. One consumer explains: "We have four cats, a fish, and a guinea pig. Our cats have to have their toys." Another says: "It took us five years to have a baby. During that time, my pets were my children. If you don't have children, then you put a lot into your pets because they fill that need to care for someone. Then when you have kids, it becomes a money factor, a time factor, and a room factor. My animals suffered a change in living standards."

The American Pet Products Manufacturers Association reports that the majority of pet owners bought a gift for their pet in the past year. Typically, gifts are purchased for either no special occasion or for Christmas.

Demographic Variables

Women were more likely purchasers of pet accessories than men, with 45 percent of women, as compared to 38 percent of men, buying these items for their household. Younger and middle-aged households are more active purchasers of pet accessories, as households aged 55 and above show a marked drop in their purchase incidence of this category of products.

The more affluent the households the more likely they are to buy pet accessories, as are those with children in the home. Nearly half of households with children bought pet accessories in the past year. Except for consumers that have not finished high school, pet accessories purchases cut across educational levels.

Key demographics of pet accessories buyers.

* Women purchase more often than men.
* Households under age 55 buy more.
* Purchase incidence rise with income levels.
* Households with children buy more pet accessories.

WHAT PEOPLE BUY: PHOTOGRAPHY EQUIPMENT AND SUPPLIES

Purchase incidence of photography equipment and supplies has experienced a rise and fall since 2000. In that year, some 38 percent of households bought photography equipment or supplies. Purchase incidence rose to 51 percent in 2001, only to drop down to some 43 percent of households in 2003.

This up-and-down trajectory may in part be explained by the pace at which consumers adopt new technology. Since 2000, the photography market has been impacted by new technology and the ready availability of affordable digital cameras, which offer a significant improvement to film-based photographs. Through digital cameras consumers have the ability to store and arrange picture images on computer disks. This is an attractive and lasting alternative for recording a family's heritage, rather than flimsy paper images stuffed in books, drawers, and scrapbooks. Presumably, the peak year for households to adopt the new technology occurred in and around 2001, with the drop since then due to fewer households having a need to upgrade to digital.

Industry Snapshot

The market for photography equipment is vibrant and benefits from technological advancements, such as digital imaging and computer storage of digital images. No longer is the family or hobbyist photographer limited to storing images on film or paper. Today, photographs are being stored as digital images in computer files, thus opening a whole realm of new possibilities in photography storage and transmission.

The retail sale of photography equipment, film, and photography supplies is about $7.5 billion, according to statistics compiled by the Bureau of Economic Analysis (see Figure 7.12). The Photo Marketing Association estimates the cost of photo finishing and processing to be about $7 billion, making the services side of the amateur photography market larger than either the product equipment ($4 billion) or film and photography supplies ($3.5 billion) segments today. However, spending on photo finishing may slide as more photographers opt out of film processing in favor of digital storage and display.

Retail Overview

While an estimated 4,600 camera and photo supply stores currently operate in the United States, these stores have been on the decline as shoppers turn to alternative outlets. In film processing, mass merchants and discounters, notably Wal-Mart, and one-hour photo shops, are drawing away a significant share of business from dedicated photography shops. In addition, mass merchants and electronic retailers are gaining more ground as merchants for the new digital-based cameras and digital imaging equipment.

Discount department stores lead as the favorite place that consumers shop for photographic equipment and supplies. More than half of households (53 percent) made purchases of these products at discount department stores in the past year. The next most widely used source, used by 31 percent of shoppers, was electronics and appliances stores. Nonstore retailers are becoming a more important source for

FIGURE 7.12

Photography Equipment and Supplies Industry Snapshot

	2000	2002	% CHG '00-'02
Total Personal Consumption in millions	$7,116	$7,462	4.9
Photographic equipment	3,808	3,993	4.9
Film and supplies	3,308	3,469	4.9

Source: Bureau of Economic Analysis

photography goods, with some 15 percent of shoppers buying from the Internet, catalogs, or television shopping channels in the past year.

There is only one store today that can lay claim to being a national specialty retailer of cameras and photo processing—Ritz Camera Centers. For years, Ritz with some 1,000 stores and an estimated $500 million in annual sales, held the lead over archrival Wolf Camera, with 530 stores and $467 million in sales. What made the competition even more intense was that both stores were owned by cousins and descendants of commercial photography pioneer Benjamin Ritz.

But in 2001, the family rift was mended when David Ritz, chief executive of Ritz Camera Centers, rescued his cousin Chuck Wolf's Wolf Camera from bankruptcy in an $85 million acquisition deal. Privately held Ritz Camera Centers today boast over 1,200 stores in 48 states and estimated revenues of $1.34 billion.

Ritz Camera faces stiff competition from both the mass merchants and the electronic giants, like Best Buy and Circuit City, in the camera market. They also are challenged by the growing obsolescence of film processing due to the digital revolution. Ritz Camera's strategy to maintain growth is to fully embrace the new technology. Besides selling new digital cameras, which can run up to $7,000, Ritz is installing new equipment in all stores to make high-quality prints from a customer's memory card or media storage disk. Ritz also operates Internet sites where customers can buy cameras, film, and accessories as well as read product reviews and share digital photos.

Purchase Drivers

Driving the purchase of new photographic equipment is innovation in technology. With the price of digital cameras coming down and more households having access to a computer, consumers are upgrading their old cameras with the latest digital models. As one young mother explains: "I really wanted a digital camera. I asked my husband for one for my birthday, but I knew he wouldn't get it. So I went out and bought it for myself. I want to record all the stages of growth of my baby. It's important, but my husband doesn't see it like I do."

In a recent survey among 950 consumers, Unity Marketing found that about 54 percent of households reported having a digital still camera. This survey also uncovered how consumers view their picture-taking activities. Some 44 percent agreed with the following statements describing their participation in photography: "I enjoy taking pictures. I do so throughout the year, not only for special occasions. I like having a lot of pictures."

On the other hand, about one-third of consumers were less involved with picture taking and agreed with these statements: "I take pictures occasionally on holidays and special occasions. Sometimes taking pictures is a bother."

Only 14 percent of consumers reported they rarely take pictures.

Demographic Variables

Women show a slightly higher propensity to buy photography equipment and/or supplies for their households than men. This is a class of goods that is likely to be purchased by all age groups, except the most aged. White households, as opposed to black and/or Hispanic households, are more active buying photography equipment and suppliers.

Purchase incidence in this category rises with income. Households with incomes of $50,000 or more are most likely to purchase photography equipment and supplies, as are larger households and those with children. Educational attainment is linked to purchase incidence, as more educated consumers buy more.

Key demographics of photography equipment buyers.

- Women are more likely to buy these products for their households.
- Except for the most aged, consumers of all ages, from 18 to 64, are likely to purchase.
- White households buy more.
- Larger households and those with children buy more.
- Purchase incidence rises with income and educational attainment.

WHAT PEOPLE BUY: PRERECORDED VIDEOS, MUSIC, DVDS, ETC.

In the 2003 survey, the category of prerecorded videos, music, DVDs, etc. dropped out of first place as the most widely purchased entertainment product to second place after books, magazines, and newsletters. In the most recent year, prerecorded entertainment media were purchased by 62 percent of households, down from 79 percent in 2001. This category has been negatively impacted by Internet-based services that allow consumers to download their favorite music, giving consumers the new ability to program their own musical entertainment experiences without having to buy prerecorded media. The ability to select and custom program one's own entertainment is a strong draw to many consumers.

Industry Snapshot

Total retail sales of prerecorded videos and music reached $32.9 billion in 2002, up 11.7 percent from 2000's level of $29.5 billion (see Figure 7.13). Technological changes account for the ups and downs of sales in this product category. As digital DVDs replace analog prerecorded videos as the consumers' media of choice for home entertainment, consumers are also using the Internet to transfer music to their home systems without paying producers royalties. Due to these shifts, retail sales of both prerecorded videos *and* music recordings are down. But because retail sales of DVDs have tripled since 2000, the overall prerecorded entertainment category has continued to grow.

There is still tremendous room for growth in the sales of prerecorded DVDs. While penetration of videocassette recorders (VCRs) today stands at 91 percent of all television households, DVD players are only available in 36 percent of TV households, or 38.8 million out of the nation's 106.7 million television-equipped homes. As the price of DVD players has dropped to an average of $140, shipments of DVD players to dealers are rising exponentially. In 2000, the Motion Picture Association of America (MPAA) reported that 8.5 million DVD players were shipped. The number of DVD players shipped more than doubled by 2002 when 17 million units were delivered to retailers.

Once consumers get their new DVD players home, their appetite for movies to play on DVD is quickened, so the studios are responding with

FIGURE 7.13
Prerecorded Media Industry Snapshot

	2000	2002	% CHG '00-'02
Total Personal Consumption in billions	$29.47	$32.92	11.7
DVDs	3.95	13.16	233
Videos	11.20	7.15	−36.1
Music	14.32	12.61	−12.0

Source: Motion Picture Association of America, Recording Industry of America, Unity Marketing

more new titles. Today some 20,000 titles are available on DVD, up from 8,500 in 2000. And an astonishing 685 million prerecorded DVDs were shipped to retailers in 2002, nearly four times as many (182.4 million) as were shipped in 2000. With an estimated average price of $20.78, the U.S. market for prerecorded DVDs totaled $13.2 billion at retail in 2002.

While the story of prerecorded DVDs is up, up, and away, the now-obsolete video market is on the decline. During the 1998 sales year, shipments of prerecorded videocassette titles peaked at 657.8 million units. It's been going down ever since, reaching 433.2 million in 2002. With an estimated average retail price of $16.50, the total market for prerecorded videocassettes was $7.15 billion in 2002, according to data from the MPAA.

Retail sales of recorded music on all media plateaued in 1999 at $14.6 billion in retail sales, according to statistics compiled by the Recording Industry Association of America (RIAA), and have been sliding ever since. In 2002 retail sales of music was $12.6 billion, a drop of 13.5 percent overall. Much of the decline in retail sales is attributed to what the industry calls "piracy" (i.e., the illegal downloading and sharing of music files from the Internet). The industry today is taking aggressive legal action to put an end to this practice. Over 90 percent of the industry's sales are attributed to CDs.

Retail Overview

For prerecorded videos and music, discount department stores are the most popular destination, visited by 63 percent of consumers in the past year. This is followed by electronics and appliance stores, shopped by 54 percent of consumers. Sporting goods, hobby, book, and music stores came in third, with 34 percent of consumers making these stores their destination to buy prerecorded media. No other traditional store category was chosen nearly as often as these three.

Nonstore retailers, including Internet, catalogs, and TV shopping, are taking a bite out of traditional stores for these products. Nearly one-fourth of shoppers (23 percent) bought prerecorded entertainment media from nontraditional retail outlets.

The big story in the retail market for prerecorded videos, music, and DVDs is the shift out of specialty outlets devoted to either video or music media into mass merchants and discounters that stock the latest releases at discount prices. For example, the RIAA reports that 2002 was the first year that more music purchases were made at non-music-only stores, like mass merchants and electronics specialty stores. On the other hand, record store purchases decreased to 36.8 percent in 2002.

For the video retailers, the loss of video rental revenue is hurting their bottom line because more shoppers opt to buy, rather than rent, videos and DVDs as retail prices decline. While the national chains like Blockbuster are holding their own against the discounters like Wal-Mart, Target, and Best Buy, who offer new releases for $16 as opposed to Blockbuster's $20, smaller, independent mom-and-pop video stores are closing in unprecedented numbers (see Figure 7.14).

Blockbuster, with more than 8,500 stores and 48 million customer accounts, is exploring the strategic advantage that having movie titles for rent gives them over discounters. Their new marketing program called "Rent It! Like It! Buy It!" offers renters a previously viewed version of a DVD for only $9.99. They also offer a free rental with every purchase of a new DVD and are testing a flat rate for unlimited 30-day rentals. The company has ambitious goals: To become the customers' complete source for movies and games in the format of their choice—rental or retail, new or used.

Purchase Drivers

While new competition is appearing from the Internet and various services that permit downloading of music, in the movies category consumers continue to want the added convenience of owning prerecorded DVDs and videos, rather than renting them in the video stores. "I always

FIGURE 7.14
Prerecorded Media Market Share Leaders

	2002 SALES
Blockbuster (8,500 stores)	$5.56 billion
Musicland Stores/Sam Goody (1,195 stores)	1.89 billion
Hollywood Entertainment (about 1,800 stores)	1.5 billion
Trans World Entertainment (850 stores)	1.4 billion
MTS/Tower Records/Video (120 stores)	983 million
Wherehouse Entertainment (about 150 stores)	604 million
Virgin Entertainment (about 25 stores)	300 million

Source: 2002 *Directory of Computer & Electronics Retailers by Chain Store Guide*

forget to take our videos back to the rental store. I end up spending more on rental than I would if I just bought the tape," one focus group respondent confided. Besides convenience, many consumers want to keep up with technological advances, which bring better quality recordings and improved pleasure. Entertainment and pleasure are essential benefits this category provides. Music especially influences mood, so it offers emotion-moderating effects. Finally, children are major users of prerecorded music and videos. For them, repeated watching and listening is a pleasure, whereas adults often get bored with frequent viewing.

Most families consider entertainment DVDs, videos, and recorded music an indulgence, but not too extravagant. The barriers against continued purchase of the category are falling as prices moderate, and the desire to save time and be more efficient makes buying, rather than renting a video or DVD, a more attractive option.

Demographic Variables

The purchase of prerecorded entertainment media is a gender-neutral category with just about as many men purchasing these products as women. This category strongly skews toward a more youthful audience, with the youngest consumers the most likely to make a purchase in this category. Purchase incidence steadily declines with age.

Household income level is an important predictor of likelihood to purchase prerecorded videos and music. Purchase incidence of products in this category dramatically increases among households with income of $35,000 a year and above. Purchase incidence also increases steadily with education level.

Household size is a key to purchase incidence. A household with three or more people and one with the presence of children is an important predictor of purchases in this category.

Key demographics of buyers of prerecorded videos, music, and DVDs.

- It is a gender-neutral market.
- Skews toward a youthful market, with purchase incidence declining with age.
- Household size and presence of children are strong factors predicting purchase.
- Rising income and educational levels favor purchase.

WHAT PEOPLE BUY: SPORTING GOODS AND EXERCISE EQUIPMENT

Since 2000, consumer purchase incidence of sporting goods and exercise equipment has been on the rise. In 2003, nearly half of U.S. households (48 percent) reported buying either sporting goods or exercise equipment and supplies, compared to 43 percent in 2001 and 36 percent in 2000.

This finding signals that consumers are getting concerned about health and fitness, as does research from the National Sporting Goods Association about the sports in which consumers choose to participate. For example, exercise walking was the number one most widely enjoyed sport during 2002. More than 82.2 million Americans age 7 or older walked for exercise at least once. Other popular sports in order of participation were camping overnight (55.4 million), swimming (54.7 million), exercising with equipment (50.2 million), and fishing (44.2 million). New concern with health and fitness is evidenced by the fact that exercising with weights is among the five fastest-growing sports in terms of participation, up 14 percent over 2001 levels. Among the other fastest-growing sports based upon participation are paintball games, up 24 percent; water skiing, up 18 percent; and hiking, up 17 percent over 2001.

Industry Snapshot

Total industry sales of sporting goods and equipment were $21.7 billion in 2002, up only 1.8 percent over 2000 levels of $21.4 (see Figure 7.15). Fueled by a concern about rising obesity levels, Americans spent $4.3 billion on exercise equipment to help them get back into shape. While expenditures on exercise rose, they spent nearly 11 percent less on golfing equipment, suggesting that Mark Twain was right in his assessment of golf as "a good walk spoiled." Nearly 80 percent of total industry revenues are from the sale of equipment within these seven categories: exercise, golf, team sports, hunting and firearms, fishing and tackle, camping, and optics.

Retail Overview

Consumers favor sporting goods stores as the best place to buy sporting goods and exercise equipment. Valuing the sports stores' much wider

FIGURE 7.15

Sporting Goods and Exercise Equipment Industry Snapshot

	2000	2002	% CHG '00-'02
Total Retail Sales in millions	$21,373.8	$21,748.3	1.8
Exercise	3,643.2	4,336.1	19.0
Golf	3,744.2	3,338.8	−10.8
Team goods and sports	2,456.0	2,530.5	3.0
Hunting and firearms	2,256.0	2,469.9	9.5
Fishing tackle	2,030.2	2,023.5	−0.3
Camping	1,344.5	1,415.0	5.2
Optics	729.1	825.7	13.2
Billiards and indoor gaming	359.0	543.1	51.3
Skiing, downhill	547.8	528.3	−3.6
Wheel sports and pogo	1,074.4	493.5	−54.1
Tennis	378.0	396.5	4.9
Skin diving and scuba gear	355.3	330.8	−6.9
Basketball	285.6	322.7	13.0
Baseball and softball	319.0	305.8	−4.1
Archery	254.4	276.4	8.6
Skiing, snowboards	234.3	244.8	4.5
Bowling	162.3	172.5	6.3
Hockey and ice skates	136.0	165.3	21.5
Football	84.9	89.9	5.9
Soccer balls	65.1	62.4	−4.1
Water skis	50.2	58.4	16.3
Skiing, cross country	33.6	37.2	10.7
Volleyball and badminton	29.3	32.2	9.9
Racquetball	42.0	28.5	−32.1
Other	759.4	720.5	−5.1

Source: National Sporting Goods Association

selection of goods, nearly 60 percent of consumers of these products made purchases in sporting goods stores. Discount department stores, where only 39 percent of shoppers frequent, have a way to go to draw the sporting enthusiast to their stores for their favorite equipment. Traditional department stores trail with only 16 percent of shoppers using these stores for sporting goods.

With 3,600 stores and sales of $4.4 billion, Foot Locker is the leader in the category with an emphasis on athletic footwear and apparel through their Foot Locker, Champs Sports, and Eastbay brands (see Figure 7.16). Sports Authority, after merging with Gart Sports in 2003, became number two in the category with $1.4 billion in sales and just fewer than 400

FIGURE 7.16
Sporting Goods Market Share Leaders

	2002 SALES
Foot Locker (3,600 stores)	$4.4 billion
Sports Authority (385 stores)	1.4 billion
Dick's Sporting Goods (140 stores)	1.1 billion
Bass Pro Shops (15 stores)	1.1 billion
Academy Sports (60 stores)	775 million
Recreational Equipment/REI (60 stores)	700 million
Big 5 Sporting Goods (275 stores)	668 million
Galyan's (35 stores)	483 million
Modell's Sporting Goods (90 stores)	465 million

Source: 2002 *Directory of Apparel Specialty Stores by Chain Store Guide*

stores nationwide. Dick's Sporting Goods follows with about 100 stores and $843 million in revenues.

These specialty retailers, along with others like Galyan's, Bass Pro Shops, Orvis Company, Cabela's, and Eastern Mountain Sports, have kept the "sport" first and foremost in their store design and shopping experience and so have been able to maintain their specialty edge. For example, Galyan's signature two-story climbing wall has made their 20 stores a destination for climbing enthusiasts all over the country. The company's senior vice president of marketing, Ed Whitehead, explains: "It's become an icon for us. We really refer to it as our town center." They also sponsor seminars, athlete appearances, and even basketball shooting contests.

Purchase Drivers

Sports provide the participant a sense of accomplishment and well-being, health benefits, and stress relief. Sports can become compelling hobbies in which one or all members of the family participate. Practitioners of various sports have to purchase the right equipment to be a "player"—the right clubs, shoes, clothes, accessories, and so forth. Men, in particular, like competitive sports including the competitive purchase of sporting accessories. "My husband is really involved in buying sporting goods. It's a luxury and very expensive. Most sports are expensive. But my husband really needs it as an outlet. It's his time with the guys, without the stress of the office. He works hard at the hobby. And it gives him health benefits." But what is stress relief for one can be stress inducing for another: "To me sports and exercise is a stress. It means sweating and working hard."

One consumer explains how she and her family cut back on certain discretionary expenses to allow them to pursue their passion for skiing. "We drive old cars, but we get to ski all winter long. It is all about what you and your family think is important. We don't care if people are impressed by the car we drive, but we have a whole ton of fun on the ski slopes. There are trade-offs. What is one family's idea of fun isn't the same as another's. Some want a pool in the backyard. For us it's the time spent skiing."

Demographic Variables

In this category men are more active purchasers than women, with 53 percent of men buying sporting equipment, compared to 43 percent of women. This is a category for the younger consumer. Although consumers up to age 54 are fairly active buyers in this category, the youngest consumers, aged 18 to 24, have the highest purchase incidence of any age group. In this category, white and Hispanic consumers are much more likely to purchase than are black Americans.

As income rises, so does a consumer's likelihood of purchasing sporting goods and exercise equipment. Those at the highest income levels are more active purchasers than the lower-income households. The more highly educated households, those with some college or more, are also more active buyers of sporting goods. Household size is also an important determinant of purchase. Households of three or more people, as well as those with children, are the most likely to make purchases in this category.

Key demographics of sporting goods and exercise equipment buyers.

- Men buy more actively.
- This category skews toward a more youthful consumer, although purchase incidence is strong through age 54.
- White and Hispanic households buy more actively than blacks.
- Rising income and educational levels favor purchase.
- Households with children buy more often.

WHAT PEOPLE BUY: TOYS, DOLLS, AND GAMES

The purchase incidence of toys, games, and dolls has been up and down since 2000, ranging from 45 percent in 2000 to 54 percent in 2001 and 50 percent in 2003. While children represent the core user market for toys, more adults are buying toys, not just for kids, but for their own playtime. Toys are popular adult collectibles, and more toy companies are recognizing that adults, just like their kids, want to play with toys.

Industry Snapshot

American consumers spent more than $43.8 billion on toys in 2002, according to statistics compiled by the U.S. Bureau of Economic Analysis (see Figure 7.17). There is an expanding market for toys, as evidenced by growth of 5.6 percent since 2000 when personal consumption was $41.5 billion. Notoriously given to boom-and-bust cycles, the toy industry's biggest categories in 2002 according to classifications used by the Toy Industry Association, were video games, with sales of $14.8 billion;

FIGURE 7.17

Toys, Games, and Dolls Industry Snapshot

	2000	2002	% CHG '00-'02
Total Personal Consumption in millions	$41,510	$48,825	5.6
Video games	9,879	14,786	49.7
Infant and preschool	3,445	4,019	16.7
Dolls	4,358	3,478	−20.2
Arts and crafts	4,483	3,125	−30.3
Vehicles	3,404	3,008	−11.6
Games and puzzles	3,196	2,999	−6.2
Plush	2,988	2,226	−25.5
Action figures and accessories	1,577	1,801	14.2
Sports toys		1,413	
Building sets		1,076	
Ride-ons	2,200	811	−63.2
Pretend play		793	
Learning and exploration		531	
Trading cards and accessories		408	
Models and accessories		362	
All other toys	5,978	2,987	−50.0

Source: Bureau of Economic Analysis; Toy Industry Association; Unity Marketing

infant and preschool toys, $4 billion; dolls, $3.5 billion; arts and crafts, $3.1 billion; vehicles, $3 billion; and games and puzzles, $3 billion.

Retail Overview

While Toys R Us, with some 1,600 stores and $11 billion in sales, is a prime mover of toys at retail, Wal-Mart stores are recognized as the nation's number one retailer of toys. As a result, the mass merchant and discounter channel of distribution commands an estimated 39 percent of the total retail market for toys, according to the NPD Group who compiles statistics for the Toy Industry Association. National toy stores, including Toys R Us, K-B Toys, and FAO—which resulted from the merger of Zany Brainy and the FAO Schwarz specialty stores—hold about 20 percent share of the market (see Figure 7.18).

With Wal-Mart replacing Toys R Us as the nation's largest retailer of toys, it is not surprising that toy shoppers today favor the discount department stores as the place to buy. Nearly three-fourths (72 percent) of toy buyers bought these products from discount department stores. Trailing far behind with just under one-third (31 percent) of toy shoppers are other specialty stores, which includes the category of toy stores. Traditional department stores are next, patronized by nearly one-fourth (23 percent) of toy shoppers.

Competition in toy retailing has been particularly fierce in the past three years as Toys R Us and Wal-Mart battle it out for market share leader. A major casualty of the "toy wars" is the luxury-positioned FAO Company. After filing and emerging from bankruptcy in early 2003, the company once again filed for bankruptcy protection in the midst of the 2003 holiday shopping season. FAO plans to sell off its FAO Schwarz and Right Start toy-store chains, while liquidating the Zany Brainy stores.

FIGURE 7.18
Toy Retail Market Share Leaders

	2002 SALES
Toys R Us (1,600 stores)	$11 billion
K-B Toys (1,325 stores)	2 billion
FAO/Zany Brainy (about 100 stores)	460 million

Source: 2002 *Directory of Discount and General Merchandisers by Chain Store Guide*

Because the retail market for toys is so highly dependent on the Christmas shopping season with about 53 percent of the industry's sales during the fourth quarter, many other retailers get into the toy game only seasonally. Card, gift, and stationery stores, department stores, grocery and drug stores, mail order, and e-tailers together take about 20 percent of the total toy market. Due to the dominance of national retailers in the toy business, the traditional mom-and-pop toy stores are facing a squeeze and today command less than 5 percent of toy industry sales.

Purchase Drivers

American parents cannot do enough for their kids! That is the simple reason behind the steady growth in the toy market. The toy industry enjoyed many years of growth as the baby boom generation progressed through its prime childbearing years. However, in 2003, with the leading edge of the baby boom generation reaching age 57 and the trailing edge now at age 38, the toy industry faces challenging times as boomers' kids progress beyond the age of toys and the much smaller GenX cohort enters its family formation and childbearing years. The total number of households under age 45 will decline from 2000 to 2010—down 3 percent among the age group 18 to 24; 7 percent for the group aged 25 to 34; and 14 percent for the group aged 35 to 44.

However, there is a second wave of baby boomer spending on toys coming soon as their grandchildren arrive. The babies of the baby boomer generation are called the millennial generation whose birth years extend from 1977 to about 1994. The leading edge of the millennial generation today is 27, the age associated with first marriage. As this generation starts to marry and have children of their own, proud boomer-aged grandparents will lavish spending on age-appropriate toys for the new generation.

Demographic Variables

Toys are more likely to be purchased by women than men, with their purchase incidence reaching 56 percent in 2003, compared to 43 percent for men. Consumers aged 25 to 44 are far and away the most likely to purchase items in this category, as these ages represent the prime childbearing and rearing age ranges. Purchase incidence drops off after age 45. Middle-income households making between $35,000 and $50,000 annually are the most likely to purchase toys, games, and dolls.

Household size and presence of children are major predictors of purchase. Not surprising, households with children are two times as likely to purchase toys, games, and dolls than are households with no children. All education levels are equally likely to make purchases in this category.

Key demographics of buyers of toys, dolls, and games.

- Women take the lead in this category.
- Prime market for toys is ages 25 to 44.
- Middle-income households, between $35,000 and $50,000, buy more.
- Children in the home are a key predictor, along with larger household size.

WHAT PEOPLE BUY: TELEVISIONS, RADIOS, VCRS, DVD PLAYERS, ETC.

Most television, radio, VCR, and DVD player purchases are made today to replace or upgrade existing equipment. New flat screen and plasma TVs and DVD players represent the latest technological innovations drawing shoppers into the stores for new entertainment equipment. Nearly all (99 percent) of U.S. households own a color television, while 71 percent own two or more TVs. VCR and DVD player ownership is almost as high, with about 90 percent of households having a VCR or DVD player.

Today the digital DVD is being used more as a video recording medium, thus encouraging consumers to upgrade their older VCR player for the latest and greatest digital DVD player. With a purchase incidence of 38 percent in 2000, purchase incidence of TVs, radios, VCRs, and DVD players rose in 2001 to 46 percent of households only to drop back down to 38 percent of households in 2003.

Industry Snapshot

With consumer purchases of $26.5 billion in 2002, the market for televisions and other video equipment is robust (see Figure 7.19). Like computers and audio equipment, upgrades in technology, such as today's large-sized plasma screen televisions that are so flat they can be mounted on the wall like a painting, tend to drive consumers into the stores to

FIGURE 7.19

Television, Radio, VCR, and DVD Player Industry Snapshot

	2000	2002	% CHG '00-'02
Total Personal Consumption in millions	$25,148	$26,461	5.2
Televisions	14,422	15,365	6.5
Video equipment and media	10,726	11,097	3.5

Source: Bureau of Economic Analysis

upgrade their old TV sets with newer models. For consumers, it is all about enhancing the television experience and today shoppers can find an enormously wide range of viewing options that improve upon the traditional 21-inch color console set.

Retailer Overview

With nearly equal purchase incidence, shoppers are as likely to shop for new TVs and other entertainment players in discount department stores as in specialty electronics and appliance stores. Some 52 percent of shoppers made purchases for these products in a discount department store, while 51 percent bought at electronics and appliance stores.

Traditional department stores have a small, but meaningful, share of shoppers in this category of goods, with some 14 percent buying entertainment players in these stores. Shoppers want to see in person the player media they buy, so only 7 percent of shoppers make purchases of this class of goods through nonstore channels such as Internet, mail order, or television shopping.

Product cycle is the key to successful electronic appliance retailing, including televisions. The product cycle includes the pattern of new consumer electronic introductions and the rate at which they gain consumer acceptance. Without new products to promote, retailers can only sell replacement items to their customers, which is not enough to sustain growth, especially because the price of consumer electronic products continue to fall after their initial introduction. A new electronic product, like the plasma screen televisions, sell at a premium and tend to draw shoppers into the stores to see what all the fuss is about.

Today, analysts see the product cycle as very strong with the potential of wireless technology, HDTV, and plasma televisions just beginning to climb on the typical consumer's radar. "The product cycle should remain strong for the next three to five years," says analyst Ken Gassman of Davenport & Company. "There are brand new technologies hitting the stores that everyone has to have, like with the VCR revolution of the 1980s."

Because television retailing mirrors that of audio and stereo equipment, for a discussion of market share leaders at retail see the audio equipment section.

Purchase Drivers

Like computers, technological innovation in the recording and display of video images is a major driver for growth. DVDs are rapidly replacing videocassettes as the recording medium of choice for video images, thus motivating U.S. households to upgrade their video playback equipment to be compatible with DVDs.

Television too is changing with digital technology. The new flat-screen and plasma television display technology brings improved display of digitally stored images, as well as cable and satellite digital transmission. Consumers are also buying wide-screen television sets, enhanced with new sound technology that projects such a large image that consumers can re-create a movie theater experience in their own homes. As one focus group respondent explained: "My husband just bought a wide-screen television set. It was actually a practical purchase since we have had two television sets stolen in the past. My husband bought the big wide-screen television because thieves wouldn't be able to get it out the door. We also have the only wide-screen television in the neighborhood, so it is a WOW when people come over. My husband likes to watch sports." I suspect that television thieves have mastered the skill of stealing the much more expensive large wide-screen television sets, but this wife seemed convinced that her husband was making a practical decision when he bought the new set to enjoy the football games and show off to his friends.

Demographic Variables

A gender-neutral category, most households view expenditures in entertainment equipment as a joint purchase, so men and women are about equally likely to buy. This is a category of goods that tends to skew toward a more youthful market. As the age of the consumer increases, the likelihood that they will make a purchase of a television, radio, VCR, or DVD player decreases.

Black American households have a statistically significant increased purchase incidence, as compared with white or Hispanic households. Except for a spike at the highest income level, purchase incidence is fairly equal across the income ranges.

A key determinant of purchase of this category of products is household size and/or presence of children in the home. Households with three or more people and those with children are most likely to buy. Likelihood of purchase in this category cuts equally across education levels.

Key demographics of buyers of televisions, radios, VCRs, DVD players, etc.

- This is a gender-neutral category.
- Purchase incidence skews toward younger households.
- Black Americans are more active buyers.
- All incomes buy, but higher-income households buy more.
- Households with children buy more.

8

WHAT PEOPLE BUY
Home Furnishings and Home Décor

OVERVIEW

About a quarter of American's $7.385 trillion in personal consumption expenditures is spent on their homes. Spending on the four walls that shelter us topped $1.145 trillion in 2002, and spending on household operations, which includes all home furnishings, cleaning products, stationery and writing supplies, utility expenditures, and domestic services was $748.3 billion. Housing expenditures are rising faster than spending on household operations, as rock-bottom mortgage rates have encouraged more Americans to either buy into the housing market for the first time or trade up to larger, more expensive homes.

An intriguing factoid out of the government's latest numbers on household spending is that after the cost of electricity, which we all know is going through the roof, the fastest-growing household expenditure category in 2002 was cleaning and polishing preparations, which advanced 8.4 percent to reach $66.8 billion. We can learn something as we consider why people buy things they don't need. What's happening in so many other categories of consumer goods is taking

> Consumers' expectations are rising and they want an enhanced cleaning experience.

hold in the home cleaning category. Consumers' expectations are rising and they want an enhanced cleaning experience. The regular everyday brands of household cleaners won't do anymore. Consumers demand more cleaning power with less effort, which ultimately means a better value. Marketers are responding by enhancing existing brands through better performance or creating totally new products that deliver a cleaning experience never available before. Products like the new Swiffer floor mop from Proctor & Gamble, or the range of cleaning products sold via television infomercials from Orange Glo—including Oxiclean, Orange Glo, and Kaboom—or the Mr. Clean Magic Eraser, which promises to erase away grimy wall stains, are positioned as twenty-first-century cleaning solutions. Because these products really deliver the goods, the companies will gain a loyal shopper who is willing to pay two, three, or even five times the price of the store brand for the extra cleaning performance.

END OF COCOONING DOESN'T MEAN END OF SPENDING ON THE HOME

For the past 20 years or so, home marketers have enjoyed a time of remarkable growth as the nation's consumers devoted their time, attention, and budgets, to home-related purchasing. Cocooning and nesting and all that these concepts imply were the dominant cultural trend. Because all ships rise with a rising tide, many home marketers and retailers enjoyed an extended period of strong and predictable growth.

With the dawn of a new century, some major home players began to sputter, but corporate inefficiencies and management misdirection could be blamed for these problems. As other, better-managed companies began to feel the pinch of reduced consumer spending, a slowing economy and negative impact from September 11 were credited. But something more fundamental was changing in the marketplace, and that is that consumers today are emerging from their cocoons and looking to reconnect with the external world.

Like all things, the cocooning trend must come to an end. It is in its death throes now and only the home marketers who recognize the signs and plan for a future without the spur of cocooning will thrive, even survive.

In January 2003, the *New York Times* reported that Bloomingdale's and its owner, Federated Department Stores, are "gambling

> Consumers today are emerging from their cocoons and looking to reconnect with the external world.

> Today's consumers are looking for ways to scale down, throw out, and otherwise eliminate clutter from their homes.

that the salvation for retail in 2003 is going to come from home furnishings." Bloomingdale's invested more than $40 million to open a 140,000-square-foot home furnishings store in Chicago in an abandoned Shriners temple. Federated likely has a winner in this concept, due to its impressive size and the intense attention it is receiving from upper management. Just because the cocooning trend is over doesn't mean that consumers aren't going to buy things for their home. In fact, Bloomingdale's with its upper-income, luxury niche is likely to attract just the kind of customers—that is the mature baby boom generation of affluent shoppers—to make a go of it.

But home furnishings alone are not going to be any marketer's or retailer's "salvation" anymore. It is going to be harder and harder for home furnishings retailers and marketers to get consumers to invite new furniture pieces or purely decorative home furnishings objects into their homes. Today's consumers are looking for ways to scale down, throw out, and otherwise eliminate clutter from their homes.

While consumers are spending less money on major furniture pieces and decorative accessories, they are "hungry" for more and better tools, equipment, and accessories to enhance their living experiences in the home. For example, gourmet cooking and dining is an experience that more and more Americans desire to pursue in their home kitchens. As a result, they are willing to buy all kinds of things they don't need but will enhance the cooking and dining experience. This characterizes consumer psychology for so many discretionary and luxury products. That is, consumers buy things, whether it is a new All-Clad sauté pan, Lenox china place setting, Viking stove, or Waterford candlestick, to achieve a feeling, an experience. Therefore, the thing that people buy becomes the means to an end, and the end is a feeling. In order for home marketers to prosper in the years ahead, they must understand this new experiential emphasis and make it part of their strategy.

When it comes to home décor, the primary value is no longer how good it looks. Rather, with an experiential twist, it is about how it feels,

> The thing that people buy becomes the means to an end, and the end is a feeling.

how it flows, how it lives, and, most important, how it enhances the quality of one's home life. That is why clutter is anathema today. Too many things take away from one's pleasure and enjoyment in the home, rather than enhancing the experience.

OVERVIEW: HOME FURNISHING AND HOME DÉCOR PURCHASE INCIDENCE

In 2003, greeting cards and stationery were the most widely purchased category of home goods, bought by 83 percent of households (see Figure 8.1). Candles were next, with a purchase incidence of 62 percent. Christmas and seasonal decorations were the third most popular home category, bought by 61 percent of U.S. households in the previous year.

Some key trends in consumers' appetite for home furnishing and décor emerge when comparing the three years' survey findings on purchase incidence of 19 key home categories:

- *Stationery purchase is up, as consumers buy more paper products.* Greeting cards are the most purchased product within stationery, but the entire category of stationery and paper products is gaining new attention among consumers. Over 80 percent of consumers bought any stationery and/or greeting cards in the past year, making stationery the number one most purchased home product.

FIGURE 8.1

Home Purchase Incidence

	2000	2001	2003
Greeting cards and stationery	79%	72%	83%
Candles	54	65	62
Christmas and seasonal décor	50	55	61
Flowers, seeds, and shrubs	50	59	56
Kitchenware	46	58	56
Home textiles	51	60	52
Aromatherapy and scents	39	42	49
Picture frames	40	52	48
Baskets, boxes, and vases*			42
Vases, urns, and pots		30	
Garden equipment and décor	41	47	42
Art, prints, and pictures	21	27	42
Furniture and occasional furniture	35	41	41
Florals, indoor	38	43	41
Wall décor	22	25	38
Window coverings			37
Collectibles	31	34	36
Lamps and lighting	24	33	30
Figurines and sculptures	19	20	22
Tabletop china, etc.	16	26	16

*Category expanded in 2003

Today the ultimate luxury form of communications is a handwritten note.

Consumers' desire to connect emotionally in a more meaningful way has led to increased sales of personal notes. New luxury stationery made of high fiber paper with enhanced textural values is also drawing new consumers to buy. Today the ultimate luxury form of communications is a handwritten note.

- *Seasonal decorations are a key focus for consumers.* The purchase incidence of Christmas and other seasonal decorations experienced an upward shift, from 55 percent in 2001 to 61 percent in 2003. This interest in decorating the home for various holidays and events is part of the new connecting trend, which has taken hold most strongly in the post-9/11 culture. Consumers are returning to more values-based consumption and seeking to reach out and reconnect with their families, their communities, their social networks. Decorating the exterior of the home is one way that consumers are expressing this connecting trend. From the patriotic to the whimsical, consumers desire to decorate their homes and express their feelings and values externally. This is a major trend that has positive impacts for marketers and retailers of home products.
- *Consumers' interest in scent growing.* While candle purchase incidence is flat, even declining slightly, consumers' interest in alternative household scenting products, such as potpourri, steamers, and sprays, is growing. With purchase incidence up from 42 percent in 2001 to 49 percent in 2003, consumers are expressing a desire to enhance the sensual environment in the home through scent. By turning away from the candle alternative, they are signaling a desire for safer, more healthful alternatives in household scenting options with concerns about indoor air pollution, open flames, burning petroleum-based waxes, and possible leaded wicks becoming more of an issue for consumers.
- *Decorating turns from the tabletop and mantle to the walls.* Consumer purchases of pictures, art and prints, and wall décor show a strong upward trend in 2003 compared to previous years. Consumers are turning their attention to the walls to decorate.
- *New emphasis is placed on storage alternatives.* Because the 2003 survey grouped baskets and tins along with vases and other decorative storage items, no direct comparison can be made to the previous year's survey. However, 42 percent of the consumers surveyed reported buying decorative storage items.

- *Downward trending categories, home tex-tiles and tabletop china, signal anti-clutter mood.* While the purchase incidence of most other categories in home were basically flat or characterized by only a point or two downward shift, two

> Consumers are expressing a desire to enhance the sensual environment in the home through scent.

categories included in the survey point to a significant drop in purchase incidence. Home textiles, including rugs, throws, pillows, and table linens, dropped from being purchase by 60 percent of consumers in 2001 to 52 percent in 2003. This is one of those cat-egories consumers associate with "clutter," so they are buying less of it than before. Tabletop china, crystal, silver, and other dinner-ware also experienced a downward shift in purchase incidence, from 26 percent in 2001 to 16 percent in 2003. This is an impor-tant category for entertaining and a traditionally popular category for wedding gifts. In interpreting this downward shift it may indi-cate that young brides are choosing other categories for their bridal registry, as well as consumers having all the tabletop "stuff" they need for their current standard of living.

Through the rest of this chapter we will examine in more detail each of the home product categories.

WHAT PEOPLE BUY: AROMATHERAPY AND SCENTED HOUSEHOLD PRODUCTS

Purchase incidence of aromatherapy and scented household prod-ucts rose sharply in 2003 to reach 49 percent, up from 42 percent of U.S. households in 2001. Consumers are turning away from candles as the primary delivery option for household scent toward other alternatives, such as potpourri, steamers, and sprays. By lighting fewer candles, they are expressing a desire for safer, more healthful alternatives for home fragrance. Concerns about indoor air pollution, open flames, burning petroleum-based waxes, and possible leaded wicks are becoming an im-portant issue for consumers.

Because scents are so intimately tied to emotions, aromatherapy and other scented products enhance the atmosphere of the home with pleas-ant, emotionally evocative scents.

Industry Snapshot

The home-fragrance market, excluding candles, reached nearly $2 billion in retail sales in 2002, with over half of industry sales, or $1.1 billion, attributed to the category of home-fragrance diffusers (see Figure 8.2). Either battery-operated or electrically driven, diffusers give a measured release of fragrance at regular intervals. Room sprays totaled $393 million in retail sales, while potpourri reached $228 million. Manufacturer S.C. Johnson, a private company with sales estimated in excess of $5 billion, markets home-fragrance products under the Glade brand name and is the market share leader in the home-fragrance category. Home fragrances have also become an important brand extension category for the perfume and personal fragrance marketers. By adding home scents to their product lines, they deliver a 360-degree home and personal scenting experience to their customers.

Retail Overview

Now that aromatherapy products are bought by nearly half of all U.S. households, the category has moved beyond narrow specialty store distribution into the mass channels. In a recent Unity Marketing survey, the most popular stores where some 50 percent of shoppers bought aromatherapy products in the past year were discount department stores. Other retail outlets where at least one in five shoppers bought these products include traditional department stores (32 percent), other specialty stores, including candle and personal care specialty stores (29 percent), drug stores (25 percent), and grocery stores (21 percent). Note:

FIGURE 8.2

Aromatherapy and Household Scents Industry Snapshot

	2000	2002	% CHG '00-'02
Total Personal Consumption in millions	$1,833.2	$1,992.5	8.7
Diffusers	980.5	1,107.0	12.9
Room sprays	383.7	392.5	2.3
Potpourri	213.2	228.3	7.1
Specialty room	170.5	177.7	4.2
Specialty wardrobe	85.3	87.0	2.0

Source: Kline & Company; Euromonitor; Unity Marketing

these percentages don't add up to 100 percent due to shoppers visiting different types of stores throughout the year to buy these products.

Purchase Drivers

Consumers buy aromatherapy and scented household products for much the same reason they buy candles. While purchase incidence of candles is waning, consumers are turning to other, potentially less hazardous, more healthful ways of using scent to enhance one's mood. In describing her purchase of aromatherapy products, one woman told us: "I buy anything scented lilac. It's my favorite scent. I feel good when I walk into my house and it smells like lilac." Scents have powerful effects on consumers' emotions, and more manufacturers are looking at opportunities to enhance the appeal of their products through the addition of aromas.

Demographic Variables

Women lead in purchasing aromatherapy products, with 56 percent of women reporting a purchase, compared with 41 percent of men. This category has a strong youthful skew, with purchase incidence highest among the households aged 25 to 34. Purchase incidence is elevated for householders aged 18 to 24 and 35 to 54, and drops sharply at age 55. Ethnically neutral, white, black, and Hispanic households buy aromatherapy products at about the same rate.

There is little variation in the purchase incidence of aromatherapy in terms of household income. Household size and presence of children make a difference, with larger-sized households of two or more individuals and those with children purchasing more.

Key demographics of buyers of aromatherapy and scents.

- This is a women-led category.
- Income makes little difference in purchase incidence.
- Incidence skews to households under age 35, but households to age 65 are fairly active.
- Large households and those with children buy more.

WHAT PEOPLE BUY: ART, PRINTS, LITHOGRAPHS

Just over 40 percent of households (42 percent) bought some kind of art in 2003, up significantly from the purchase incidence in 2001. With consumers turning their attention to the walls for decorating, they are responding to new availability of ready-to-hang art at retail outlets ranging from mass merchants and discounters to home specialty stores. No longer are consumers required to seek decorative art in out-of-the-way galleries and art dealers, or pay exorbitant prices to custom frame a print. Already-framed art, as well as the explosion of specialty framing boutiques that offer affordable and quick custom frames, have opened the art market to the masses.

Industry Snapshot

The consumer market for art reached $27.6 billion in 2002, up 8.4 percent over sales in 2000. The fastest growing category in art is already-framed art, which grew nearly 30 percent in the past two years (see Figure 8.3). While already-framed art is up, the sales of unframed prints declined by 17 percent as consumers opt for the one-stop shop convenience of already-framed art.

Retail Overview

The art market is rapidly becoming a mass market. Preframed prints are available at all sorts of outlets, including Wal-Mart, Target, and Kmart, as well as at national specialty home furnishings chains, such as Bed Bath & Beyond, Bombay Company, Pier 1, and Linens 'n Things. Over the

FIGURE 8.3
Art Industry Snapshot

	2000	2002	% CHG '00-'02
Total Personal Consumption in millions	$25,489.80	$27,632.30	8.4
Already-framed prints	6,768.60	8,583.80	26.8
Unframed prints	5,255.00	4,357.30	−17.1
Custom-framed art*	5,215.20	5,663.80	8.6
Original art	8,251.00	9,027.40	9.4

Source: Unity Marketing

past several years Kirkland's has emerged as an important retailer of high-quality, already-framed art. With approximately 250 stores nationwide situated in mall locations, Kirkland's offers its customers high-quality art at affordable prices. The company generates about one-fourth of its total $307 million in sales from art and wall décor and says in its annual report that its diverse mix of home décor items, with most selling for under $50, are perceived by their customers as "affordable luxuries."

The custom-framing segment of the art market is also in transition with the introduction of custom-framing services in craft stores nationwide. No longer the exclusive purview of art galleries and specialty framing stores, custom framing services are now available at nationwide craft chains, like Michael's, A.C. Moore, Hobby Lobby, and Jo-Ann Stores (see Figure 8.4). Because the crafters offer limited framing choices at significantly lower prices than the specialty mom-and-pop art framing stores, they are drawing a mass audience to art framing. They also have been instrumental in introducing the concept of using shadow-box frames to display three-dimensional collectibles and crafts to a wider audience, proving that custom-framing isn't just for two-dimensional artwork any more.

While all this activity is going on at the mass level, a more clearly differentiated market at the luxury end is emerging among connoisseurs. Sales of original art, defined as one-of-a-kind work, such as watercolor, oil painting, pencil sketch, and chalk drawing, are growing. Original art is more available and accessible than ever before to today's art buyer. Moreover, recent advances in art reproduction technologies, such as printing on canvas and Giclée, have the greatest appeal to the upper end of the art-buying market. Today's art buyers are more sophisticated and better educated, so they can truly appreciate the value of owning a one-of-a-kind piece.

FIGURE 8.4
Art & Framing Market Share Leaders

	2002 SALES
Michaels w/Aaron Brothers (923 stores)	$2.5 billion
Jo-Ann Stores (959 stores)	1.5 billion
Hobby Lobby (272 stores)	1.0 billion
Bombay Company (420 stores)	494 million
A.C. Moore Arts & Crafts (70 stores)	393 million
Kirklands (250 stores)	307 million
Deck the Walls/The Great Frame Up (about 100 stores)	100 million

Source: Unity Marketing

Purchase Drivers

For some consumers, art is something they put on their walls to match the color of their sofa, but for others the art they select is an important outlet for personal self-expression. That's why more than half of the art buyers in a recent survey agreed with the following statement: "When choosing art for my home, the way the piece makes me feel is more important than whether it matches the décor in my home."

But whether shoppers buy art to decorate or for emotional reasons, the fact is once the piece is hung, it becomes part of the architecture of the room, like the windows and doors. One focus group respondent told us: "I have kept the same pictures my entire 35 years of marriage, longer than I have kept anything else in my home. I buy something and if it fits, it stays."

Others, however, collect art and use it to create a mood in the home. One respondent who collects art explains: "I appreciate the creativity of the artist. I have both originals and prints. When I go to art shows, I am amazed. It is a real lift to see the art. I enjoy it so much." Another respondent with a passion for mountain lions displays a series of prints in her home: "We have a collection of mountain lion prints. It is a focal point of our home. When people come into the house, they see our art and find it interesting and want to talk about it."

Art adds decorative value and provides a focal point, but it also colors the emotional mood in the home. As this respondent put it: "Art is like a candle. It makes you feel good. I feel good when there are things hanging in my house that I really like."

Demographic Variables

Art is a gender-neutral category, purchased by men and women at the same rate. Art purchases are slightly elevated among younger consumers aged 18 to 34, with purchase incidence declining slightly after age 35. As in so many other categories, purchase incidence tanks after age 65. Art-purchasing households tend to have higher incomes, with those households making $50,000 or more per year reporting the highest purchase incidence. Household composition has little impact on the purchase of art, with two-person households, three-person households, and those with children purchasing at about the same rate.

Contributing to the growth in the art market is an increasingly educated consumer market. This also correlates strongly with increased household income levels. Because 28 percent of adult Americans older than age 25 have completed four or more years of college, up from 24 percent in 1990, the prospects for the art market look bright for the years ahead. Purchase incidence rises with education, and households with completed college degrees and those with higher levels of educational attainment have the highest purchase incidence.

Key demographics of buyers of art, prints, and pictures.

- This is a gender-neutral category.
- Purchase incidence rises with income and education.
- Incidence skews toward ages 18 to 34.
- Household composition is not a factor.

WHAT PEOPLE BUY: BASKETS, BOXES, VASES, POTS, AND DECORATIVE HOLDERS

Just over 40 percent of consumers (42 percent) in 2003 purchased baskets, boxes, vases, pots, and other decorative holders. With the definition of this category expanded from the last survey, the whole range of functional storage accessories are becoming more important in home décor, offering both decorative values as well as the functional benefit of holding flowers, plants, or other items.

Industry Snapshot

Baskets, boxes, vases, and pots are part of the $16.2 billion home decorative segment of the giftware market. Total sales of decorative boxes and tins were $1.1 billion in 2002, up 26 percent over retail sales in 2000 (see Figure 8.5). Vases, urns, and pots represent about $650 million in retail sales, while the retail sales of decorative baskets are in the range of $2.3 billion. Total retail sales of the category reached $4 billion in 2002.

Retail Overview

When shoppers go looking for decorative household storage, including vases and pots, they turn first to discount department stores. Traditional department stores are the second most popular alternative,

FIGURE 8.5

Baskets, Boxes, Vases, Pots Industry Snapshot

	2000	2002	% CHG '00-'02
Total Personal Consumption in millions	$1,834.3	$4,040.3	
Baskets	n.a.	2,289.0	
Boxes and tins	875.8	1,102.7	25.9
Vases, pots, and urns	958.5	648.6	−32.3

Source: Unity Marketing

followed closely by other specialty stores, including gift stores, florists, office supply stores, and others.

As demand for innovative and decorative household storage solutions grows, specialty retailers are targeting this need. Williams-Sonoma has a chain of 12 Hold Everything stores along with a catalog by the same name. Another chain called Organized Living operates about 25 stores nationwide. Longaberger Baskets makes handcrafted wooden baskets their specialty, which are sold only through home parties and sales consultants.

The nation's home furnishings specialty chains, such as Linens 'n Things, Bed Bath & Beyond, Pier 1, Pottery Barn, Crate & Barrel, and Kirklands, are also getting into this area in response to consumer's demand for help in eliminating clutter and getting organized.

Purchase Drivers

The most significant trend impacting the home today is the end of cocooning. The same home that two years ago looked cozy and comfortable with every nook and cranny filled, today looks cluttered and disorganized. To the rescue come legions of baskets, boxes, and other storage solutions that help the homeowner eliminate the mess. It is getting harder and harder to persuade shoppers to invite purely decorative objects into the home. That only makes for more clutter. Today consumers have a new and growing demand for storage boxes and baskets that can be put to use for organizing household clutter. Though baskets and tins serve a practical function, they are decorative as well. While shoppers today wouldn't think of buying a purely decorative figurine, they are perfectly willing to buy a decorative vase to display on the shelf, as long as it is used with a real floral bouquet.

Demographic Variables

Women take the lead in buying baskets, boxes, vases, and other decorative storage items. In terms of age, no spikes appear that would mark a prime age-group target for this category. Rather, consumers up through age 65 have about the same purchase incidence for baskets and boxes. People living in metropolitan areas are more active buying these items than rural folk, but with space tight in city apartments this finding isn't surprising.

The higher-income houses, especially those making $75,000 or more, have the highest reported purchase incidence of this category. Household size also relates to purchase incidence, as two- and three-person households are far more active buyers than are single-person households.

Key demographics of buyers of baskets, boxes, vases, urns, and pots.

- Women take the lead in buying.
- The highest-income households buy more.
- No specific age is prime.
- Larger households are bigger consumers.

WHAT PEOPLE BUY: CANDLES AND CANDLE ACCESSORIES

Sixty-two percent of U.S. households purchased candles in 2003, down slightly from the 65 percent who purchased in 2001. That makes candles the second most widely purchased home product category, after stationery and greeting cards. With nearly two-thirds of American households buying candles in 2003, there is little new growth available in the marketplace. The simple fact is the candle market has reached a plateau and further growth will be hard for marketers and retailers to come by easily.

Industry Snapshot

Since 2000, retail sales of candles have dropped 12.2 percent, while sales of candle accessory items, such as displays, candlesticks, decorative jar lids, and lighting and extinguishing accessories, have grown 44 percent (see Figure 8.6). Overall the sales of candles and candle accessories were about even in 2002 with sales in 2000.

FIGURE 8.6
Candle and Accessories Industry Snapshot

	2000	2002	% CHG '00-'02
Total Personal Consumption in millions	$2,836.0	$2,783.0	−1.9
Candles	2,313.5	2,031.6	−12.2
Accessories	522.5	751.4	43.8

Source: Unity Marketing

Retail Overview

Some of the decline in retail sales of candles since 2000 has been due to the rapid expansion of candles beyond the specialty retailer channels, where higher prices are common, into the discount and mass merchant channels, which reward value pricing. Whereas seven years ago or so the premium brands of candles were almost exclusively distributed in specialty-retail and gift boutiques, today mass merchants, grocery, drug, and other mass-market outlets have reached a 40 percent share of market and become the single largest distribution channel for candles.

In terms of specialty retail, the brand leaders are Yankee Candle, Intimate Brand's White Barn Candle, and Blyth's Partylite and Colonial Candle of Cape Cod brands. Yankee Candle operates 250 specialty stores in mall locations and distributes its line through 14,000 specialty gift retailers. They also are distributed nationally through Bed Bath & Beyond and Linens 'n Things home stores. White Barn Candle has 130 dedicated specialty stores and is the candle house brand for the 1,600 stores of its corporate sister, Bath & Body Works. Partylite candles are exclusively distributed through 33,000 independent sales consultants who host parties and build excitement for the brand. Finally Blyth's Colonial Candle brand gives Yankee Candle a run for its money in the gift stores.

Purchase Drivers

Candles represent an indulgence item that gives consumers an emotional lift and only costs pocket change to buy—the perfect antidote for fending off the blues. As a consumer product, candles are unique. Burning a candle has a magical, transforming effect. One focus group respondent said: "Every woman looks beautiful in candlelight." Its flame mesmerizes, as this respondent describes: "I love to watch a candle burning. It's very relaxing to watch how they burn down." Its scent comforts and it sparks romance. Candles work on many different sensory levels to calm and refresh. A burning candle hearkens back to hearth and home. Candles are also a favorite gift item for holidays and throughout the year, as consumers seek gifts that will help them connect emotionally with loved ones and friends. One described the choice of candles as a perfect gift: "Everybody loves candles and you can get a really nice quality candle for $20 to $25, the price I like to spend on gifts."

Lighting a candle often signals a break from the ordinary and a time to relax. For some people, it is almost a ritual. A respondent explains that every time she sits down in her home office to work, she lights a candle: "I love candles and I always burn candles especially when I am working. When I light my candle on my desk, it means I am ready to work." Candles also support bathing and cleaning rituals, with a candlelit bath representing the ultimate in luxury. The fresh scent that candles impart in the home conveys cleanliness: "It reflects on your home, if it smells good. A burning candle gives a scent that tells how you keep your home and make it more enjoyable." For consumers, the role of scent in burning candles is very important, as three-fourths of all candles consumed are scented.

Yet there is a dark side to candles and that comes from the combustion of petroleum-based waxes. Indoor air pollution is becoming a concern, and while candles have a healthful glow, they can be a major source of indoor air pollutants, smoke, and dirt. I learned firsthand about the negative effects of over exuberant candle burning. Last year we had to repaint our living room as the soot from candles left tell-tale stains on the ceiling and walls. At our home now, candles are only an occasional indulgence.

Demographic Variables

Women are more likely to report candle purchases for their home, with 70 percent saying they or someone in their household bought a candle in the past year. However, with 53 percent of men reporting the same, this is hardly a female-only category. Despite their lower overall reported purchase, men represent a market for candles as they both purchase and influence the purchase of candles, especially when romance is on the agenda.

Candle purchase is higher among the more youthful consumers, aged 44 and younger. Purchase incidence declines with age with the lowest overall purchase incidence among those 65 years and above. Candles also appeal to all ethnic groups, with blacks and Hispanics buying candles at a slightly higher incidence than white households.

As household income rises, so does candle purchase incidence. The biggest jump in purchase incidence is found among the $35,000-to-$49,999 income range with 70 percent of these households reporting purchase. This elevated purchase incidence continues with rising income. Larger households buy more candles, with two-or-more-person households and those with children buying more candles than people living alone.

Key demographics of buyers of candles.

- This is a female-dominated category, with strong male participation.
- There is a youthful skew in purchase incidence that falls after age 45.
- Middle to the highest incomes, $35,000 or more, buy more.
- All racial and ethnic groups purchase.
- Households with children buy more.
- Large households buy more.

WHAT PEOPLE BUY: CHRISTMAS AND OTHER SEASONAL DECORATIONS

Christmas is the pinnacle of all holiday decorating, but thanks to Martha Stewart and other home-decorating mavens' tutoring, Americans have expanded the number of holidays for which they go "all out" and decorate their homes. Over 60 percent of American households (61 percent) purchased Christmas decorations or other seasonal decorations in 2003, up from 55 percent purchase incidence in 2001. While no statistics are available about the exact number of homes that decorate for each major holiday, the holidays that are key for home decorating are Valentine's Day, Easter, Fourth of July, Halloween, Thanksgiving, and, of course, Christmas. This is the third most widely purchased home product category.

Industry Overview

Retail sales of seasonal decorations totaled $4.7 billion in 2002, up about 4 percent over retail sales in 2000. The Christmas holiday accounts for the biggest share of decoration sales, or 62 percent of the total (see Figure 8.7). The fastest-growing category within Christmas decorations is "collectible" Christmas. These collectible ornaments usually are larger in size with special features and sell at premium prices, reaching $30 per ornament and above.

The Christmas tree is the center of holiday decorating in most American households. The National Christmas Tree Association estimated that 79.5 million households displayed a tree in their homes in 2002, down from the 82.5 million households that had a tree the previous year. As a result of the decline in homes displaying Christmas trees, the Association sees competition coming not just from the 70 percent or so of households that display an artificial tree, but from the nearly one-third of American households that decide against the decorating hassle associated with a tree of any kind. As the population ages and children depart the nest, tree-centered Christmas decorating is likely to continue to tumble.

But while Christmas decorating may slow, consumers' desire to dress up their homes for holidays throughout the year is on the upswing. This is a category of household clutter for which people still clamor, at least for the time being. Thanksgiving and harvest home decorating grew most rapidly since 2000, as consumers turned away from the more ghostly, ghoulish decorations associated with Halloween in the after shock of September 11. But the Halloween season of 2003 saw many American households returning to the darker side of Halloween decorating, so that will likely be a growth category in the future.

FIGURE 8.7

Christmas and Seasonal Decorations Industry Snapshot

	2000	2002	% CHG '00-'02
Total Personal Consumption in millions	$4,479.5	$4,646.6	3.7
Christmas décor	2,559.3	2,892.7	13.0
Tree and trim	1,935.7	2,058.9	6.4
Collectible Christmas	623.6	833.8	33.7
Thanksgiving/harvest	501.2	571.9	14.1
Easter	470.0	495.7	5.4
Halloween	755.8	457.5	–39.5
Outdoor décor	n.a.	190.6	
Other	1,921.8	38.1	–80.2

Source: Unity Marketing

Retail Overview

The majority of shoppers rely upon discount department stores for new seasonal decorations. But when they want something a little bit special, they often turn to the nation's 1,500 year-round specialty Christmas shops. The "granddaddy" of all Christmas stores is Bronner's located in Frankenmuth, Michigan. Bronner's is a virtual Santa's village covering 27 acres and buildings that enclose the equivalent of 5.5 football fields. Over two million visitors visited the store during 2003 and bought 1.3 million ornaments. And Bronner's doesn't limit its offerings to Christmas only, but "features trims and gifts for all seasons, reasons, and budgets."

The passion with which we decorate and celebrate the Christmas season is a uniquely American phenomenon. Department 56's Judith Price, director of collector relations, explains: "When you go to Europe, even to our Canadian neighbors to the north, you don't see the extravagant outdoor displays or the kind of over-the-top gift giving that we experience here in the States. The way we celebrate Christmas is a purely American holiday and reflects the blending of so many other cultures' traditions that have been brought over by wave after wave of immigrants." Department 56 is a $200 million company that has staked its fortunes on the uniquely American Christmas celebration. Best known for its elaborate lighted villages, the company also sells a full range of Christmas ornaments and trim through specialty retailers nationwide, as well as in three company-owned stores.

Purchase Drivers

Christmas decorating is a much-loved family tradition. While some families go in for the full outdoor display, others center their decorating on the tree and hearth. Bringing out the holiday decorations usually marks the "official" beginning of a family's holiday celebration. Many families maintain a collection of ornaments and decorations for years, annually adding new items to their collection to mark the passage of each year.

Nostalgia for Christmas past is a key driver for purchases of new items used to decorate. Consumers want to recreate those special celebrations remembered from childhood. Tapping into this trend for nostalgia, the Christopher Radko company has reintroduced the Shiny-Brite line of ornaments, re-creating vintage Christmas decorations produced in the 1940s and 1950s. Shiny-Brite was first made by Corning before World War II.

The latest versions hail from China and are based upon vintage designs. A string of authentic bubble lights, rarely seen today but remembered from the childhood of many boomers, caps the new collection.

Demographic Variables

Women tend to take the lead in holiday decorating traditions, so purchase incidence of Christmas and other seasonal decorations is higher among women (64 percent) than men (58 percent). Purchase incidence of Christmas decorations peaks between the ages of 25 and 54. White and Hispanic households are slightly more likely to buy decorations than are black households.

Higher-income households of $50,000 and above tend to purchase more decorations. Household size and the presence of children in the home strongly relates with purchasing decorations. Larger households and those with children have a much higher purchase incidence of Christmas decorations.

Key demographics of buyers of Christmas and seasonal décor.

- Purchase incidence peaks between ages 25 and 54, after which it drops.
- Larger households buy more.
- Presence of children increases incidence.
- This is a female-led category.

WHAT PEOPLE BUY: COLLECTIBLES

In 2003, about one-third of households reported buying collectibles in the past year. This percentage has been about flat since 2001, when 34 percent bought the same. Merriam-Webster's dictionary defines a *collectible* as:

> *An object that is collected by fanciers; especially: one other than such traditionally collectible items as art, stamps, coins, and antiques.*

With little guidance provided by the type of object that is considered collectible, the key to the definition of the term is that it is something—anything—that a fancier brings together into one grouping or place. The focus then is on the verb or act of collecting, and not that which is collected (i.e., the noun or the thing). Even the most disenfranchised members of our society, homeless people, carry "collections" of objects around with them. In some strange way, these objects, whether they are tin cans or just cast-offs from others, connect the street person with the life they led before. It represents some normalcy and a connection with "home" in an otherwise dysfunctional lifestyle.

Industry Snapshot

While the term *collectible* often refers to a vintage item that is not yet 100 years old and thus transformed into an antique on its centennial anniversary, there is a segment of the giftware industry that defines itself by the collectibles term and is represented by a trade association, The Gift & Collectibles Guild. Its members include companies that "design decorative objects, gifts, and limited-edition artwork and collectibles." Ever since the Beanie Babies collecting fad subsided, it has been a rough period for this industry that manufactures and markets new, as opposed to vintage, items for collecting. Overall industry sales are down by 17 percent in the past two years, with most categories, such as figurines, collectible dolls, and plush, dropping sharply (see Figure 8.8).

FIGURE 8.8
Collectibles Industry Snapshot

	2000	2002	% CHG '00-'02
Total Personal Consumption in millions	$7,140.4	$5,955.9	−16.6
Figurines and sculptures	2,370.8	1,548.5	−34.7
Ornaments	623.6	833.8	33.7
Dolls, collectible	929.9	684.9	−26.3
Plush toys, collectible	752.7	595.6	−20.9
Villages	398.4	327.6	−17.8
Crystal accessories	n.a.	279.9	
Boxes, music and nonmusic	366.9	268.0	−27.0
Plates	214.9	208.5	−3.0
Cottages	170.2	198.5	16.6
Die-cast, collectible	562.6	178.7	−68.2
Steins	116.6	89.3	−23.4
Other	633.8	744.5	17.5

Source: Unity Marketing

As the collectibles industry takes its licks, some companies are beginning to fold under the pressure. The Franklin Mint, one of the more prominent collectibles industry leaders in the roaring 1980s and 1990s, just laid off approximately two-thirds of its work force and closed its company stores as it restructures its business around the die-cast collecting segment. In its announcement, the company claimed: "The biggest problem we had was not getting the new collectors into the fold. The current business model is not working." In other words, nobody wants the stuff anymore. And The Franklin Mint is not alone in these difficulties. The Bradford Group, another direct sales company based in Niles, Illinois, has also undergone layoffs in the past year. Other public companies that have traditionally focused on collectibles are steadily seeing sales slide quarter after quarter, including Boyd's; Department 56; Enesco, home of Precious Moments; Media Arts, of Thomas Kinkade fame; and Middleton Doll Company.

Retail Overview

Collectors turn first to specialty stores to buy new items to add to their collections. About 35 percent reported they shopped in these types of stores to buy collectibles in the past year. They also looked to mail order, the Internet, and other nonstore channels, with about 28 percent reporting purchase through these sources. Rounding out the top three channels for collectibles purchases are discount department stores, where 21 percent of collectors shopped last year, with women in particular having a preference for the discount stores.

The online auction company eBay has truly turned the retailing of collectibles on its ear. Starting out with just a few categories of collectibles, today eBay boasts trade listings of 18,000 categories of merchandise available for sale and 62 million registered users. Being 100 percent market driven, eBay is able to respond immediately to the shifts and turns in collector's preferences, unlike traditional marketing companies, such as The Franklin Mint, that must make manufacturing decisions one to two years in advance. A few years ago eBay radar picked up that collectors were starting to list real cars under the die-cast heading, because that was the closest category where a real car could fit. Responding in a flash, eBay added a real car trading platform and today the sale of true collector cars, not miniature die-cast models, is one of their most profitable and fastest-growing sectors.

Purchase Drivers

Since 1996, the sales of primary market collectibles (i.e., new products that are manufactured and marketed solely for the enjoyment of the adult collector) have followed a roller-coaster trajectory of rapidly rising sales followed by an even more dramatic fall. Only collectible ornaments, a category gaining momentum with the consumer's interest in seasonal decorations, achieved significant growth in 2002.

The age of cocooning, defined by trend watcher Faith Popcorn back in the '80s and which lasted roughly until the end of the twentieth century, was a good period for collecting. Cocooning was all about feathering one's nest by gathering and collecting things to fill up one's emotional empty spaces. Collecting and collectibles were a favorite way consumers expressed their cocooning drives. But with the end of cocooning, consumers are turning away from accumulating more things and looking to reconnect in a meaningful way with the outside world. While an estimated one-third of consumers still collect, they are turning their collecting interests to other things besides what a consumer in a recent focus group called "dustibles." Collecting today is about collecting real things, not inauthentic items manufactured in China solely for collecting purposes.

With a shift toward authenticity, collectors are collecting vintage items, available in antique stores, on the secondary market, at auctions, and through Internet services like eBay. Consequently, the definition of what is a collectible is beginning to shift from an object that is "fancied" to one that has potential investment value. Today when you say something is collectible, it implies that someday it may be worth serious money. The emergence of eBay, *Antiques Roadshow,* and other venues that focus on finding lost treasures in the attic have given rise to this shift in definition.

Demographic Variables

Men and women report an equal incidence of purchasing collectibles in their households. Collectibles purchasing peaks in two age ranges: among the youngest consumers aged 18 to 24 and those aged 45 to 54. Traditionally, collecting has been a hobby associated with consumers in their empty-nesting years. However, today's younger consumers, particularly young men and women intrigued with the possibilities of finding desirable collectible items on the Internet, are pursuing collecting actively.

Buying collectibles is a practice associated with the highest-income households of $75,000 and above. Two-person-and-larger households are more likely to buy collectibles, although the presence of children in the home doesn't increase incidence.

Key demographics of buyers of collectibles.

* This category is gender neutral.
* More affluent households buy more.
* Two age segments—18 to 24 and 45 to 54—buy more.
* Two-person and larger households buy more.

WHAT PEOPLE BUY: FIGURINES AND SCULPTURES

About one-fifth of households reported buying a figurine or sculpture in 2003, about the same as in 2001. A popular gift item for collectors, figurines often carry a greeting or social expression that makes them perfectly suited to gifting or as a remembrance. Figurines have been popular collectibles in the past, with lines such as Precious Moments and Hummel passed from generation to generation. But today, figurine collectibles are looked upon with disdain by many as something that one's grandmother liked, but not something for me.

Industry Snapshot

Figurines were at once the largest category within the contemporary or manufactured collectibles market, yet their sales are falling the fastest. In 2000, figurine sales at retail were $2.4 billion, but they dropped 35 percent to $1.6 billion in 2002. Traditionally, figurines have been made from porcelain or china and fired in ovens, thus making them a craft of skilled artisans and expensive to produce. The history of the invention of porcelain and the founding of the Meissen Porcelain Manufacture in Dresden, Germany, in the eighteenth century is fascinating reading in a book called *The Arcanum* by Janet Gleeson.

Compared to porcelain figurines, cold-cast figurines are not even a branch on the same family tree. Once inexpensive cold-cast molding became widely available in factories in the far east, so named because cold-cast figurines are made of material that cures without firing in an oven, the cost of entry into the figurine market was so low—too low—that many companies that never should have gotten into the business did so. The result was too much boring product that looked just like everybody else's.

Whereas the porcelain figurine business kept its artistic traditions and higher price tag, cold-cast was just a little too common and often times too cute. Today, the companies that have held fast to their porcelain and china crafting, like Lladro, Goebel, Lenox, Royal Doulton, and Herend, are staying the course, while the cold-cast folks are falling by the wayside.

Purchase Drivers

For consumers this is a category that was generally associated only with collectors and not appropriate to give to anyone but a collector. One respondent in a focus group coined the term *dustible* to describe figurines. This term caught fire with the rest of the group. This name indicates that figurines are more trouble than they are worth, requiring that they be dusted and kept up. Figurines today are considered irrelevant by the vast majority of consumers, and only of interest to those who already have a collecting interest, as one person said: "Figurines are more of a collectible thing. You have to know what they like and what they're collecting." When asked about buying a figurine as a gift, one consumer said: "I wouldn't buy one for someone because they'd probably just put it in their closet and never see it again."

Demographic Variables

This is a gender-neutral category with about the same percentage of women and men buying them. Figurine purchasing spans all ages, with the exception of consumers older than age 65. Black American households have a higher purchase incidence of figurines than do white or Hispanic. That may be partly due to some very nicely rendered product lines by artists like Thomas Blackshear from Willitts Design that celebrate African-American heritage and ancestry. Purchase incidence of figurines crosses all income levels, while households with children and two or more individuals tend to purchase at a higher rate.

Key demographics of buyers of figurines and sculptures.

- This is a gender-neutral category.
- All income households purchase evenly.
- Black Americans purchase more.
- All ages, except 65 and older, purchase evenly.

WHAT PEOPLE BUY: FLORALS AND GREENERY FOR INDOOR USE

Forty-one percent of households purchased florals and plants for indoor use during 2003, down slightly from 44 percent in 2001. Cut flowers are a popular gift item, especially for Valentine's Day.

Industry Snapshot

The retail market for cut flowers and florist items is said to be $15 billion by *Chain Store Age* magazine.

In total, sales of flowers, seeds, and potted plants (including both indoor and outdoor plants) was $18.2 billion in 2002, according to personal consumption data from the U.S. Bureau of Economic Analysis. This represents a 1.4 percent increase over sales of $17.9 billion in 2000.

Retail Overview

There are about 24,000 florists in the United States, according to statistics compiled by the Department of Census, but no national store-based retailer of note. Consumer brands FTD and Teleflora are actually wholesalers that distribute through the existing independent retail network. But more and more flowers are available to shoppers everywhere, from the grocery store, Wal-Mart, and the corner convenience store to the garden center and nursery. So where cut flowers were once a specialized product that you had to search out, today they are commonplace.

As the flower market opens up, more marketers are exploring ways to bypass the retailer altogether and deliver flowers directly to the consumer. 1-800-FLOWERS was an early innovator of delivering flowers directly. The company was founded in 1986 by Jim McCann who operated

FIGURE 8.9

Flowers, Seeds, and Potted Plants Industry Snapshot

	2000	2002	% CHG '00-'02
Total Personal Consumption in millions	$17,974	$18,219	1.4

Source: Bureau of Economic Analysis

a chain of 14 flower shops in the New York area. Smartly anticipating the future, he bought the rights to the 1-800-FLOWERS phone number and so an innovative direct-to-consumer technology-enabled national florist business was born. Today it is a $566 million company selling cut flowers, plants, and a wide selection of gift items through its Web site, toll-free hotline, direct mail catalogs, and more than 100 franchised and company-owned stores.

Purchase Drivers

Self-purchasers in this category tend to be indoor gardening enthusiasts. Indoor gardening allows the homeowner to bring the outdoors in, decorating the home with plants. Indoor gardening can be as simple as an African violet on the windowsill, or as elaborate as greenhouses equipped with grow lights, hydroponic culture, and special heating systems.

The National Gardening Association estimates that 46 percent of American households participate in some aspect of indoor gardening. That makes indoor plants the second most popular and participated-in gardening activity after lawn care.

But beyond indoor gardening, flowers and plants are an extremely popular gift item, accounting for much of the purchasing by men. Valentine's Day, Mother's Day, Easter, Christmas, housewarmings, anniversaries, and romance occasions are the primary gifting holidays and occasions for flowers and plants.

Demographic Variables

Men tend to buy flowers for gifts, while women are the primary consumers of indoor greenery. All ages, even seniors age 65 and above, buy florals and indoor plants.

Florals and indoor greenery are more widely bought by middle-to-upper-income households, those that make $50,000 and above. Also linked with higher purchase incidence is greater educational attainment. So if one is thinking of starting a floral business, a location near a college would be ideal. Purchase incidence rises with household size, as households with two or more individuals buy more in this category. The presence of children in the home, however, has little impact on purchase incidence.

Key demographics of buyers of florals for indoor use.

- Men buy flowers and women buy indoor plants.
- Households with income of $50,000 and above buy more.
- Larger households buy more, but there is no impact from the presence of children.
- All ages from the youngest to seniors buy flowers and indoor greenery.

WHAT PEOPLE BUY: FLOWERS, SEEDS, SHRUBS, AND TREES FOR OUTDOOR LANDSCAPING

More than half of American households (56 percent) bought flowers, seeds, shrubs, and trees for outdoor landscaping in 2003, down just slightly from 59 percent in 2002. Outdoor gardening is a passion for many, and a necessity for others. The American Gardening Association reports that 80 percent of U.S. households participate in some garden-related activity that usually results in the expenditure of money for tools, equipment, greenery, and supplies.

With home ownership at two-thirds of the population, few have the luxury of escaping some gardening expenditure. After all, if you leave your home empty for a few weeks, it will only get dusty. But leave your lawn or garden alone for the same amount of time and you've got a major project to contend with when you get home. The lawn and garden are always in the state of "becoming," transforming themselves from the manicured and orderly look the gardener desires to the abundant, chaotic, lushness that nature strives to achieve.

Industry Snapshot

Consumer spending on flowers, seeds, and potted plants (i.e., garden "software") totaled $18.2 billion in 2002, up 1.4 percent over $17.9 billion in 2000, according to the Bureau of Economic Analysis (see Figure 8.13). However, that statistic tells only part of the story of America's passion for gardening. The National Gardening Association estimates that Americans spent in total $39.6 billion on their lawns and gardens in 2002, a 5 percent increase over spending of $37.7 billion in 2001. That includes gardening equipment and decorative items (i.e., garden "hardware") discussed in more detail later.

Retail Overview

The Department of Commerce classifies the bulk of garden retail sales within the broad building materials and garden equipment dealers category. In 2002, building materials and garden equipment dealers posted total retail sales of $300.9 billion on 9 percent growth over 2000 results of $276.2 billion (see Figure 8.10). But while the building materials segment, which includes sales by The Home Depot, Lowe's, and other home centers, grew 9.8 percent overall, the garden equipment and supplies side, much smaller by comparison, posted only 5.8 percent growth over 2000 results. These numbers tell the story of garden retail: The home centers like The Home Depot and Lowe's are drawing more and more sales out of the specialty garden center market. The winners in the gardening retail business include The Home Depot with 1,500 stores and 40 EXPO Design Center stores and sales in calendar year 2002 in excess of $58.3 billion; and Lowe's, the number-two home center chain, with 850 superstores in 45 states, and sales in 2002 of $26.5 billion.

The National Gardening Association's 2001 consumer survey confirms this finding. The top source for households to buy garden-related products in 2001 was home centers, used by 38 percent of garden consumers. While lawn and garden centers and nurseries were the second most frequently used source by 36 percent of garden-consuming households, the mass merchants and discounters are also increasing their share of consumer sales, ranked number three with 35 percent of the market for garden purchases in 2001.

Purchase Drivers

Spending on outdoor landscaping is often seen as an investment that increases the value of the home, and thus gives consumers justifica-

FIGURE 8.10

Building Materials and Garden Retailers Industry Snapshot

	2000	2002	% CHG '00-'02
Total Personal Consumption in millions	$276,163	$300,932	9.0
Building materials dealers	241,053	264,751	9.8
Hardware stores	15,363	15,295	−0.4
Garden suppliers	19,747	20,886	5.8

Source: Department of Census, Monthly Retail Census

tion to spend more to improve the lawn, patio, and outdoor areas. With consumers emerging from the indoor cocoon, they are turning their decorating energy outdoors with increased spending on both plant materials and decorative accents.

Gardening demands physical labor and therefore is a great way to relieve stress. As one focus group respondent explains: "Gardening is my husband's stress relief. Every year he puts in a garden, and it saves his sanity. He likes to work in the yard." Besides offering exercise, gardening appeals to people because it makes their yards look better, more attractive, and more inviting. Another respondent who is devoted to her yard says: "I love showing off my yard. I love to have friends over and to eat on the patio. I like them to admire my garden. I like to get praise and appreciation for my work and for them to recognize my accomplishment. Gardening is hard work."

For some, maintaining their yard to the standards of the neighborhood is a factor, but most do it solely for personal enjoyment. Another respondent explains: "I just bought a lilac bush. I have always loved lilac—it's my favorite fragrance. Of course, it will make my yard look nicer, but I bought it for me." Another says: "I grew up on a farm, so I look at gardening as a necessity. It gives pleasure, relieves stress. After all, your house has to look as good as everyone else's in the neighborhood."

However, what can be stress relieving for one can be stress inducing for another. Some view the need to keep their yard up with their neighbors' yards as one more obligation: "I find it stressful. It is something I have to do, and it has to get done. It's not something I want to do."

Demographic Variables

With about 56 percent of households reporting they bought flowers, seeds, shrubs, and trees for outdoor landscaping in the past year, men and women participate in gardening purchases about equally. This is a category where the purchase incidence rises with age. Those aged 35 to 54 purchase more plant material for their gardens than younger and older consumers. White and Hispanic households spend more on plants for outdoor landscaping than blacks. Rising incomes, especially those of $75,000 and above, education levels, and household size all correlate with rising purchase incidence for the garden.

Key demographics of buyers of flowers, seeds, and shrubs.

- Men and women are equally involved.

- Peak participation is between ages 35 and 54.
- Purchase incidence rises with income and is the highest among $75,000 households and above.
- Home ownership leads to greater incidence.
- Households with two or more people buy more.
- Higher educational levels leads to greater incidence.

WHAT PEOPLE BUY: FURNITURE AND OCCASIONAL FURNITURE

Purchase incidence of furniture was the same in 2003 (41 percent) as in 2001. The purchase of furniture can range from inexpensive occasional tables and ready-to-assemble and unfinished furniture to major furniture acquisitions that are often bought on credit and paid for over time.

Industry Snapshot

Personal consumption of furniture, including mattresses and box springs, reached $69.8 billion in 2002, up 3.2 percent over 2000 levels of $67.6 billion (see Figure 8.11). The key growth categories in furniture were kitchen and dinning room furniture and outdoor furniture. Infant furniture, wall units and cabinets, and occasional furniture also were

FIGURE 8.11

Total Furniture and Mattresses Industry Snapshot

	2000	2002	% CHG '00-'02
Total Personal Consumption in millions	$67,596.0	$69,777.0	3.23
Mattresses and box springs	9,152.3	9,200.3	0.52
Other bedroom furniture	11,959.0	11,881.6	−0.65
Sofas	15,426.9	14,837.7	−3.82
Living room chairs	7,586.2	6,818.1	−10.13
Living room tables	2,974.6	3,135.2	5.40
Kitchen, dining room furniture	8,039.6	10,655.7	32.54
Infant furniture	1,076.3	1,123.3	4.37
Outdoor furniture	2,623.4	2,919.5	11.29
Wall units, cabinets, occasional furniture	8,757.7	9,205.5	5.11

Source: U.S. Department of Commerce, Bureau of Economic Affairs; Bureau of Labor Statistics Consumer Expenditure Survey Diary, 2002

growth categories in 2002. During that year, sales were off for major furniture pieces, as consumer demand for occasional and smaller investment pieces was up.

Retail Overview

The furniture industry has been undergoing a retrenchment in the past several years. Furniture retailing is evolving, with many large chains of independently owned furniture stores, such as Heilig-Meyers, going out of business or through bankruptcy and major reorganization, such as Levitz. National specialty chains, including Pottery Barn, Restoration Hardware, Pier 1, and Bombay Company, are also capturing a greater share of the furniture market, offering affordably priced imports manufactured to their specifications. Many branded furniture companies, facing the loss of retail furniture stores, are opening dedicated, often franchised gallery stores to ensure continued distribution at the consumer level. La-Z-Boy, for example, has built a chain of 300 dedicated furniture stores and launched 315 in-store galleries to showcase the company's furniture line. La-Z-Boy is following in the footsteps of furniture manufacturer Ethan Allen, which has long controlled retail distribution through their own chain of 300 stores.

But while the long-established, well-respected Ethan Allen watches its sales erode below the $1 billion mark in 2003, the upstart Rooms to Go, with only 90 stores, has taken over the position of the nation's number-one furniture retailer with sales estimated at $1.3 billion. As its name implies, the concept of Rooms to Go is simple and perfect for our time. It offers instant decorating solutions one room at a time in moderately priced packages that include the furniture and decorative accessories. It has recently expanded the concept to target tweens and teens with 20 Rooms to Go Kids stores. The specialty child, tween, and teen market is also getting attention from Pottery Barn through new niche-focused catalogs and targeted stores cropping up in malls across the country.

According to the Census Department's monthly retail census, retail sales at traditional furniture stores, such as Ethan Allen and Rooms to Go, totaled $52.6 billion in 2002, up 4 percent over 2000 results (see Figure 8.12). Home furnishings stores that sell a wider selection of more decorative home furnishings, such as Pottery Barn, Bed Bath & Beyond, Bombay Company, and Pier 1 to name a few, generated retail sales of $42.4 million, an increase of only 3.1 percent over 2000.

FIGURE 8.12

Retail Furniture and Home Furnishings Stores

	2000	2002	% CHG '00-'02
Total retail in millions	$91,662	$94,978	3.6
Furniture stores	50,539	52,563	4.0
Home furnishings stores	41,123	42,415	3.1

Source: Department of Census, Monthly Retail Census

Purchase Drivers

While consumers frequently turn to less expensive decorative acces-sories to update their room décor, they often buy furniture to replace a worn-out piece. After all, upholstered furniture gets worn before case goods and wooden furniture do. But when consumers go out to replace a worn-out chair or sofa, shoppers often end up making a cascade of ad-ditional furniture purchases. With the justifier of replacing an existing item, they don't want to stop there but want to create a whole new look for the room, so they add curtains, rugs, tables, and all the rest.

Moving and buying a new home is another primary motivator for consumers to get out and shop for furniture. The past few years have been very positive for the housing market as mortgage interest rates have dropped, thus giving consumers extra cash to trade up to larger, more expensive homes with more rooms to furnish.

Often thought of as a necessity, one focus group respondent views all furniture purchases as discretionary: "We have all the basics [furni-ture] that we need. I view all [furniture purchases] as discretionary. I just bought a grandfather clock. It is fun. It is the first thing you see when you walk into the house." After moving to the Midwest from Florida, one respondent needed to change her home décor to be more compatible with the local neighborhood: "We used to live in Florida and had very con-temporary furnishings. Then we moved to Ohio, and it didn't have the same feeling. We needed to buy all new furniture to match our new home."

Demographic Variables

Furniture purchases often represent major household expenditures, so that men and women are equally involved in the purchase. Men, in fact, report a higher purchase incidence of furniture (44 percent) than women do (39 percent). Furniture buying tends to skew toward a more youthful market, with households aged 18 to 24 reporting the highest purchase incidence. Furniture purchasing remains elevated through age 54 and then declines sharply among those aged 55 and older.

Purchase incidence is highest among households with incomes of $75,000 and above, though it is elevated too for the $50,000-to-$75,000-income households. Larger households of two or more members and those with children have a higher purchase incidence of furniture than do single-person households and those without children.

Key demographics of buyers of furniture and occasional furniture.

- Furniture purchases are considered joint purchases.
- Purchase incidence rises with income, with the highest income households buying the most.
- Incidence skews toward a youthful market, and drops after age 55.
- Larger households and those with children buy more.

WHAT PEOPLE BUY: GARDEN EQUIPMENT AND DECORATIVE ITEMS FOR THE GARDEN AND PATIO

With consumers spending more money on landscaping and their lawns, it is not surprising the purchase incidence of garden equipment, furniture, and décor is strong as well. Purchase incidence of garden equipment, furniture, and decorative items for the garden (i.e., garden hardware) was 42 percent in 2003, down slightly from results of 47 percent in 2001.

Industry Snapshot

As discussed previously, The National Gardening Association estimates that Americans spent in total $39.6 billion on their lawns and gardens in 2002, a 17 percent increase over spending of $33.5 billion in 2000 (see Figure 8.13). If we subtract spending on plant material from the total, we find that consumer spending on gardening hardware—products, tools, fertilizer, equipment, decorative accents, and other nonliving materials that enhance the gardening experience or gardening environment—is $21.4 billion, up 38.1 percent over 2000 sales. That makes garden equipment, accessories, and décor the fastest growing category in the garden market today.

FIGURE 8.13

Lawn and Garden Industry Snapshot

	2000	2002	% CHG '00-'02
Total Personal Consumption in billions	$33.5	$39.6	18.2
Plant Material	18.0	18.2	1.4
Garden Hardware	15.5	21.4	38.1

Source: Bureau of Economic Analysis; National Gardening Association Consumer Survey, 2002

Retail Overview

Retailers that attract gardening enthusiasts for plant material also tend to attract them for equipment and garden decorations, so The Home Depot and Lowe's are major retailers of gardening hardware, used by 63 percent of shoppers. Discount department stores are also major providers of this class of products to consumers. In fact, consumers are more likely to buy garden hardware (27 percent) from the discounters than they are to buy plant material (19 percent).

In terms of specialty retailers, the top name in garden décor is Smith & Hawken. The company targets the upscale market with 45 specialty retail stores in 20 states and a direct mail catalog and Internet site for gardening enthusiasts. It specializes in well-designed garden décor, furniture, tools, and garden containers, along with garden apparel, housewares, plants, bulbs, and books. The company had sales of about $100 million and recently partnered with Saks to add garden boutiques into more than 240 Saks stores nationwide.

Purchase Drivers

Spending on one category for the home frequently results in additional spending in other categories, justified by the original purchase. It is no different with consumers' spending on the garden. The upgrade of plants, landscaping, or the lawn often results in the purchase of garden equipment, furniture, and decorations to match the new, improved outdoor look. As one consumer explained: "We just put in a finished patio and new sidewalk, so we needed plants to complement that. Then we needed patio furniture to complement that. It gives me a feeling of accomplishment."

Grills are a frequently named utilitarian purchase for the garden, with the grill providing the owner with a new way to cook. One woman told us: "My husband is crazy about grills. We already have four grills. The gas grill is for me because I love the convenience and don't want to build a fire. My husband likes to cook regularly and use hickory. Now he wants to buy a smoker, not just one, but two, so one smoker can be at home and another one at the campground. I think we have enough already. I ask him how often he will use a smoker. Once a year is what I say, so why buy two?"

Demographic Variables

Men and women report about the same purchase incidence of garden equipment and accessories, suggesting that both men and women are equally involved with such purchases. Like the purchase of outdoor plants and landscaping, the purchase incidence is highest among more mature households, aged 35 to 54. While there are no meaningful regional differences in purchase incidence, white households are more likely to purchase than black households.

Purchase incidence is concentrated among the middle-to-upper-income ranges. Home ownership seems to be an important link. Purchase incidence is highest among the most affluent, with incomes of $75,000 or more. Greater educational attainment is also linked to increased purchase incidence. Larger households and those with children are more likely to buy garden equipment and accessories than single-person households and those without children.

Key demographics of buyers of garden equipment and décor.

- This category is gender neutral.
- Households with incomes of $35,000 or more, especially $75,000 and above, purchase more.
- Purchase incidence is highest among households aged 35 to 54.
- Larger households and those with children buy more.
- White households are more likely than black households to buy.

WHAT PEOPLE BUY: GREETING CARDS AND PERSONAL STATIONERY

Greeting cards and personal stationery are the most widely purchased home products. More than 80 percent (83 percent) of American households purchased greeting cards and personal stationery in 2003. This represents a significant increase over the 72 percent purchase incidence found in 2001. Today paper products are really hot with dynamic growth in the purchase of specialty luxury papers for writing and crafts. The burgeoning scrapbooking hobby is also drawing more people to a passion for paper.

The new connecting trend is the primary driver in growth in the stationery market. Connecting relates to consumers' need to establish connections with others through all forms and methods of personal communications. The stationery and greeting cards market is benefiting, as consumers embrace the handwritten note as the ultimate in luxury communications.

Industry Snapshot

Total industry sales of greeting cards and stationery were $14.2 billion, up a modest 3.4 percent over 2000 sales of $13.8 (see Figure 8.14). But the story in this category is mixed. Sales of greeting cards, the industry's mainstay, have been flat for the past several years. Greeting card companies' top line sales are being negatively impacted by rampant discounting and deflationary pressures, as mass merchants and discounters now capture a growing share of the greeting card market with discount and off-priced cards and stationery items.

Industry giant Hallmark is beginning to feel the pinch. In its U.S. greeting card and stationery business, Hallmark reports its 2002 sales

FIGURE 8.14

Greeting Card and Stationery Industry Snapshot

	2000	2002	% CHG '00-'02
Total Personal Consumption in millions	$13,771	$14,240	3.4
Greeting cards	7,161	7,195	0.5
Scrapbooks	n.a.	1,175	
Social stationery	996	1,064	6.9
Gift bags and wrapping paper	1,253	1,149	−8.3
Books and albums	689	720	4.6
Calendars	689	656	−4.8
Custom imprints	n.a.	386	
Party goods and other supplies	2,995	1,894	−36.8

Source: Unity Marketing

were down approximately 1 percent from the previous year. Narrowing of its distribution is partly to blame. Since 2000, the number of Hallmark Gold Crown Stores, its flagship outlets, dropped from 4,800 to 4,300 and other specialty retail outlets featuring Hallmark cards declined from 47,000 to 42,000 stores. The company claims to hold a 56 percent share of the greeting card retail market.

Also negatively impacting the traditional greeting card market is the computer revolution. The ready availability of e-mail, as well as the continuing decline of long-distance telephone rates and increase in postage fees, predisposes consumers to use more technologically advanced personal communication methods instead of old-fashioned "snail-mail" letters and greeting cards. Today, sending Christmas cards through the mail is rapidly becoming an anachronism even in business circles that were slower to abandon the practice than holiday-stressed consumers.

On the positive side, stationery suppliers have expanded their offerings to include cards and preprinted stationery suited to use in computer printers. As paper crafting and stationery continues to merge, more high-end paper suppliers are finding an eager market for their very specialized, expensive—at least by paper's standards—goods. Whether for writing, gift wrap, or crafts, luxury paper has special appeal.

Retail Overview

Today, with all the major greeting card brands, like Hallmark and American Greetings, firmly entrenched in discount channels featuring greeting cards in the 99¢-or-less price range, the mass retail market has sunk to the bottom of the pricing barrel. Mass marketers will see little revenue growth in the future if prices remain so low.

But the luxury realm of specialty paper, including handmade paper and cards, specialty stationery, and books and journals, along with luxury writing implements, is a significant growth opportunity for the future. As our world becomes more digital, with technology dominating our communications at both work and home, consumers crave to be grounded in the real world of sight, sound, emotion, and sensation. The return to handwritten notes on exquisite stationery carries the ambiance of an earlier time. Writing and receiving a beautiful handwritten note is the ultimate expression of luxury communications, when so many technology-enhanced options are readily available to us.

Through the marketing efforts of such specialty paper retailers as Papyrus, with 125 mall-based stores, and Crane & Co, both a major paper supplier and growing retailer with 20 company stores, consumers are becoming more aware of the special features and appeals of luxury paper. But if you really want to find out what's hot in the stationery business, a trip to New York–based Kate's Paperie is required. With three New York City locations in addition to the flagship store at 140 W. 57th Street, and one store in Greenwich, Connecticut, Kate's Paperie is featured in all the tourist guide books to the "Big Apple" as a must-see shopping destination. The store offers a selection of over 4,000 luxury paper products and perfectly reflects the trend toward luxury stationery and personal connecting in the market today.

Founded in 1987, Kate's Paperie reaches consumers near and far through its Web site (http://www.katespaperie.com). Beside selling a full selection of paper-related goods, from traditional stationery, such as Crane's and William Arthur, and other stationery sold by the pound, to letter press cards and unusual handmade wrapping papers, it also offers photo albums, journals, fancy ribbons, art supplies, toys, books, beautiful containers, writing implements, and everything needed to wrap and package a gift to make it really special. Its party goods selection is enough to inspire the most party-shy consumer to throw a shindig.

Custom printing, notably wedding stationery, is a specialty of the house. Kate's will custom design a wax seal or rubber stamp for invitations to add sophistication and old-world charm. How-to demonstrations and classes are an important part of marketing luxury stationery, because all but Martha Stewart really know how to wrap that special gift. Afternoon and evening how-to demonstrations are offered Tuesday, Wednesday, and Thursday on topics including Japanese pleats, party garlands, shirt wrap for dad's gift, Kimono cards, and Victorian photo holders. Consumer education is even a revenue generator for Kate's with two-hour sit-down classes offered for $55 on scrapbooking basics, decoupage picture framing, and make-your-own stationery and cards.

As paper goes up market, luxury writing instruments, too, are enjoying a renaissance. High-end writing instruments manufacturers, such as Cartier, Parker, and montegrappa, say that sales of their "fancy" pens are up some 20 percent. Part of the growth in the luxury writing category is due to the shift from fountain pens, which used to dominate high-end pens, to writer-friendly rollerball pens. For example, Colorado Pen Direct, a leading pen catalog, reports that half of its sales of pens was rollerballs, compared to only 20 percent in 1999, according to a recent story in the *Wall Street Journal.*

Purchase Drivers

Greeting cards are an essential accompaniment to a gift. In a recent Unity Marketing survey on gifting, over 60 percent of gift givers agreed with the statement: "I typically buy a greeting card to accompany a gift to give."

Greeting cards can also substitute for a gift and fulfill the need to connect with family and friends near and far.

The industry has carefully honed its image with consumers through media advertisements. The industry positions a greeting card as a more thoughtful expression of feelings than a simple note. With illustrations and ready-made poetic sentiments, greeting cards help consumers convey emotions that they might otherwise find difficult to express. Recipients frequently keep greeting cards as reminders of the sender's sentiment. With these advantages, the industry positions its greeting cards as a far better way for consumers to connect emotionally with others. For the consumer, greeting cards offer real advantages, not the least of which are saving time and effort, since expressing deep emotion is difficult for many.

Demographic Variables

The greeting card and stationery product category is a female-oriented category, with more women (90 percent) than men reporting a household purchase of greeting cards in the past year. However, men are hardly slackers when it comes to stationery purchases, as nearly three-fourths of men (74 percent) also reported buying in the category in the past year. Purchase incidence of cards and stationery cuts across all ethnicities and age ranges, but the highest overall purchase incidence is among consumers aged 45 to 54.

While the most affluent, those with household income of $75,000 or more, have the highest purchase incidence of stationery, more than 80 percent of all households of all income levels report buying stationery in the past year. Purchase incidence is linked to household size, with larger households of two or more individuals buying more stationery than those with one person.

This category is positively linked to educational level, with the more educated households buying stationery products at a higher rate than the less educated ones.

Key demographics of buyers of greeting cards and stationery.

- This is a female-dominated category, but men are active too.
- All ages purchase, but ages 45 to 54 have the highest incidence.
- Middle-to-upper-income households buy more.
- Larger households buy more.
- Higher educational achievement leads to higher incidence.

WHAT PEOPLE BUY: HOME TEXTILES

Purchase incidence of home textiles, which includes rugs, throws, pillows, and table and bed linens, dropped sharply in 2003. While purchase incidence peaked in 2001 at 60 percent, only 52 percent of households bought this class of goods in 2003. Once one of the prime categories associated with nesting and cocooning, consumers' new anti-clutter approach to home décor is turning them off this once-vibrant category.

Industry Snapshot

In 2002, total household spending on home textiles and rugs and floor coverings was $53.9 billion, distributed as shown in Figure 8.15. This represents a modest 1.8 percent increase over 2000 industry sales of $53 billion.

FIGURE 8.15
Home Textiles and Rugs Industry Snapshot

	2000	2002	% CHG '00-'02
Total Personal Consumption in millions	$52,948	$53,875	1.8
Total home textiles	36,465	37,399	2.56
Bathroom linens	4,596	5,270	14.68
Bedroom linens	15,421	16,512	7.07
Kitchen and dining room linens	1,058	1,234	16.66
Curtains and draperies	9,480	7,526	−20.61
Slipcovers and decorative pillows	828	963	16.24
Sewing materials for home	4,389	5,171	17.82
Other linens	689	719	4.36
Rugs and floor coverings	16,483	16,476	−0.04

Source: Bureau of Economic Analysis; Bureau of Labor Statistics Consumer Expenditure Survey Diary

Changes in retail distribution of home textiles have drawn sales out of department stores. The rise of national specialty retail chains focusing exclusively on home furnishings has attracted new consumers in search of home textiles. Today, home furnishings stores generate nearly 30 percent of home textile sales.

Retail Overview

Two national chains dominate the discussion of home textiles today: Bed Bath & Beyond, a $3.7 billion group of over 500 stores headquartered in Union, New Jersey; and Linens 'n Things, with $2.2 billion in annual sales and 390 stores. Both chains are positioned along similar lines, offering a wide selection of name-brand linens and housewares at discount prices. Shopping in one store provides a déjà vu experience with the other, yet they strive futilely to achieve differentiation.

But Wal-Mart and its discount department store competitors are bringing in the really serious money in home textiles today. Wal-Mart is the nation's largest retailer of home textiles, the position it claims in almost any product category it decides to pursue seriously. Embattled Kmart has stayed afloat largely due to the phenomenal good fortune of signing Martha Stewart and her Martha Stewart Everyday home textiles line. Target continues to attract attention as the most luxurious of the discounters. In Unity Marketing's latest survey, 44 percent of home textile shoppers made purchases at discount department stores, while only 17 percent bought these products from a home furnishings specialty chain like Bed Bath & Beyond.

Another notable player in home textiles is Tuesday Morning. An off-price retailer generating $729 million, Tuesday Morning takes a novel approach to its business as a major closeout retailer of upscale home furnishings with strength in the home textile arena, gifts, and related items. Its 526 stores are all located in off-beat and decidedly nonprime locations. The stores are open only during periodic "sales events," each of which starts on a Tuesday morning, thus its name, and lasts from three to five weeks. The stores close for the months of January and July and in between sales events to stock up on new merchandise for the next big event.

Purchase Drivers

Rather than investing in major furniture pieces as they have in the past, consumers are turning to decorative accessories to change the décor of their homes. Home textiles—including rugs, throws, pillows, table linens, and curtains—offer an affordable, fun way to update the home. With the ready availability of name-brand textiles at discount prices, many consumers view new sheets, pillowcases, comforters, and duvets for their bedroom as indulgences, rather than major expenditures. "I have an addiction to decorating any room. I especially like TJ Maxx or Marshall's, where I can find a lot of really good deals. I just bought a great rug on sale at TJ Maxx. I wasn't looking for it specifically, but I saw it and had to have it," one focus group respondent told us.

Demographic Variables

Women take the lead in home textile purchases, with 58 percent of women compared to 45 percent of men reporting a household purchase in the category in 2003. All age groups through age 64 maintain a fairly strong purchase incidence, peaking among households aged 25 to 34, corresponding with the household-formation years, and those aged 45 to 54, associated with the empty-nesting period.

Except for the lowest-income households, this is a category that is widely purchased across all income levels, with the most affluent households, those making $75,000 and above, purchasing most often. Household size and presence of children in the home relates to increased purchase incidence, as larger households and those with children buy more frequently.

Key demographics of buyers of home textiles.

- Women are prime consumers.
- Peak buying ages for this category are 25 to 34 and 45 to 54.
- Middle-to-upper-income households buy more, especially the most affluent.
- Large households buy more.
- Households with children buy more.

WHAT PEOPLE BUY: KITCHENWARE AND ACCESSORIES

Some 56 percent of U.S. households bought kitchenware and housewares in 2003, about even with the 58 percent that did the same in 2001.

A category that is often perceived as a household necessity, consumers are encouraged to buy when retailers and marketers give them a reason to replace existing kitchen accessories with the latest models that give new functionality or ease of use. For example, OXO, a division of World Kitchen, is a model of a housewares company that gives consumers a good reason to buy. They have designed and developed a line of can openers, slicers, dicers, peelers, and other manual utensils that provide a measurably better consumer experience in the kitchen. Their ergonomic designs simply fit the human hand better than anything else out there. That gives consumers a well-justified reason to throw out all the old stuff cluttering the kitchen utensil drawer and replace them with new OXO products that, as its Web site says, "feel great, look great, and perform with excellence."

Industry Snapshot

Total spending on kitchenware and housewares, including tabletop and dinnerware products, was $37.1 billion in 2002, up from $35.6 billion in 2000 (see Figure 8.16). That represents a 4.1 percent increase in spending on kitchenware products. Small appliances, many of them devoted to kitchen duty, grew 7.9 percent over the two years, while sales of traditional kitchenware, utensils, cooking equipment, and tabletop grew more slowly—only 3.6 percent in the same period.

FIGURE 8.16

Total Kitchenware and Housewares Industry Snapshot

	2000	2002	% CHG '00-'02
Total Personal Consumption in millions	$35,635	$37,104	4.1
Total housewares	30,993	32,097	3.6
Plastic dinnerware	1,581	1,622	2.6
China and other dinnerware	9,298	9,597	3.2
Flatware	3,936	3,915	-0.5
Glassware	4,029	4,184	3.8
Silver serving pieces	465	455	-2.2
Other serving pieces	1,457	1,488	2.1
Nonelectric cookware	10,228	10,847	6.1
Total small appliances	4,642	5,007	7.9

Source: Bureau of Economic Analysis; Bureau of Labor Statistics Consumer Expenditure Survey Diary

Salton with sales of $922.5 million in 2002, is a major player in kitchen appliances sold under the Salton name, as well as George Foreman, Toastmaster, Juiceman, Farberware, Melitta, White-Westinghouse, Kenmore, Breadman, Maxim, and others. Every year its product designers dream up new special features to add to their appliances to render last year's model obsolete, so shoppers are justified replacing a perfectly serviceable indoor grill, toaster, juicer, or breadmaker with the latest and greatest. The company's newest strategy is to expand into the bed and bath category with new personal-care appliances that appeal to the company's existing health-conscious consumers.

Retail Overview

Kitchenware and housewares are widely available at every discount department store, traditional department store, hardware store, and virtually every grocery store. Even convenience stores get into the act selling bottle and can openers and other necessities for off-hours household emergencies. The retail market share leaders, however, are the discounters, including the big three—Wal-Mart, Kmart, and Target. In Unity Marketing's latest survey, some 44 percent of shoppers made purchases of these items in discount stores (see Figure 8.17). Traditional department stores, such as Sears, JCPenney, and others, followed close behind, servicing 40 percent of shoppers. Nonstore retailers, including television shopping, the Internet, and mail order catalogs, are a growing source for these goods, with some 10 percent of shoppers making kitchenware purchases without crossing the threshold of a store.

FIGURE 8.17

Housewares Market Share Leaders

	EST. SALES 2002
Wal-Mart (4,775 stores)	$10.3 billion
Kmart (1,500 stores)	3.6 billion
Target (1,100 stores)	2.6 billion
Federated Department Stores (450 stores)	1.4 billion
Sears (about 2, 200 stores)	1.4 billion
Bed Bath & Beyond (500 stores)	1.3 million
May Company (450 stores)	1.1 billion
Williams-Sonoma (480 stores)	950 million

Source: HFN magazine

Purchase Drivers

Often viewed as a necessity rather than a discretionary purchase, a significant amount of spending on kitchenware is for storage containers to store all the other unnecessary "stuff" people buy, accumulate, and collect. Along with a clean house, people crave an organized house. As one focus group respondent explained: "With all the men [i.e., husband and three sons] in my house, everything is a mess. I would love to have it better organized. There would be less stress if it was better organized. Right now, it is all ripped apart."

In servicing the need to store the things we buy, Newell-Rubbermaid, a $7.5 billion company, which generates nearly 70 percent of total company sales in housewares products, is on to something. The company has been uniquely successful at taking generic everyday housewares and making them more special, more highly positioned, and more in demand among consumers, through branding. Their housewares brand portfolio includes Rubbermaid, Levolor, Calaphon, Pyrex, and Kirsch. The company has moved up-market in recent acquisitions, such as Paper Mate/Parker, Burnes of Boston, Graco, and Little Tikes. By adding more exclusive brands to its portfolio, the company is making a strategic move toward selling products that satisfy consumers' emotional as well as physical and practical needs.

Demographic Variables

Being a gender-neutral category, men and women report purchasing kitchenware and housewares accessories nearly equally. Younger consumers under age 35 are the leading buyers in this category, but purchase incidence remains relatively high through age 65 when purchase incidence drops sharply.

Purchase incidence is fairly even across all income levels, but rises sharply among the most affluent households, those of $75,000 and above. Clearly the more affluent have less need to get a couple of more years use out of older appliances and kitchenware and so can respond to marketer's pitches for "new and improved." These consumers also have been investing in kitchen remodeling in unprecedented numbers. After an investment of $25,000 to $50,000 on new appliances, cabinets, countertops, and fixtures, what is a thousand or two more spent on getting new small appliances, cookware, and utensils to update the whole cooking experience?

Household size and presence of children in the home relate to purchase incidence, as the larger households and those with children under age 18 in the home express a greater need to buy kitchenware and other housewares.

Key demographics of buyers of kitchenware.

- Men and women are equally involved.
- Trend is toward consumers under age 35.
- Highest-income households buy more.
- Larger households buy more.
- Presence of children increases incidence.

WHAT PEOPLE BUY: LAMPS AND LIGHTING ACCESSORIES

Just under one-third of households (30 percent) bought lamps and lighting accessories in 2003, about equal to the purchase incidence in 2001. While lighting is an essential component of everyday life, it also serves a decorative function, with lamps being a key decorative accessory. The effects of lighting are a key element for creating a mood of peacefulness and harmony in the home. People buy lamps and lighting as much for need as desire, making them essential yet discretionary.

Industry Snapshot

The lamps category is tracked along with the personal consumption of clocks and other durable furnishings by the Bureau of Economic Analysis (see Figure 8.18). In 2002, the sales of lamps and lighting accessories, along with other durables, totaled $32.6 billion, an increase of 3.6 percent over sales of $31.5 billion in 2000.

FIGURE 8.18

Lamps, Clocks, and Other Durable Furnishings Industry Snapshot

	2000	2002	% CHG '00-'02
Total Personal Consumption in millions	$31,493	$32,616	3.6

Source: Bureau of Economic Analysis

Retail Overview

As in so many other categories of home furnishings, lamps are widely available at many different types of outlets, including discount department stores, traditional department stores, hardware stores, home furnishings stores, and specialty stores. But unlike so many other home products, the discount department stores have less of a stranglehold on sales in the category. Only 31 percent of lamp buyers reported shopping for lamps in discount stores in the past year, according to Unity Marketing's latest survey. Some 26 percent shopped at traditional department stores, while 24 percent went to furniture and home furnishings stores for these items. Rounding out the top retail sources, 22 percent turned to their local hardware store or home improvement center to buy lamps. (Please note: Shoppers could shop in different types of stores throughout the year, so percentages do not add to 100 percent.)

Purchase Drivers

New lamps and lighting can change the look and feel of a room, yet often consumers buy them as part of a more extensive makeover. As seen in other home décor purchases, one purchase—say a new chair or a new rug—made to replace a worn-out item often results in a cascade of additional home purchases justified by the original purchase. Since lamps are mechanical, replacing a broken or worn-out lamp can become the driving force behind more extensive household purchases. One respondent's example illustrates this point perfectly: "All our furniture is hand-me-downs, but I needed new lamps for the family room. Then I needed to get new furniture there, too. It was long overdue."

Demographic Variables

Men and women participate equally in the purchase of lamps and lighting accessories for their home. The peak age for the purchase of lamps and lighting, ages 18 to 24, corresponds with the household-formation years, but purchase remains strong through age 54, then drops off sharply after age 55.

Households with incomes of $50,000 or more report the highest incidence for purchasing lamps and lighting accessories. The presence of children in the home and household size doesn't markedly impact purchase incidence of lamps and lights.

Key demographics of buyers of lamps and lighting.

- This is a gender-neutral category.
- Purchase incidence rises with income, as households with incomes of $50,000 or more buy more.
- Peak purchase age is 18 to 24, but remains strong through age 54.

WHAT PEOPLE BUY: PICTURE FRAMES

In 2003, just under half of U.S. households (48 percent) bought picture frames, a slight decline from the 52 percent found in 2001. With more people buying digital cameras and thus having new pictures to display in their homes and offices, the picture frame industry has responded by offering new designs in frames that add visual interest and contribute to the overall presentation. Appreciative consumers are spending more on picture frames as a result.

Industry Snapshot

Gift picture frames, intended to frame snapshots and smaller pictures and sold mainly in gift shops and gift departments of department stores and mass merchants, represented over a $1.3 billion market in 2002. Sales of gift picture frames have remained steady since 2000, according to Unity Marketing's *Gifts and Decorative Accents Report, 2003* (see Figure 8.19).

Retail Overview

Ubiquitous at retail, picture frames are found in mass merchants, traditional department stores, housewares and home furnishings stores,

FIGURE 8.19

Picture Frames Industry Snapshot

	2000	2002	% CHG '00-'02
Retail Sales in millions	$1,339	$1,297	–3.1

Source: Unity Marketing, Gifts and Decorative Accents Report, 2003

gift stores, and in many of the nation's 4,500 specialty photography stores. But the places where the majority of shoppers (50 percent) turn to buy new frames are discount department stores. For example, Wal-Mart's photo-finishing department offers to enlarge one the shopper's photographs and put it in a special frame for one low packaged price. Traditional department stores are the next most widely shopped source, selected by 34 percent of shoppers.

Purchase Drivers

Who doesn't have pictures of family and friends displayed on their mantel, end tables, or book shelves? Picture frames satisfy a universal need for people to create personal mementos and remembrances. This makes picture frames a popular gift item, presented to remember life events, as one consumer said: "I think they make great gifts. I've done this with wedding gifts. I'll get a silver photo album and have their name put on it."

Until fairly recently, the focus of picture frame manufacturers was to simply "frame" a picture, with the picture being the center of attention. However, a few years ago, picture frame companies discovered that the frame itself could add interest to the display and they started to offer more fashionable, stylized frames. Consumers gobbled them up as they found that distinctive frames added value to their prized and cherished pictures.

Demographic Variables

Young women are the most likely shoppers to buy picture frames. Some 53 percent of women purchased frames in the past year, compared to 44 percent of men, showing that women take the lead in purchasing frames for their homes. Purchase incidence is highest among the most youthful households, aged 18 to 34. However, purchase incidence remains strong among ages 35 to 64, and drops sharply after age 65.

Rising income relates to rising picture frame purchasing incidence, with purchasing highest among households with incomes of $50,000 and above. The presence of children in the home has a significant impact on the purchase incidence of picture frames, with only 43 percent of households without children purchasing, compared to 57 percent of those with children. Having three or more people living in the home also relates to increased picture frame purchase.

Key demographics of buyers of picture frames.

- Purchasers are more likely to be female.
- Purchase incidence rises with rising income, with households of $50,000 and above being the most active.
- Households with children and those with three or more members buy more.
- Younger households aged 18 to 34 buy more.

WHAT PEOPLE BUY: TABLETOP CHINA, CRYSTAL, SILVER, STERLING FLATWARE, AND OTHER DINNERWARE

Purchase incidence of tabletop products was 16 percent in 2003, about even with results of the 2000 survey, after jumping sharply in 2001 to 26 percent. With purchase incidence going up and down, it is likely to be driven by home entertaining and other special occasion needs, including wedding occasions where tabletop is popular.

For example, more specialty retailers are merchandising their dinnerware departments with specially themed groupings that are offered as a more prestigious option than paper plates for entertaining or other special occasions. The patterns are clearly not intended for permanent, long-term use. A recent trip to Pier 1 found a whole range of very attractively priced, color-coordinated tabletop items for spring, including dinnerware, chargers, stemware, napkin rings, and table linens, perfectly suited to setting a spring-fling table, but clearly not appropriate for year-round use. So instead of going to Wal-Mart and spending $10 on tacky paper places, you can go to Pier 1 and drop a $100 but set your party table in much more style.

More sophisticated consumers are expanding their selection of dinnerware from everyday and formal patterns by buying different dinnerware patterns to match the season, holiday, or special mood of the occasion. For many tabletop companies, their holiday dinnerware patterns, such as the classic Christmas tree pattern from Spode and Lenox's holiday pattern, are suited only to use from the day after Thanksgiving until New Year's, but the holiday lines are among their company's strongest sellers. Home-decorating mavens, notably Martha Stewart, have promoted the trend to mix and match different dinnerware patterns by teaching consumers how to pull off the tricky business of setting the table with a more polished style.

Industry Snapshot

With retail sales tracked in the housewares category by the Bureau of Economic Analysis, sales of tabletop dinnerware, including china and other dinnerware, glassware, and flatware, including sterling silver and crystal, totaled $19.6 billion, up 2.4 percent over sales of $19.2 billion in 2000 (see Figure 8.20). Tabletop items are also popular gifts for weddings and housewarming occasions.

Retail Overview

Traditional department stores, rather than the discount department stores, are the primary source for shoppers in this category. Some 39 percent of tabletop buyers turned to a traditional department store to buy this class of goods. On the other hand, discount department stores garnered 28 percent of the shoppers, as other specialty stores drew 21 percent. Nonstore retailers, including the Internet, television, and direct mail, are a growing outlet for tabletop capturing 12 percent of tabletop purchasers in the past year.

The tabletop industry is finding new outlets for its products as consumers turn to the national specialty home furnishings chains for tabletop and dinnerware. Crate & Barrel, Williams-Sonoma, and Pottery Barn rank among the top 25 tabletop retailers nationwide. Department stores continue their stronghold on the bridal market, but specialty stores are also joining the game, as many, such as Pier 1, have already instituted bridal registries within their stores. At mass-market retailers, Martha

FIGURE 8.20

Tabletop Dinnerware, Flatware, Glassware, and Serving Industry Snapshot

	2000	2002	% CHG '00-'02
Total Personal Consumption in millions	$19,185	$19,638	2.4
China and other dinnerware	9,298	9,597	3.2
Flatware	3,936	3,915	−0.5
Glassware	4,029	4,184	3.8
Silver serving pieces	465	455	−2.2
Other serving pieces	1,457	1,488	2.1

Source: Bureau of Economic Analysis; Bureau of Labor Statistics Consumer Expenditure Survey Diary

Stewart's Everyday at Kmart and Michael Grave's work with Target are at-tracting a new clientele for tabletop.

Purchase Drivers

The market for tabletop, particularly what is called the "upstairs" market for fine china, crystal, and sterling, has been traditionally associ-ated with the bridal market. Each year 2.2 to 2.5 million Americans get married. As a result, the bridal market for tabletop has been stable since 1970. The bridal market is expected to grow over the next five to ten years, as the millennial generation (i.e., the babies of the baby boomers born from 1977 to about 1994 and numbering 71 million in all) reaches young adulthood and first marriage.

With tabletop manufacturers primarily focused on department stores as an outlet for their bridal business, the continued decline in de-partment stores as a retailing force is likely to have a negative impact on the tabletop industry as well. Today's brides are turning to specialty re-tailers offering patterns and styles that are a better match with their more casual lifestyles. As a result, the traditional fine china and dinner-ware companies are losing their connection with their key target market. One young married woman said: "I have a lot of stuff I got as wedding gifts. All it does is sit in the china cabinet and gather dust. It looks nice, but with the kids, I find we use paper plates when we have parties." An-other describes it this way: "You get married and you pick what you want. Then you put it away and use it once a year. It is nice to have for holi-days or special occasions, but it is something you do once and then it fades. I was all excited when I got it, but after the first year, it's no big deal anymore."

After age 35 or so, women often return to the tabletop market to re-place their original bridal patterns with styles more suited to whom they have become. One table devotee put it this way: "Tabletop is all about your stage in life. I have had china ever since we were married, but it doesn't fit me anymore. I only use it at Christmas. I love to set a nice table, but I prefer something different today." A passion for tabletop may strike more mature consumers as they venture back into the market to find new styles: "Tabletop is my passion. I love good crystal and setting a really nice table. I have four different china patterns that I use on dif-ferent occasions. Tabletop is my hobby."

Demographic Variables

The purchase of tabletop china, dinnerware, crystal, and sterling and stainless flatware is usually a joint decision, with men and women reporting a nearly equal purchase incidence in the past year. In 2003, there are two peak age periods for the purchase of tabletop: the youngest consumers, aged 18 to 24, setting up house, and the empty-nesters, aged 45 to 54. Purchase incidence of tabletop drops sharply after age 65. Hispanic households had the highest purchase incidence of tabletop, due primarily to the emphasis the Latino culture places on food and family gatherings.

Rising household income is linked to purchase, with the more affluent households of $50,000 and above more active buying tabletop. For this category, the presence of children or size of household is not linked to purchase incidence.

Key demographics of buyers of tabletop china, etc.

- This category is gender neutral.
- Higher-income households, those of $50,000 and above, buy more.
- The two prime markets are households aged 18 to 24 and 45 to 54.
- Hispanics buy more.

WHAT PEOPLE BUY: WALL DÉCOR

Consumers have two main choices when it comes to decorating their walls: either they display art or they use other types of wall décor, including sconces, mirrors, and tapestries. Purchase incidence of wall décor shot up in 2003, from one-fourth of American households purchasing wall décor in 2001 to 38 percent in 2003. As a new anti-clutter approach to home decorating is sweeping the country, consumers are turning their decorating attention away from the tabletops, mantles, and bookshelves toward the walls. With purchase incidence of both art and wall décor rising in 2003, the home's walls can be adorned without appearing too cluttered.

Industry Snapshot

The retail sales of wall décor, including sconces, mirrors, and mirror and picture frames, reached $6.2 billion, up 13.1 percent over sales of $5.5 billion in 2000 (see Figure 8.21). This vibrant category is enjoying

FIGURE 8.21
Wall Décor Industry Overview

	2000	2002	% CHG '00-'02
Personal Consumption in millions	$5,523	$6,244	13.1

Source: Unity Marketing

growth as national specialty home furnishings chains, such as Pottery Barn, Restoration Hardware, Williams-Sonoma, Pier 1, Bombay Company, Bed Bath & Beyond, and Linens 'n Things bring a more upscale design sensibility to the category.

Retail Overview

Wherever framed pictures are sold you'll likely find wall décor, while many places that don't sell pictures may well carry decorative items for the wall, such as sconces, mirrors, shelves, and other accents. Cornerstone Brand's Ballard Design catalog offers an eclectic mix of furniture along with decorative accessories. Wall décor gets major play in their book as an important element of the finely decorated home.

Purchase Drivers

Blank walls beg to be decorated. This is the main reason why consumers purchase wall décor. In a recent Unity Marketing nationwide survey among a representative sample of women shoppers, about half of the consumers said their homes had fully decorated walls, leaving another half of the households in the country a likely target market for wall decorations.

The ready availability of more fashion-forward designs has opened new possibilities for wall decoration. Mirrors are always popular, but new designs that feature mirrors with shelves offer decorating and display possibilities for vases, statues, and figurines. Wall sconces are a popular decorative item to use with candles, offering lighting possibilities beyond the tabletop.

For those considering an entrance or expansion into what is a booming category of home decorating, there is an important caveat to keep in mind. Once consumers hang things up on their walls, those things tend to stay put and become like the architectural elements of windows and doors. Whereas consumers give themselves permission to move, trade in and out, and otherwise rearrange objects displayed on tables and other flat surfaces, they don't feel so empowered when it comes to the walls. Unless there is an open space on the wall that needs to be filled, the consumer is very unlikely to take something else down and to put something new up.

Demographic Variables

Wall décor is a female-skewing category, with only 34 percent of men, as opposed to 41 percent of women, reporting a household purchase. The market for wall décor is more youthful, with consumers under 45 years of age reporting the highest purchase incidence. Purchase incidence declines with advancing age, suggesting that this decorative category has its strongest appeal to the young who are setting up new homes. The highest-income households buy more wall décor as do larger households and those with children.

Key demographics of buyers of wall décor.

- Women are more likely to purchase in this category.
- Higher income households, those of $50,000 and above, buy more.
- Households aged 18 to 44 buy more.
- Larger households and those with children buy more.

WHAT PEOPLE BUY: WINDOW COVERINGS

As a new category added to the 2003 consumer survey, window coverings, blinds, curtains, and other window treatments are an essential part of most home remodeling projects, big or small. Some 37 percent of households made a purchase of window coverings in the past year. With consumers avidly tuning into such do-it-yourself decorating shows as The Learning Channel's *Trading Spaces* and *While You Were Out,* they are learning all about the easy, quick, and cost-effective decorating possibilities available through window treatments.

Industry Overview

With retail sales of fabric window treatments tracked in the textiles category, the sales of durable window coverings, including blinds, rods, and other window hardware, totaled $5.6 billion in 2002, up 2.6 percent over sales in 2000, according to statistics compiled by the U.S. Bureau of Economic Analysis.

Netherlands-based Hunter Douglas is a worldwide leader in the window covering business. With a wide selection of product offerings from wood blinds, shades, even powered models, Hunter Douglas targets the more upscale shoppers with distribution through designers and specialty outlets, as well as national retailers like The Home Depot, Fortunoffs, and JCPenney.

Retail Overview

When thinking about covering their windows, shoppers turn primarily to three types of stores: discount department stores (used by 36 percent of shoppers in 2003), traditional department stores (34 percent), and home improvement and hardware stores (25 percent). Specialty retail is also focusing on the window treatment business. Canadian-based Blinds to Go is a chain of 100 superstores devoted exclusively to blinds and other window treatments. Country Curtains, headquartered in Stockbridge, Massachesetts, offers their exclusive line of down-home designs through 25 stores, a direct mail catalog, and the Internet.

Because many window treatments must be custom made, mail order and Internet providers are finding new avenues to reach consumers. Cataloger and Internet provider Smith+Noble specializes in selling its own line of custom window blinds, shutters, shades, and panels. Blindsexpress.com

FIGURE 8.22
Window Coverings Industry Overview

	2000	2002	% CHG '00-'02
Total Personal Consumption in millions	$14,921	$13,106	−12.2
Blinds, rods, and other window durables	5,441	5,580	2.6
Curtains and draperies	9,480	7,526	−20.6

Source: Bureau of Economic Analysis

offers name brands including Hunter Douglas, Levolor, and Kirsch at discount prices. It also teams with NBI Inc. to provide custom blind installation virtually anywhere in the country, thus giving shoppers confidence to buy products from an Internet supplier that often require expert installation.

Purchase Drivers

Window coverings are an important category within home products and one to which many consumers buying new homes or involved in redecorating pay attention. Describing the role of window coverings, a consumer said: "It is the way these make you feel. They finish the room, and set the mood of the home. It's not a brand, it's a look. It makes the house a home. It makes it your own."

The quality of window coverings is largely signaled by touch and feel for fabrics and by the brand name for window hardware. In a recent focus group, a consumer said: "I just bought Hunter Douglas silhouettes. They were $2,000 per window. I've seen Hunter Douglas advertised and a lot of my friends have them. Hunter Douglas is very well known." A key pleasure driver for consumers in this category is the opportunity it gives them to express themselves and their creativity, and to make the home unique by how they select and style the window coverings. For one consumer, window coverings are a key factor in achieving a luxurious look and feel to her home: "The fabrics are luxury to me, as is the color. It doesn't matter where you get it or how much you pay as long as it reflects your solution. So you can have luxury if you didn't spend a lot of money. I try not to put a price on luxury. It's what it does for you as a person."

Demographic Variables

Just less than 40 percent (37 percent) of U.S. households bought window coverings in the past year. A gender-neutral category, it is often one where couples make a joint purchase. While purchase incidence peaks among buyers aged 18 to 24, consumers through age 54 are fairly active in this category; however, purchase incidence drops among those over age 55. Households in all income ranges have a need for window coverings and so purchase incidence cuts across all incomes. The presence of children in the home and households with three or more members are more likely to buy window coverings than others.

Key demographics of buyers of window coverings.

- This is a gender-neutral category representing a joint purchase decision.
- All incomes purchase evenly.
- Younger households aged 18 to 24 buy more, and consumers through age 54 are still active.
- Larger households and those with children buy more.

9

TRENDS THAT IMPACT
WHY PEOPLE BUY THINGS
THEY DON'T NEED

What does the future hold for companies in the business of manufacturing, marketing, and selling discretionary products—those things that people desire but don't need? How can these new insights about why people buy things they don't need help the companies selling the product categories analyzed in Chapters 6, 7, and 8 sell more of their products? How can companies divine the future for the sales of discretionary products and develop plans for action that will increase sales and build market share? The following sections will help to answer these questions.

KEY TRENDS SHAPING THE FUTURE
OF THE CONSUMER MARKET

Tracking trends is one method many businesses use to foresee the future. Futurists—people who predict trends for businesses—make good copy sources in the media or as guests on television shows as they weave tales of what the future will look like. Who isn't fascinated when Faith Popcorn presents her vision of the evolving future coined in catchy names and phrases?

I am no futurist, but my company, Unity Marketing, does help our clients see what the future holds for their companies and how to maxi-

These trends were developing throughout the consumer psyche long before September 11, but that terrible, life-changing event has in many ways accelerated the rate of change.

mize the opportunities that are just over the horizon. We use the same tools most futurists use—wide-ranging environmental scanning, including print and electronic media scans, continuous qualitative and quantitative market research, and ongoing dialogue with key business leaders. However, the results are often different and more specific to the client's business because we focus exclusively on consumer behavior and psychology in the context of industries that market discretionary products.

Here are the key trends we are sharing with our clients today about what the future holds for their businesses. First, we will look at three demographic shifts in the population that are setting the stage for the continued evolution of the consuming trends on the horizon. These trends were developing throughout the consumer psyche long before September 11, but that terrible, life-changing event has in many ways accelerated the rate of change. It has made these trends a more prominent and more potent force in the U.S. economy.

Demographic Shift: Aging Population

Today the gigantic baby boom generation, roughly 76 million strong, is slowly advancing through its middle age and into maturity. In 2004, the vanguard of the boomer generation, born in 1946, reached age 58 while the trailing-edge boomers, born in 1964, celebrated their 40th birthdays. In the year 2011, the boomer vanguard will slip beyond age 65, marking

FIGURE 9.1
Household Projections by Age, 2000–2010 (in Millions)

	2000	2005	2010	% CHANGE 2000–2010
Total	$104.1	$108.9	$114.8	10.3
Under age 25	5.9	5.4	5.7	−3.4
25–34	18.8	15.6	17.5	−6.9
35–44	24.0	22.6	20.5	−14.2
45–54	20.2	23.9	26.3	25.2
55–64	13.6	17.3	20.7	52.2
65 and older	21.6	23.1	25.1	16.2

Source: U.S. Bureau of the Census

the entrance into their senior years. By 2029, the entire baby boom generation will officially be "seniors." The boomer generation has had a profound influence on every socioeconomic and political trend they have touched, usually due to sheer numbers alone. In our democratic culture, a generation of that many

> As they age into their senior years, the boomers' influence will continue to be felt in strong and lasting ways

people is bound to have a significant impact on everything it touches. As they age into their senior years, the boomers' influence will continue to be felt in strong and lasting ways.

In the next decade, the total number of U.S. households will grow by 10.3 percent, from 104.1 million in 2000 to 115.8 million in 2010 (see Figure 9.1). Due to the aging of the boomers, over that period the number of younger households headed by someone under age 45 will decline while the number of older households will continue to expand. The next generation with the comparable size and thus potential to impact the culture as strongly as the boomers is the millennial generation, comprised of the boomers' children, born between 1977 and 1994.

FIGURE 9.2
Household Characteristics

	AVERAGE INCOME	AVERAGE HOUSEHOLD SIZE	AVERAGE NUMBER OF CHILDREN
Total	$43,051	2.5	0.7
Under 25	18,276	1.8	0.4
25–34	42,470	2.9	1.1
35–44	53,579	3.2	1.3
45–54	59,822	2.7	0.6
55–64	49,436	2.2	0.2
65 and older	28,581	1.7	0.1
	AVERAGE NUMBER OF EARNERS	HOME-OWNERS	SOME COLLEGE
Total	1.3	65%	55%
Under 25	1.3	13	64
25–34	1.5	45	60
35–44	1.7	67	59
45–54	1.8	77	62
55–64	1.3	80	50
65 and older	0.4	80	38

Source: U.S. Bureau of the Census

Marketers who are planning for the future need to assess the impact of the aging population on their marketplace.

The two fastest-growing household age segments will be those aged 55 to 64 (52.2 percent growth) and 45 to 54 (26.2 percent). In most of the discretionary-product categories examined in Chapters 6, 7, and 8, we observed a marked change in consumer purchasing behavior starting at about age 55 and well established by age 65. This dramatic change in spending, combined with growth in the number of mature households, signals shifts in demand for most discretionary products.

Today, marketers who are planning for the future need to assess the impact of the aging population on their marketplace. Each company should understand how the aging of the population will affect spending behavior. When today's 35-to-44-year-olds reach age 45 to 54, will they behave the same as they did when they were younger or more like the 45-to-54-year-olds preceding them? The answer to this question will have profound implications for discretionary product marketers, because consumer purchases of discretionary products start to slow after age 55 and drop sharply at age 65.

FIGURE 9.3

Key Demographics Related to Aging

- Highest income: Households aged 45 to 54 have the highest average income, $59,822, followed by those aged 35 to 44, $53,579.

- Largest households: Those aged 35 to 44 have 3.2 individuals on average.

- Largest number of children: Households aged 35 to 44 have the largest number of children at 1.3, followed closely by those aged 25 to 34.

- Most earners: Households aged 45 to 54 have the highest number of individual wage earners (1.8), followed closely by those aged 35 to 44 (1.7), and those aged 25 to 34 (1.5).

- Home ownership rises with age: Households headed by persons aged 45 and older report the highest percentage of home ownership.

- More-educated: Only 38 percent of Americans older than age 65 have completed at least some college, compared with 62 percent of those 45 to 54. The most highly educated age group in our society is those under 25, where 64 percent have at least some college.

FUTURE TRENDS

While the baby boomers age, the babies of the baby boomers, called the *millennial generation,* which numbers about 71 million people born between 1977 and about 1994, will begin to advance into adulthood. This demographic shift will result in two huge generational waves—baby boomers in the upper end and millennials at the lower end—bracketing the trough represented by the 41 million strong GenerationX in the middle. The result: The overall consumer economy will polarize, with significant growth at the luxury end targeting the affluent, empty-nesting baby boomers and strong demand for economy priced goods for the millennials who will be setting up homes, having families, and facing the challenge of stretching a small paycheck across the demands of a growing family. This polarized consumer economy will be a totally new experience for marketers and retailers, because the consumer story for the past century has been all about the great big growing middle class. Now the consumer economic action will be directed toward the opposite ends of the spectrum.

So along with the significant growth prospects at the luxury and low-priced economy end, the future also holds a paradoxical twist. The affluent baby boomer consumers who can afford to pay full price for their luxuries will inevitably reach down to take advantage of the incredible bargain offerings for those less economically endowed. Even more interesting, the millennials with limited budgets and growing families will reach up to buy those high-priced luxury items to which they aspire.

We are already seeing this trend of "class" luxury consumers reaching down to mass and the "mass" moderate income folks extending to "class" today. In two consecutive years of surveys among the luxury consumers, we found that in every product category but one—luxury cosmetics and beauty products—the majority of shoppers bought their last luxury item on sale or at a discount. The luxury consumers are savvy shoppers and they know how to find a bargain. When you find a $300 jacket on sale for $150, you get an experiential thrill that means you are a winner in the shopping game. Likewise, the new book, *Trading Up: The New American Luxury,* by Michael Silverstein and Neil Fiske, documents the trend of the masses trading up to the classes by scrimping and saving in one category of their life in order to buy luxury in another. So the hip-hop generation has embraced the Burberry

> The luxury consumers are savvy shoppers and they know how to find a bargain.

FIGURE 9.4
Best Market for Discretionary Products

- Consumer households aged 35 to 44 spend slightly less on household furnishings ($1,590 on average).

- A greater percentage of the total spending of households aged 35 to 44 is for housing (33.2 percent) and food (14.3 percent), because they have more family members.

- Households aged 45 to 54 have the highest income, spend the most in general, spend the most in the household furnishings and equipment categories ($1,980 on average), and spend the most on gifts to others outside the household ($1,690).

- Consumer households aged 55 to 64 have the third highest average income ($49,436). Their spending on household furnishings ($1,779) and gifts ($1,537) is exceeded only by the 45 to 54 age group.

Source: Bureau of Labor Statistics, Consumer Expenditures Survey

plaid and young professional women invest in Manolo Blahnik shoes while they buy their dress suits on sale at Banana Republic.

Demographic Shift: Rising Education Level

The average educational level of American consumers is on the rise, and our government's continued emphasis on public education foreshadows a continuation of this trend. Younger people in particular are far more educated than the older population. The most highly educated age group in our society is those under age 25, where 64 percent have some college or more educational attainment. Many consumer marketers have largely overlooked the potential impact of this key demographic shift. Linked to income levels, educational attainment plays a larger role in consumer behavior than many marketers recognize.

More educated consumers have very different needs and expectations of the products they buy and the brands they support than less educated consumers do. More educated consumers come equipped with a more highly developed and complex set of consuming values, and they know how to research and evaluate information to guide their decision making. Remember the tsu-

> More educated consumers come equipped with a more highly developed and complex set of consuming values.

nami impact that Ralph Nader and his book *Unsafe at Any Speed* had on the U.S. car industry? He single-handedly had more to do with the shaping of the modern cars we drive than any other individual, company, or industry leader. Think what might happen to any consumer industry if a twenty-first-century "Ralph Nader" examined its product safety, the welfare of its workers, its contribution to society, its protection of the environment, or even its support of governments or regimes that allow terrorist organizations to exist within their borders. A more educated consumer population may well present new challenges, especially for companies and industries that may not be as "politically correct" as others. Companies can no longer afford to sidestep the safety of their products or react defensively if some product has a flaw or fails completely. Consumers today are just too smart. At the same time, they are more informed and educated in how to manage risks, and they are far more security conscious. Abraham Lincoln said: "You can fool all the people some of the time, and some all of the time, but you cannot fool all the people all the time." Today, with the rising educational levels of the population, it is getting harder and harder to fool them at all.

The benefits of more educated consumers. A more highly educated consumer market represents a challenge to some companies, but for others, it brings wonderful new opportunities. Branding is all about establishing an emotional connection between the product or brand and the consumer. You can communicate with a more educated consumer on a deeper, conceptual level. More-sophisticated, better-educated consumers are receptive to complex branding messages. They have the intellectual tools to absorb such messages and internalize them. In fact, more educated consumers demand information about their favorite products, companies, and brands. They need information to make their consuming decisions.

In certain categories, such as electronics, computers, art, and books, education level is linked to increased purchase incidence. Marketers of these products can anticipate a prosperous future, as a growing market of sophisticated, educationally enhanced consumers demands more of these products. Look at how a company like Gateway has taken the opportunity to sell to better educated customers through a campaign that uses humor and irony.

> Branding is all about establishing an emotional connection between the product or brand and the consumer.

GATEWAY COMPUTER
Subtle irony sells computers.

Frank Purdue said: "It takes a tough man to make a tender chicken." Ted Waitt, CEO of Gateway Computers, is proving it takes a "smart" cow to tell a "dumb" man how to sell computers.

Any high-tech CEO who lets himself play straight man to a talking cow is supersmart in my book. Using irony in product marketing messages has been a big "no-no," because it takes a sophisticated audience to be able to understand it and see through it. However, Waitt and the smart, talking cow reinterpreted the dynamics of the Bugs Bunny-Elmer Fudd relationship, and in doing so worked marvelously together in communicating their marketing message about the latest and greatest computer gadgetry from Gateway. This series of ads talked to Gateway's sophisticated, educated, entertainment-literate audience.

It is so humbling and so refreshing to see Waitt let the cow be the smart guy and such a wonderful counterpoint to his high-tech CEO cohorts. I personally cannot see Bill Gates or Michael Dell playing second fiddle to a cow, but I would like them more if they did.

What these ads said to me as a consumer is that Gateway is really, truly

a different computer company. If Ted Waitt can take directions from the cow, then I, techno-illiterate that I am, can go to the Gateway store and get good direction and advice. I do not need to know anything about computers to buy a Gateway. The cow knows, and that is all that matters. Brilliant, brilliant marketing!

Demographic Shift: Minority Majority

In California, non-Hispanic whites are already a minority. Within the next 60 years, that will be true throughout the United States. White Americans of non-Hispanic origin will fall below 50 percent of the population, while Hispanics, blacks, and other ethnic groups together will represent the national majority. Called the "minority majority" trend, it will bring big changes to our country's cultural, political, economic, and consumer landscape.

> While emotions are universal and cross all cultural divides, the ways people from different cultures express those emotions differ.

While we do not brand one culture bad and another one good, we recognize that people from different cultures behave differently. With America being the melting pot of the world, ethnic stereotypes are part of our cultural mythology. Anglos are reserved, Scots are frugal, French are romantic, Italians are demonstrative, Germans are stubborn, and so forth. The foundations of those ethnic stereotypes are the shared cultural values, expectations, and behavior patterns that children absorb as they grow up in a culture. While emotions are universal and cross all cultural divides, the ways people from different cultures express those emotions differ. Because people make discretionary purchases for emotional reasons, we need to understand how people with different cultural origins express those emotions as consumers. It is in these differences that opportunities and challenges will abound for discretionary marketers in America over the next 60 or so years. In our examination of consumers' purchasing behavior, we found some, but not a lot of differences based on ethnic heritage. For example, black Americans place a higher priority on education than non-Hispanic whites do as a justifier for discretionary purchases, and they also purchase TVs and other electronic equipment at a higher rate. While few ethnic distinctions were uncovered in this research, we expect more differences in ethnic consumer behavior to be expressed in the next half-century as the minority majority trend expands.

The discretionary product categories that are highly tradition bound, such as Christmas and seasonal decorations, home décor, housewares, and tabletop, are expected to be the most affected by the minority majority trend. The whole business of tabletop dinnerware, for example, is predicted to be strongly influenced by the rise of the Hispanic population and their different culturally based needs and expectations for dinnerware and tableware. Just like every culture has its unique cuisine, every culture has its own way of dining, setting the table, serving, and participating in the meal. Today's tabletop industry, especially its mar-

> The discretionary product categories that are highly tradition bound are expected to be the most affected by the minority majority trend.

FIGURE 9.5

Population Projections, 2000–2050

		PERCENT OF POPULATION BY HISPANIC AND NON-HISPANIC ORIGIN		
	Hispanic	Non-Hispanic White	Non-Hispanic Black	Non-Hispanic Other
2000	11.8%	71.4%	11.2%	4.6%
2010	14.6	67.3	12.5	5.6
2020	17.0	63.8	12.8	6.5
2030	19.4	60.1	13.0	7.5
2040	21.9	56.3	13.1	8.6
2050	24.3	52.8	13.2	9.7

Source: U.S. Census Bureau, Population Reports, May 2000

keters of fine china, traces its heritage to eighteenth- and nineteenth-century upper-crust England, and it clings to that heritage even today. But how many contemporary American consumers aspire to dine as nineteenth-century English landed gentry did?

There is a great opportunity for tabletop and housewares companies to market to the growing ethnically diverse America. However, they need to research and understand each culture's unique dining heritage in order to market contemporary products that reflect that heritage. There is a strong risk for established tabletop companies that they will fall by the wayside if they do not figure out how to bridge the cultural divide and reach out to the emerging minority majority consumers.

CONSUMER TRENDS

Having explored the cultural shifts that are giving rise to the trends, here are the major trends on the horizon that will have the strongest impact on discretionary product manufacturers.

Shift from Buying Things to Buying Experiences

Part of our popular cultural mythology says that when people reach middle age they undergo a personal identity crisis, the "midlife crisis," that often is played out in the consumer marketplace. Stereotypically, a man may address his midlife crisis by buying a little red sports car or, more sinisterly, by trading in his middle-aged wife for a new, younger model. A woman may get a facelift, dye her hair, find a younger man, or, empowered by "menopausal zest," find new energy to pursue a career or hobby. When grandchildren come along, the new grandparents may shower presents and gifts on their grandchildren to make up for some of the inadequacies that their children may have faced when they were growing up because money was tighter. This is the life stage that the

> With the attitude of "been there, done that" about buying more things, boomers will turn away from a consuming focus on things to a hunger for experiences and personal development.

boomer generation is now approaching en masse, and it will change the fortunes of many companies that sell and market to people who buy things they don't need.

In their middle years, the members of the baby boom generation will face the inevitability of their mortality. In doing so, they will try to make up for lost time and the things they may have missed by directing their energy and money toward experiences and away from the continued acquisition of material things. With the attitude of "been there, done that" about buying more things, boomers will turn away from a consuming focus on things to a hunger for experiences and personal development. Service industries that satisfy the mature boomer's craving for personal enhancement will fare well after 2010. These include travel providers, especially adventure travel modified for aging boomers' health and fitness levels; health and beauty spas; and colleges and adult-education experiences, including training, such as cooking or language schools. Consumers will turn away from a focus on the thing consumed (i.e., the noun) to the experience (i.e., the verb).

G e t t i n g   I t   R i g h t

VIKING RANGE CORPORATION
Viking's new take on experiential retailing.

With the luxury end of the major appliances industry accounting for an estimated $5 billion of the total industry's $31.6 billion in 2001 sales, Viking Range Corporation claimed to be the first to offer "professional" ranges to the homeowner in 1987.

Since that first commercial-type range, the company now offers a complete line of home appliances for the kitchen, as well as outdoor products for the pool and patio.

Recognizing that selling luxury extends far beyond the thing (i.e., the appliance) to selling the whole experience (i.e., a professional-quality dining experience in the home), Viking launched its first Viking Culinary Arts Center in Memphis, Tennesee, in 1999 as a center for training home cooks. It then acquired HomeChef, a 27-year-old San Francisco–based cooking school, in November 2000, and so aggressively launched itself into experience marketing. Today, the company operates eight Viking Culinary Arts Centers in Georgia, Missouri, New York, Ohio, Pennsylvania, Tennessee, and Texas and four Viking HomeChef locations in California.

The Viking Culinary Arts Center concept is a simple and an organic extension of its flagship appliance brand. "Viking products have always been designed for the true epicurean enthusiast, and the Viking Culinary Arts Center is a way for Viking to really connect with our consumers," explains Joe Sherman, president and CEO of Viking Culinary Arts Center. "It is a natural extension of the Viking brand because now consumers can come in to test drive Viking products before choosing which to buy."

But the center is far more than a place to "test drive" your new stove. It's part gourmet theater-in-the-round where world-class chefs prepare their signature dishes in state-of-the-art demonstration kitchens. All decked out with overhead video monitors, each participant has a clear overhead view of the cooking surfaces.

Another aspect of the Viking Culinary Arts Center concept is a hands-on cooking school. Students can choose between one-, three-, or five-day classes and work on cooking stations outfitted with Viking professional appliances. The curriculum covers everything from basic baking techniques to preparing a restaurant-quality gourmet meal.

And no Viking Culinary Arts Center would be complete without the retail store, where consumers can purchase the tools they need to create their new recipes. The stores sell only professional-type, high-caliber equipment, from spoons and spatulas to complete cookware sets, along with gourmet food ingredients from sea salt to Belgian chocolate and pasta sauce. While Viking major appliances are not available in the store, consumers are referred to their local dealer.

The three aspects of the center—cooking theater, cooking school, and store—provide, as the company's Web site describes, "a unique venue where Viking consumers can fuel their passion for cooking and experi-

ence the full Viking product line in action."
There is also an "evangelical" aspect to this
program. In effect, it helps create the ideal
target market for Viking in the future. The
thinking goes that a better-educated, more-
sophisticated home cook will be better able
to discern the ultimate benefits of a Viking
appliance over other brands.

> From *things* to *experience*,
> that is the motto for the
> future for marketers and
> retailers that sell things
> people don't need.

From *things* to *experience*, that is the motto for the future for marketers and retailers that sell things people don't need. Ultimately, all emotionally driven purchasing is about buying a thing to achieve a feeling,
enhance an experience, or get an emotional lift. The Viking Culinary
Arts Center is an example of a product-based marketer fully embracing
the challenges of experiential retailing. As Fred Carl, the president of
Viking says: "The Culinary Arts Center was developed around the concept that Viking wants to provide our consumers with the best cooking
experience possible. That includes not only the appliances they cook on,
but the techniques and cooking tools they use."

As boomers pursue new experiential passions, they will need tools,
equipment, and accessories to support them in their new pursuits. Discretionary product providers can position themselves for success by providing new products to enhance boomers' experiences and adventures.
Durable-goods providers, such as automobile manufacturers, will fill such
a need as will those who manufacture and
market sporting goods, personal-care items,
books, housewares, and entertainment. For
example, boomers will need new recreational
vehicles to take them on their new adventures.
I predict they will eschew the big, bulky, luxurious RV models so admired by today's mature generation. Instead, they will favor more
simplified, environmentally friendly models
that can take them off the highway. Think
modified VW bus concept crossed with an
SUV, equipped with a bed, kitchen, and bath,
with a powerful engine and four-wheel drive.

> The future focus in
> consumer behavior will
> be about buying the
> experience, so manufac-
> turers and marketers
> must think beyond the
> features and benefits of
> the product they are
> selling, to how that
> product supports or
> enhances an experience.

The future focus in consumer behavior will be about buying the experience, so manufacturers and marketers must think beyond the features and benefits of the product they are selling, to how that product supports or enhances an experience. If you came of age in the 1960s as I did, you will remember the strong anti-materialism ethic running through the youth culture. At the same time, 1960s youth hungered after new, mind-opening experiences. Some members of the boomer generation self-destructively turned to sex, drugs, and rock 'n' roll to fulfill much of this craving for experience. I sincerely hope that boomers learned from their youthful excesses, as I foresee that they will participate in a second adolescence in their senior years.

With a "been there, done that" attitude, some boomers will turn away from the pursuit of materialism and excessive consumption and save their money for adventures. New and exciting experiences in their second adolescence could include climbing Mount Everest or at least trekking to base camp. They might decide to travel to China, hike the

FIGURE 9.6

Quarterly Retail and E-commerce Sales, 1999 to 2003

	E-COMMERCE SALES IN MILLIONS	% CHANGE E-COMMERCE SALES PREVIOUS PERIOD
1999 4th Quarter	$ 5,393	(NA)
2000 1st Quarter	5,772	6.1
2nd Quarter	6,250	9.2
3rd Quarter	7,079	13.3
4th Quarter	9,248	30.6
Total 2000	**28,349**	**(NA)**
2001 1st Quarter	8,009	−13.4
2ndQuarter	7,904	−1.3
3rd Quarter	7,894	−0.1
4th Quarter	10,788	36.7
Total 2002	**34,595**	**22.0**
2002 1st Quarter	9,470	−12.2
2nd Quarter	9,761	3.1
3rd Quarter	10,465	7.2
4th Quarter	13,770	31.6
Total 2002	**43,466**	**25.6**
2003 1st Quarter	11,928	−13.4
2nd Quarter	12,464	4.5
3rd Quarter	13,284	6.6
4th Quarter	17,226	29.7
Total 2003	**54,902**	**26.3**

Source: Department of Commerce, U.S. Census Bureau

Appalachian Trail, learn to cook in Paris, or get an advanced degree in English literature. Some may take up painting or photography; set off cross country on a Harley; or learn to fly, sky dive, or balloon. Closer to home, others may take up a second language, join a theater group, form a "garage" band, or, like me, take piano lessons after 30-odd years without touching a keyboard.

> With a "been there, done that" attitude, some boomers will turn away from the pursuit of materialism and excessive consumption and save their money for adventures.

Oh, did I mention that I had to buy a piano to play so I could take those piano lessons? Pretty soon, I will be ready to buy the baby grand I really wanted but felt was a little too extravagant before I knew whether I could recover my piano-playing skills. The Steinway Company and my music store will be thrilled.

Consumer Trend: Consumers Will Crave Reality

Our society is undergoing a digital revolution. More of the equipment we interact with daily—our office computers, cellular phones, microwave ovens, digital televisions, entertainment systems, radios, and even our cars—are digitized and virtually unknowable to ordinary human beings. Where one might have conceptually understood how an analog telephone, television set, or precomputerized car operated, today you need a degree in computer science or electrical engineering to even begin to comprehend how digital models work. Operating many of these machines presents a challenge to the techno-illiterates. I cannot set the timer on my microwave oven or program the VCR to tape a show without getting out the manuals, but luckily, I have two sons who can do those things for me.

The Internet is playing a bigger role in our lives. School children today learn about computers right along with their lessons in reading, writing, and arithmetic. They are exposed to the Internet, too, with 95 percent of U.S. schools having Internet access in 1999, according to the U.S. Center for Education Statistics. Internet use is rising dramatically across the entire population, with the average number of hours spent per person per year on the Internet rising from 74 hours in 1998 to 122 hours in 2000, a 65 percent increase. In 2000, roughly 43 percent of the adult population used the Internet in the past 30 days, according to a survey reported by Mediamark Research. The Internet is also playing an increased role in the commercial side of consumers' lives.

The Internet's rapid growth as a commercial powerhouse will have profound influences on the way people shop in the years to come.

Today, close to two-thirds of adult Americans access the Internet, as compared to 47 percent back in 2000, according to research from the Pew Research Center. Today, the Internet is becoming a central hub for communications (e-mail is the most widely used Internet application, while instant messaging, or IM, brings an entirely new way to communicate among youthful Internet users who are its main users today), information and research (searching the Internet for news, health, or cultural information has grown by 50 percent since 2000), and commerce (the number of people who have made purchases online grew by 63 percent since 2000, with online travel services posting some of the greatest gains in e-commerce activity).

As the Internet assumes a growing role in the commercial side of consumers' lives, they spent $54.9 billion over the Internet in 2003, a 26.3 percent increase from 2002. While this is only 1.6 percent of total retail sales, the Internet's rapid growth as a commercial powerhouse will have profound influences on the way people shop in the years to come.

As our contemporary American society becomes more "virtual," with consumers turning to computers and the Internet for their work, social interaction, entertainment, and shopping, there will be a swing back to the "real" world. Consumers will crave reality. We live and will always live in a real world bounded by time and space and governed by the physical laws of the universe. As our world goes more cyber, consumers will feel the need to surround themselves with things that will bring them back to reality. This will manifest itself in many different areas of our lives, from how we dress, to how we decorate our homes, play, and entertain ourselves.

As we turn away from buying things and focus more of our spending on experiences, nature travel and history travel will grow. What connects us with the real world more than nature? What grounds us in our cultural reality better than history? History travel, especially travel focused on Civil War sites, is already a booming business and destined to grow. History travel will encompass colonial America, Revolutionary War sites, western expansion, and native cultural attractions as well. Foreign travel will take consumers overseas to the homelands where their ancestors originated.

As our world goes more cyber, consumers will feel the need to surround themselves with things that will bring them back to reality.

Grounding through nature will express itself in the garden. Outdoor living space will grow, with consumers building elaborate garden getaways where they can shut out the modern world and enjoy the sounds, smells, and sights of nature. We will invite wildlife into our garden worlds, including birds, but hardly limited to them. We will populate our gardens with turtles, frogs, toads, peaceful snakes, squirrels, bats, even other furry mammals that will connect us better to the real world. A flock of wild turkeys roams our neighborhood. Cars stop on the road just to watch them. They are ugly creatures, looking like miniature *Jurassic Park* raptors with feathers, but fascinating nonetheless when they come to forage in our yard. I keep food on hand to throw out to them because they seem so special in a first Thanksgiving, Plymouth colony sort of way.

With an emphasis on reality, our home decorating focus will expand to include all five senses. While color and style (i.e., sight) may always dominate our home décor, consumers are broadening their focus to texture (i.e., touch), background music or sounds of running water in indoor fountains (i.e., sound), and home fragrances (i.e., smell). The sense of taste is indulged in our kitchens, now the center and focus of the home.

As we arouse and stimulate our senses through the things with which we surround ourselves, we will pay particular attention to the feel of fabrics in our upholstered furniture, rugs, pillows, throws, bed linens, curtains, towels, and kitchen and dining linens. Shoppers have always been "touchy-feely" when buying these products, but in the future they will become even more so. Consumers will demand that the fabrics they touch, sit on, and cover up with, engage them and stimulate them texturally, as well as be a pleasing color and design.

Our taste in home furnishings, including the colors we use to decorate and the art we choose for our walls, will also become more harmonious with nature, more soothing, more natural, and more beautiful. Our taste in color will not fade into pastel nothingness. Rather, we will look for stronger, bolder colors that appear in nature. Think of the bright, bold colors found in a spring garden filled with tulips, daffodils and other flowers. Moreover, we will combine colors not to contrast, but to complement. Art will turn from modern influences with its stress on shapes and colors back to more beautiful, naturalistic images. The continued popularity of the Impressionist painters foreshadows the new direction for art in the third millennium.

In the home of the future, sound will play a more central role. Music that is created to stimulate a mood or a feeling will grow in demand, as consumers enhance their home

Silence itself may become a new luxury and status symbol, with architects incorporating more sound-blocking features in new homes.

with new entertainment systems that give the effect of surround sound. Designers will figure out ways to bring the sounds of nature into our homes from simple tabletop fountains that recycle tap water to other more complex fountain designs. Expect architectural design to incorporate a Spanish influence by introducing inner courtyards with natural fountains. Silence itself may become a new luxury and status symbol, with architects incorporating more sound-blocking features in new homes.

Home fragrance will become an essential element of the home. While candles are the preferred means for home-fragrance delivery today, new more flexible mechanisms, such as heated waxes, potpourri boilers, and misters will give consumers more control of the fragrance and the mood the fragrances are intended to set. Aromatherapy technology will be applied to home fragrances and recipes for combining different scents to achieve desired emotional effects will become popular.

The trend toward realism and naturalism will also play out in fashion. We will strive to achieve multisensory looks that combine color and style with texture and scent. Cosmetics and personal-care products will satisfy our sensual cravings for indulgences. Fashion designers will experiment with new fiber technologies, even combining new manmade fibers with natural ones that achieve ultra-comfort in our clothes while enhancing feminine curves with fabric that floats and swings, rather than clings. We will look for more washable fabrics, rather than dry cleaning with all those dangerous chemicals. Consumers will have signature fragrances that are individually hand blended to capture the essence of the personality. Personal fragrances will be developed for different moods, allowing the individual to coordinate his or her signature scent with activities for the day or their feelings.

As we ground ourselves more and more in reality, we will want our "techno-toys" to have a decidedly *Jetsons,* twenty-first-century appeal. For TVs, home entertainment systems, major appliances, and computers, we will favor an ultra-high-tech look, lots of chrome and steel, lights and buttons, and sleek curves. Our desire for the ultra-high-tech look for technology products will play out in our favorite toy: the car. Today's consumers are enamored of the retro-looking Chrysler PT Cruiser, Ford Thunderbird, and the new GM Chevy Bel Air Concept Vehicle, but car design will take a decidedly high-tech turn soon. It will offer designs that look forward by looking back to the future vision of motor-vehicle transportation, as conceived in the 1940s and 1950s.

Consumer Trend: Time Is the New Shopping Currency

If the rising economy of the 1990s taught us anything, it was that anyone who is willing to get the right education and work hard at the right job can make more money. However, we also discovered that no matter how rich or poor we were, no one could add one second more to one's life. Time is the great social equalizer. We all have only 24 hours a day, 7 days a week, 365 days per year. With this discovery comes the awareness that our time is a precious and limited resource. A new priority of making the most of the limited time we have is taking over. Consumers are looking at all the ways they spend their time, including shopping, and demanding a more time-efficient, time-conscious way to shop.

The amount of time consumers are willing to shop has declined steadily over the past decade, and it can be expected to collapse even more as consumers are confronted with new concerns about safety in public places. America's Research Group found that consumers who visited two to three stores in 1990 to buy home furnishings, electronics, and major appliances, had cut the number of visits back by half a store by the end of the decade. Today, shoppers are going to only 1.8 stores to make the same purchases.

Further, as consumers retreat into the safety and comfort of their homes, they want to spend less time at the store, especially a store that is not satisfying their craving for a unique and emotionally satisfying experience. They will do more of their weekly shopping in a single shopping trip. More consumer shopping will also be done from the home, with consumers turning to the Internet, mail-order catalogs, and even party-based and other direct-selling businesses for their shopping needs.

Party plans and other forms of direct selling will be the next guerilla marketing method to grab share, while giving fits to traditional retailers in the years to come. This retailing methodology has everything going for it in today's emotional climate. You get a chance to meet and greet your friends in the comfort of a friend's home, thus providing social experiences that people desire. Over appetizers and a glass of wine, you get to look at new, interesting products presented by your friend, a spokesperson you can really trust. While seeing the new products, you can learn how to use them or display them in innovative ways, thus providing the enhancement of education and information. You gain access to special sales offers, and you can pay for

Time is the great social equalizer.

Television shopping mimics the intimacy of party plans.

the products later when they are delivered to your home. It is the perfect retailing method for the new millennium. Longaberger Baskets, Blyth's PartyLite candles, Pampered Chef, Discovery Toys, Avon, Mary Kay, and many others have known it for years, and soon many other smart marketers will be exploring opportunities to sell in this way. Word of warning: It only works with women, at least so far.

Television shopping mimics the intimacy of party plans. We are already conditioned to think of the television celebrities we invite into our homes every day as our "friends." As a result, the television shopping channels with their personally engaging show hosts will become a more powerful retailing media in the future.

Consumer Trend: The Coming Retail Crisis— Excess Retail Space

It is happening in office space today. Office real estate is facing a crisis of excess inventory. After years of building new office space coupled with overly optimistic tenants who grabbed more office space than they needed, nearly 40 million square feet of office space returned to the market in 2002, according to Torto Wheaton Research. As new office buildings remain vacant and existing tenants fail to renew their leases, rents will fall and overall office vacancy rates will rise. Even boom towns, such as Atlanta, Dallas, and Houston, faced office vacancy rates in the double digits at the start of 2002.

As the crisis grows in office real estate, another one will develop in commercial retail space. The results of overbuilding retail space in the 1990s will come home to roost soon. Today every man, woman, and child "owns" between 40 and 50 square feet of dedicated retail space. In the 1990s, about 3 square feet per person was added to total retail space inventory. With 44,500 shopping centers nationwide, 300 million square feet of new store space was added in 2000. During the 1990s, space devoted to retail grew 20 percent, twice as fast as the population. Consequently, operating profits for retailers have dropped, and the retail business has become far more competitive.

Contributing to the coming retail crisis is the shifting pattern of consumer shopping.

Contributing to the coming retail crisis is the shifting pattern of consumer shopping. Consumers are turning away from traditional department stores and shopping more at mass merchants, discounters, and warehouse marts. While the sales from general merchandisers in total rose 92 percent from 1992 to 2002, the key driver of growth in this segment was the category of other general retailers, including Wal-Mart, Kmart, Target, Costco, and Sam's Club. Posting growth of 264.3 percent from 1992 to 2002, the other general retailers comprised of discounters and warehouse clubs reached $258.3 billion in retail revenue. In the same ten-year period, traditional department stores sales grew only 23 percent, not even matching growth of the retail industry as a whole. Nonstore retailers also posted triple-digit growth from 1992 to 2002. Nonstore retailers include catalogers and mail-order marketers, television shopping, direct sales, party-plan marketers, and e-tailers. This segment rose 138.6 percent from $81.3 billion in sales in 1992 to $194 billion in 2002. Growth of these two segments—other general merchandisers and nonstore retailers—is expected to outpace that of the retail industry as a whole. These two segments will continue to grab market share by siphoning sales away from competing classes of retailers.

A bright spot in the retail marketplace has been the explosive growth of large, national specialty chains, including Bed Bath & Beyond, Linens 'n Things, Pier 1, Pottery Barn, Williams-Sonoma, Restoration Hardware, The Home Depot, Lowe's, and so forth. These national, specialty retailers are literally "eating the lunch" of small independent specialty retailers that specialize in gift and home products. Yet, the national specialty chains have an Achilles' heel that may soon start to trip them up. Many of these companies have become retail "darlings" by posting consistent annual growth rates in the range of 7 to 15 percent. However, that growth has come largely from opening new stores rather than increases in existing-store sales. The trouble is that with only about 225 U.S. cities boasting a total population of 100,000 or more, the new markets where the national specialty retailers can open is shrinking. Many of the chains have between 200 and 300 individual stores, and behemoth Pier 1 has just topped 900 outlets. Inevitably, revenue growth for these chains will return to earth as their "frontier" markets evaporate. Their new store openings will be slated for existing markets where they will start to cannibalize their own stores' sales.

The coming retail shakeout will have an impact on all retailers, large and small. Clearly, some big-name department stores will be unable to stay the course as the department store sector continues to distance itself from the shopping needs of consumers. More small independent retailers—those shops that line small-town-America's main streets—will fold as Wal-Mart, Kmart, or Target open up on the town's bypass. The

FIGURE 9.7

Retail Sales by Type of Store, 1992 and 2000, Excludes Motor Vehicles, Gasoline, and Food Service

	1992	2002	% CHG '92-'02
Furnishings and electronics	$ 97.8	$ 198.6	103.1
Building and garden	160.2	323.1	101.7
Food and beverage	371.5	508.5	36.9
Health and personal care	90.8	191.6	111.0
Clothing and accessories	120.3	178.6	48.5
Sporting goods and hobby/books	49.3	81.5	65.3
General merchandise total	248.0	476.1	92.0
Department store	177.1	217.9	23.0
Other general	70.9	258.3	264.3
Miscellaneous stores	55.8	105	88.2
Nonstore	81.3	194	138.6
Total retail trade in billions	1,275.0	2,257.1	77.0

Source: Census Bureau

national specialty chains will have to work harder for every percentage point of revenue growth, as their building expansion programs slow. They may well start to close some of the unproductive stores in favor of larger stores in growing urban or suburban centers. Many older malls will fold as consumers start to patronize the new, unenclosed, lifestyle malls that are sprouting up throughout the country. They are designed to mimic small-town ambiance, while showcasing national, upscale, and specialty chain stores.

WHAT CAN RETAILERS DO TO SURVIVE THE COMING SHAKEOUT?

The lessons of this book—understanding the reasons why people buy—apply equally to manufacturers and retail businesses in anticipating consumer behavior now and in the future. Retailers need to explore with their shoppers why people shop in their stores. What features, products, attributes, benefits, needs, and consumer desires does the store meet? In what areas does it fail to satisfy? Retailers need to dig deeper than simply "customer service" and "quality." Too many retailers imagine their point of difference is customer service or quality products, but if you sit in a room for five minutes with consumers, you discover that these terms are meaningless. Retailers have to understand the heart, mind, and emotions of their customers. They need to figure out what experiences consumers expect and desire to have while shopping in the store and then develop strategies to give them more of those experiences.

> Retailers have to understand the heart, mind, and emotions of their customers.

Customer service has to be more than answering a question, wrapping a package, or escorting the customer to an aisle. Retail salespeople need to participate in the shopping experience with their customers. They have to be shopping partners, not salespeople or clerks. They have to have authentic enthusiasm. They need to be real and honest. They need to be likeable. They need to like their customers.

Retailers can also enhance the shopping experience by providing information. Why should The Home Depot have a monopoly on teaching people how to use their products? Any retailer selling home products can figure out hundreds of ways to provide information to its customers. Just watch HGTV, The Learning Channel, or The Discovery Channel to figure out how. The same theory applies to retailers of electronics, books, pet supplies, cosmetics and personal care, fashion jewelry, gourmet foods, housewares, sporting goods, hobby items, and crafts supplies. Consumers are eager to learn about their passion and willing to participate with retailers in this process. The key to launching a successful experiential-retailing program is to provide valuable information without substituting a sales presentation for a learning experience. Consumers are too savvy today. They will immediately see through the hoax.

Finally, the retail mantra "location, location, location" will never fade. Retailers need to be where shoppers shop. When shoppers stop coming to your street, your strip center, your mall, you'd better move and fast. Today's shoppers are more time sensitive; they are not going to go out of their way and use up valuable time driving to this store and that one. They are going to look for the easiest, most time-effective way to complete their shopping. Retailers need to be where the shoppers are. We are already seeing the future of the shift in consumer shopping patterns. Retailers need to anticipate the shopping shifts in their local markets and be ready to move before it is too late.

> Consumers are eager to learn about their passion and willing to participate with retailers in this process.

10

PULLING IT ALL TOGETHER
How to Sell More

Now that we have explored the many facets of why people buy things they don't need and learned how that *why* drives and directs consumer behavior, we have a final task. We need to look at the strategies that evolve from this investigation. We need to learn how to get people to buy more of the things they don't need. Marketing guru Sergio Zyman says the chief aim of marketing is to sell more things to more people more often for more money. We need to learn how to harness the power of why in our marketing and brand-building strategies.

Marketers that use "why people buy" strategies in their marketing go beyond the purely tactical realm (i.e., price, distribution, advertising, media placement, and so forth) and into a future-oriented, long-term view of the business, the brand, and the marketplace. This future-oriented, strategic realm is where loyal consumer relationships form.

> Today's marketing watchwords, *emotional branding* and *emotion marketing*, are beginning to scratch the surface of a "why people buy" strategy.

Today's marketing watchwords, *emotional branding* and *emotion marketing*, are beginning to scratch the surface of a "why people buy" strategy. With their recognition of the emotional side of marketing and branding, marketers are becoming aware that consumer behavior is not based solely on reason and logic, but driven by the heart and the emotions. Yet the emotional realm is complex, highly individualized, and very personal; it takes a unique approach to get inside of the hearts of the consumer. Left-brain-dominated marketing executives employing left-brain-oriented research strategies to develop left-brain marketing tactics are destined to falter as they are confounded by the emotions of their marketplace. By ignoring why people buy in favor of focusing on who, what, where, when, how, and how much of consumer behavior, the left-brain-oriented marketing companies are forever going to be chasing their market.

> Future marketing success is based on marrying the two points of view, the qualitative and the quantitative, the intuitive and the rational, the right brain and the left brain.

"Why people buy"–informed marketing strategies must be supported by strong left-brain-oriented tactics and approaches, but marketing executives informed with "why people buy" insights will be able to anticipate the shifts and turns in their market. They will move just ahead of their customers, knowing where they are going to be next, and what the customers will demand when they get there. Do not misunderstand the strategy. Future marketing success is based on marrying the two points of view, the qualitative and the quantitative, the intuitive and the rational, the right brain and the left brain, the why people buy and the who, what, where, how, and how much.

Here are the basic strategies you can use to capitalize on the knowledge you gained about why people buy.

TOUCH THE EMOTIONS OF YOUR CUSTOMERS

Consumers make decisions to purchase discretionary products largely based on emotion because there is no strictly rational reason for buying something you don't need. However, even in the purchase of necessary products, consumers' emotions are engaged. After hundreds of hours spent talking to and interacting with consumers in a research setting, I know that emotion is at the foundation of people buying things they don't need. Reason is always secondary in the purchase decision.

A word of caution to marketers: If you do not think this is true, then you have been listening to the words consumers say, not the way they say them. In focus groups, I have seen men, in particular, trying to act so rational in explaining their purchasing behavior, yet when they are given an exercise designed to reveal the underlying emotions, their eyes light up and they get excited. In these settings, I have seen grown men turn into

Because consumers make purchase decisions in the emotional realm, they are highly responsive to environmental cues and clues that stimulate and communicate on an emotional level.

little boys before me. Their emotions take over, and that is where they ultimately make their purchase decisions. I even think that these men have convinced themselves they act rationally, but they prove the deception on camera in the focus group.

Because consumers make purchase decisions in the emotional realm, they are highly responsive to environmental cues and clues that stimulate and communicate on an emotional level. Marketers need to make sure that the emotional messages they send are in keeping with the emotional needs of the customers. Design of products, packaging, advertising, and logos resonate on an emotional level. Color sends strong emotional clues, so marketers need to use color effectively in packaging, as well as in the color palette of the product.

Involving shoppers with the product or the ad establishes a connection. Most companies pay too little attention to heightening consumer involvement through in-store and point-of-purchase displays. Brand and product awareness are no longer the endgame. You need to get consumers to do something with your product—pick it up, touch it, or interact in a multisensory way. That is what will imprint the brand in the shopper's consciousness and begin to establish an emotional connection with the customer.

GIVE CUSTOMERS RATIONAL JUSTIFIERS SO THEY WILL HAVE PERMISSION TO BUY

Emotions may lead, but justifiers close the deal in the subtle commercial seduction between a product and a consumer. Some products need few justifiers to get the consumer to buy. Products that give immediate emotional gratification and do not require the consumer to make any kind of sacrifice are indulgences that demand few justifiers. On the other hand, a purchase that is more costly, more utilitarian, or more luxurious and extravagant, requires elaborate justifiers to encourage the consumer to complete the sale. Marketers need to do the hard work of creating the justifiers for the customer. Far more than just presenting product benefits and features, marketers need to understand why people buy to provide mean-

Emotions may lead, but justifiers close the deal in the subtle commercial seduction between a product and a consumer.

ingful, wide-ranging justifiers that support consumers in their purchase decisions.

> Marketers need to explore deeply and completely how their products improve the quality of their customers' lives.

As discussed in Chapter 4, our research reveals that improving the quality of life is the top justifier that consumers use and the one that truly resonates at an emotional level with most of them. Marketers need to explore deeply and completely how their products improve the quality of their customers' lives, then make sure all marketing communications—advertising, packaging, and point-of-purchase—communicate the quality-of-life-enhancing values back to them.

APPEAL TO CUSTOMERS WHO ARE IN MOTION

A closely guarded secret that direct marketers have known for years is that the recent purchasers and the most frequent purchasers are the best prospects for buying again. Like eating potato chips, shoppers rarely stop after buying just one thing. One purchase leads to another and another, often with the first purchase justifying a continued spending spree. The emotionally driven consumer often behaves gluttonously, seeking more consuming satisfaction from buying more things.

Every shopper who wanders into a store, stands before a display window, reads an advertisement, or watches an ad is a prospect. They must be romanced into buying something, to come into the store, or to seek out more information about the store or the product advertised. Romance is not played out rationally like a chess game; it is conducted emotionally. Moreover, I will share another secret: Consumers want desperately to be romanced when they shop. It makes them feel special, unique, valuable, valued. Ultimately, the only way to truly romance customers is to love them. It may sound hokey as we talk in the context of the commercial relationship of a company and its customer, but everyone wants to be loved. If you really care about your customers, want the best for them, and want happiness and satisfaction for them, then you will find the right strategy. I have seen companies that disrespect their customers, do not value them, and do not understand that everything, ultimately, starts with the customer. Every company owes its being to the customer, and employees are dependent on customers for their weekly paychecks. However, some companies do not make that understanding part of their corpo-

> Consumers want desperately to be romanced when they shop.

> Truly put the customer first and watch how your sales skyrocket.

rate values. How many of us, as customers, have faced surly employees and store clerks who act as if we are in their way? These companies cannot succeed because their interaction with their customers is based on deception.

Marketers need to respond to consumers in motion to sell more. They have to think about ways to cross merchandise products creatively to open new consuming opportunities. Like the retailing of major appliances we looked at in Chapter 2, marketers need to think from the point of view of customers: what they want, what they need, and where they might want to find it. Companies need to stop making decisions based on their own myopic point of view: what the company wants to sell, where it wants to sell it, and how it wants to sell it. Tactical business decisions made from the point of view of what is best for the company, its operations, and its employees will fail. Companies must adapt their operations to the consumer, not the other way around. Truly put the customer first and watch how your sales skyrocket.

MAKE CUSTOMERS FEEL LIKE WINNERS EVERY TIME

Customers shop to satisfy emotional needs and longings, and they want their shopping experience to provide emotional satisfaction as well. When they shop, they want to feel like winners, as if they did something good, fun, and beneficial for themselves and their families, including saving money. It is more than just finding a great bargain, but when shoppers do find a super deal, it makes them feel like winners. When consumers feel they have done something outstanding, found something extraordinary, achieved some great height, or become unique, more special, more lovable, better, they feel like winners. When customers leave the store with your company's products in their shopping bags, you want them to be happy and satisfied. It is so much more than price, but few marketers go the extra step to discover new, creative ways to make customers feel like winners.

> Few marketers go the extra step to discover new, creative ways to make customers feel like winners.

Making customers feel like winners goes back to our earlier strategy of helping them enhance the quality of their lives. Make their lives special, more meaningful, more satisfying, more fulfilling. Things do not buy happiness, but things can enhance the life experience that leads to happiness. Consumers feel like winners when they can trade money, such a mundane thing, for the experience of greater happiness, fulfillment, and satisfaction.

HELP YOUR CUSTOMERS FULFILL THEIR FANTASIES

Advertising agencies have created consuming fantasies for years. They carefully select models, images, settings, scenes, and story lines to evoke an image, a feeling, and a fantasy of how one's life would be transformed through owning a product. I want to live in the world of laundry detergent commercials. In those ads, the day is always sunny and the trees are always green. There is beautiful music playing in the background and the curtains are gently swaying in a mild breeze. It is never too cold or hot in laundry-detergent world and it always smells fresh and clean. Perhaps the craft of advertising taught consumers how to create consuming fantasies, but however it started, consumers invent often-elaborate fantasies that they desire to act out through the things they buy and own.

When consumers talk about why they buy, they often explain it in terms of fantasy fulfillment. Through their consuming fantasies, they imagine how they will enhance their lives by the purchase of some thing, and how it will taste, feel, smell, look, and sound. They are visceral in their fantasies and use them to build excitement and anticipation leading toward a purchase. Marketers must tap into those consuming fantasies, understand them, and play back the fantasy imagery in marketing communications. It is part of romancing customers, relating on an emotional level, and making them feel special and loved.

ENTERTAIN, ENTERTAIN, ENTERTAIN

Consumers crave entertainment as a means to escape their mundane, ordinary, humdrum lives. Entertainment offers a respite from melancholy and feelings of hopelessness. Being entertained is more than just watching a movie or a television show; it is about engaging the mind in a fantasy that offers escape from the boring facets of daily life. Entertainment is about reaching out and connecting with other people, other realities, and another consciousness. It is pondering a painting, walking in the woods, climbing a

> Consumers invent often-elaborate fantasies that they desire to act out through the things they buy and own.

> Consumers crave enter-
> tainment as a means to
> escape their mundane,
> ordinary, humdrum lives.

mountain, attending a party, going to the mall, walking the streets of New York, or visiting an historic home. Our longing for experiences is all about being entertained.

An educated mind is an active mind, and an active mind needs mental stimulation. Marketers and retailers in the future need to plan to satisfy this need. It is a great opportunity just waiting for them. It will build lasting relationships with consumers and keep them coming back for more.

TRANSLATE THE BRAND INTO THE "WHY"

In a recent discussion with a client about why people buy his company's product and the implications for the brand, he had a "eureka" moment. He became animated and blurted out: "The 'why' is the brand!" All I could say was "exactly," as he so succinctly and eloquently expressed what I had been saying.

The promise implicit in the relationship between the brand and the consumer is why people buy. The promise includes the fantasies they have about the brand, the wishes they want fulfilled, and the way the brand enhances their quality of life. The brand must satisfy the promise, and if you as a brand manager and marketer do not really understand the promise encompassed in why people buy, then you are destined to fall short of their desires. The *why* is the contract with the consumer— the agreement that binds the brand with the consumer. If you do not intimately understand why people buy your brand, then it is only hit or miss that the brand will connect with the consumer.

In all the research and planning that the Coca-Cola Company did in developing New Coke, it apparently never researched why people buy Coke. Rather, it assumed it had something to do with consumers' thirst and their taste preferences. It conducted tactical research about what combinations of flavors were in tune with consumers because Coca-Cola executives thought that people bought Coke because of the taste. They learned that even when they got the taste formula aligned with consumers' preferences in blind taste tests, they got it dead wrong as a brand. People drink Coke because it links them with happy memories of their childhood and recalls the lovely fantasies Coke commercials have spawned over the years. Consumers have a deep love

> The promise implicit in the
> relationship between the
> brand and the consumer
> is why people buy.

of the brand and buy what the brand promises and the fantasies it fulfills, not just flavored soda water. That is the magic of a brand, and the foundation of that magic comes with understanding why people buy.

GAIN BIG VISION BY FOCUSING ON WHY PEOPLE BUY

In my work as a marketing consultant, I run into two types of clients: little-vision companies and big-vision companies. Little-vision companies want market research and advice that is tactically oriented. They have immediate marketing problems and need information to help them make tactical decisions related to product, pricing, advertising, distribution, and sales. Their focus is on the next quarter, or the next six months, or the next year. While they are caught in the day-to-day struggles of running a business, they will achieve only incremental improvements taking a little-vision approach. There is nothing wrong with incremental improvements. Every company can use incremental gains, but the marketing problems and challenges faced today are insignificant when compared with the challenges companies will confront in the future, especially if they maintain a little-vision approach to marketing. Ultimately, little-vision companies end up chasing their customers, trying desperately to keep up with them as they change, shift, and evolve.

Big-vision companies, on the other hand, are looking two, three, or five years out. They understand that tactics follow strategy. They know they have to have a strategic vision so they can create their future. Big-vision companies are not stuck on tactics or paralyzed by uncertainties. Their foresight yields exponential growth. By understanding why people buy, they can anticipate the shifts and bends in the consumer market. Hockey player Wayne Gretzky, when asked what made him play better than anyone else, responded that the other players skated to where the puck was, but that he skated to where the puck was going. This is a metaphor of how big-vision companies operate. They anticipate where their customers are going to be in the future and are waiting for consumers when they get there.

Only big-vision companies can successfully implement brand building and strategy. Little-vision companies define their brands too narrowly and too specifically for the here and now. In comparison, big-vision companies take a long-term view of the brand and its customers. Therefore, they create a brand strategy

> By understanding why people buy, they can anticipate the shifts and bends in the consumer market.

that is encompassing, timeless, and emotionally compelling. Big-vision companies understand that why people buy remains stable over time, and it is the secret to understanding consumer behavior today as well as how it will change in the future. Little-vision companies ignore completely the why, but instead focus only on consumer behavior—the who, what, where, how, when, and how much. Consequently, they will forever be second-guessing consumers and trying to catch up to them. Figure 10.1 outlines the characteristics of big-vision and little-vision companies.

Gap Inc. exemplifies how a company can go awry when it fails to infuse its marketing and branding programs with a "why people buy" strategy. Gap Inc. was doing great as an apparel retailer selling basic, high-quality casual clothes with youthful zing at a good value to a wide-ranging consumer market. It faltered when it launched the Old Navy brand. Old Navy had the same basic "why people buy" values as the Gap brand did. Old Navy was everything that Gap was, only cheaper. Old Navy and Gap became synonymous from the consumers' perspective, with Old Navy's less expensive positioning and perceived lower product quality dragging down the more high-quality, value-oriented price positioning of Gap. The company perceived that it created a point of difference by keeping Gap stores in malls and making Old Navy stores freestanding. But that was wrong! Consumers don't care where the stores are located. They just want to buy products when they think about them. Gap Inc. today is doing serious work to extricate its core Gap brand from Old Navy and establish each brand uniquely based on a "why people buy" strategy.

For too long, marketing executives have focused almost exclusively on studying consumer behavior. However, they have been using left-

FIGURE 10.1
Big Vision versus Little Vision

BIG VISION	**LITTLE VISION**
Strategic	Tactical
Long range, next two years, five years, ten years	Short term, next quarter, next year
Why people buy	What, where, how, when, how much
Exponential growth	Incremental improvements
Future vision	Rear-view mirror
Anticipate the market	Chase the market

brained tools that track the past and provide only tactical direction. While marketers know they need to get out in front of their marketplace and anticipate the changes that are occurring there, they do not know how to do it. It really is quite straightforward. You just have to ask the right question and be open to the implications when your customers answer you. That question is simple: Why do people buy?

My wish for you, and the reason I wrote this book, is that you incorporate the "why people buy" approach, thinking, and strategy into your marketing plans.

Bourdieu, Pierre, translated by Richard Nice. *Distinction: A Social Critique of the Judgement of Taste.* Cambridge, MA: Harvard University Press, 1984.

Catalano, Ellen Mohn and Nina Sonenberg. *Consuming Passions: Help for Compulsive Shoppers.* Oakland, CA: New Harbinger Publications, 1993.

Clapp, Rodney, editor. *The Consuming Passion: Christianity & the Consumer Culture.* Downers Grove, IL: InterVarsity Press, 1998.

DeGraaf, John, David Wann and Thomas H. Naylor. *Affluenza: The All-Consuming Epidemic.* San Francisco: Berrett-Koehler Publishers, Inc., 2001.

Frank, Robert H. *Luxury Fever: Money and Happiness in an Era of Excess.* Princeton, NJ: Princeton University Press, 1999.

Popcorn, Faith and Lys Marigold. *EVEolution: The Eight Truths of Marketing to Women.* New York: Hyperion, 2000.

Rosenblatt, Roger, editor. *Consuming Desires: Consumption, Culture, and the Pursuit of Happiness.* Washington, DC: Island Press, 1999.

Schorr, Juliet B. *The Overspent American: Why We Want What We Don't Need.* New York: HarperPerennial, 1998.

Schorr, Juliet B., forward by Ralph Nader. *Do Americans Shop Too Much?* Boston, MA: Beacon Press, 2000.

Schulz, Eric. *The Marketing Game: How the World's Best Companies Play to Win*. Holbrook, MA: Adams Media Corporation, 2001.

Twitchell, James B. *Lead Us into Temptation: The Triumph of American Materialism*. New York: Columbia University Press, 1999.

Underhill, Paco. *Why We Buy: The Science of Shopping*. New York: Simon & Schuster, 1999.

Veblen, Thorstein. *The Theory of the Leisure Class*. New York: Penguin Books, 1899.

Zyman, Sergio. *The End of Marketing as We Know It*. New York: Harper Business, 2000.

A nationally recognized expert in consumer marketing and psychology, Pamela N. Danziger founded her marketing research and consulting firm, Unity Marketing, in 1992. Her expertise lies in understanding the whys that underlie consumer behavior, and how companies can use insights based on consumer psychology to predict the future of their marketplace.

Frequently called on by the media to comment on consumer shopping trends, she has appeared on NBC's *Today Show,* the CBS News *Sunday Morning* show, Fox News, NPR's *Marketplace,* and CNNfN, and is quoted regularly by *The Wall Street Journal, The New York Times, Washington Post, Los Angeles Times, Chicago Tribune, American Demographics, Forbes, USA Today, Brandweek, Associated Press,* and others.

Luxury companies both here and abroad rely on Unity Marketing for insight and statistics on the luxury market. Among the luxury leaders that Pam advises on the changing luxury market are LVMH, Richemont, Pinault Printemps Redoute, Lenox, Starwood Hotels, Crystal Cruises, Nissan, Bulgari, Gold Council, Polo Ralph Lauren, Herend Porcelain, Bernaudaud, Waterford/Wedgwood, Target Stores, and Stueben Glass.

Pam is currently working on her next book, *Let Them Eat Cake: Marketing Luxury to the Masses—as Well as the Classes.* She holds a BA degree from Pennsylvania State University, as well as a Master of Library Science degree from the University of Maryland. Prior to founding Unity Marketing, she worked for a major Washington trade association and Bell Communications Research. Her last job was at the Franklin Mint, where she was director of competitive analysis, gathering marketing information to identify trends in the collectibles market.

Pam Danziger
Unity Marketing
Phone: 717-336-1600
Fax: 717-336-1601
http://www.unitymarketingonline.com
Pam@UnityMarketingonline.com

Share the message!

Bulk discounts
Discounts start at only 10 copies. Save up to 55% off
retail price.

Custom publishing
Private label a cover with your organization's name
and logo. Or, tailor information to your needs with
a custom pamphlet that highlights specific chapters.

Ancillaries
Workshop outlines, videos, and other products are
available on select titles.

Dynamic speakers
Engaging authors are available to share their expertise
and insight at your event.

Call Dearborn Trade Special Sales at 1-800-245-BOOK (2665)
or e-mail trade@dearborn.com

Dearborn™
Trade Publishing
A **Kaplan Professional** Company